WARTIME STANDARD SHIPS

WARTIME
STANDARD SHIPS

NICK ROBINS

Foreword by
Nick Ramsay

Seaforth
PUBLISHING

Copyright © Nick Robins 2017

First published in Great Britain in 2017 by
Seaforth Publishing,
A division of Pen & Sword Books Ltd,
47 Church Street,
Barnsley S70 2AS

www.seaforthpublishing.com

British Library Cataloguing in Publication Data
A catalogue record for this book is available from the British Library

ISBN 978 1 84832 376 6 (HARDBACK)
ISBN 978 1 84832 378 0 (EPUB)
ISBN 978 1 84832 377 3 (KINDLE)

Designed by Neil Sayer
Printed and bound in India by Replika Press Pvt Ltd

CONTENTS

PREFACE

Key to the Allied strategy in both world wars in the twentieth century was a massive programme of merchant shipbuilding. The ships were built to standard designs with increasing emphasis on prefabrication and a progression towards welded hulls. The National-type cargo ships of the First World War were the first prefabricated ships. The best known of all types of wartime standard ships, of course, were the Liberty ships and their successors, the better-equipped Victory ships, both built in the United States in the Second World War. Standard ships were not only built for the Allies: Germany and Japan also had standard merchant shipbuilding programmes during the Second World War.

Collectively, the politicians, senior naval officers, naval architects and engineers who sanctioned and designed the various classes of standard ships provide an interesting background to the ships themselves. So too do the shipbuilders and the shipyard workers, although the success of the ships was down to the skill and bravery of their wartime crews. That so many of the wartime standard merchant ships survived the two world wars, and then maintained long and successful civilian careers, reflects the superior design of the ships and their fitness for the duties perceived of them.

Some of the story has been told piecemeal in a range of diverse books and articles, a few with extensive fleet lists. However, the complete history of the twentieth-century wartime-built standard merchant ship has not previously been written. This volume records that history within its appropriate political and military background.

The text has benefited immensely from technical editing by retired naval architect Ian Ramsay. Ian has also contributed valuable text, as has former Marine Superintendent of the Harrison Line, Captain Michael Jones. Captain Jones writes first-hand of his experience with Liberty ships. Ellie Everhart also helped with the editing process. Julian Mannering, at Seaforth Publishing, guided the book through its planning stage and saw it through production.

Dr Nick Robins
April 2017

FOREWORD

In both world wars, there arose a pressing need for merchant tonnage, to supplement existing ships but, more importantly, to replace ships that had been sunk due to enemy action. This need gave rise to a series of Standard Ships in both wars. Due to the constraints caused by scarce resources there was no time for intensive research, design and model testing of suitable hulls for minimum resistance and optimum propulsive efficiency. Consequently, existing proven merchant ship types were selected as prototypes and the original production drawings were reconfigured to accommodate the individual plant and layout limitations of each of the selected builders. This was done for every type of standard ship selected: a sort of lowest common denominator basis.

In the Great War, the British shipbuilding industry became over-committed to the building programmes for warships, naval auxiliaries and merchant ships. It also suffered from a shortage of skilled labour caused by so many of the younger workers having volunteered for active service in the early years of the war. To remedy this within the United Kingdom, it was decided that use should be made of the structural steel and bridge-building industries which were able to prepare and fabricate relatively straightforward components, provided that none of the plates needed to be rolled or furnaced to a complex ship shape.

This decision resulted in the 'N' (or National) Type Standard Ship whose design was based on the quite unconventional feature that the ship's frames (or ribs) were straight and without any of the usual ship-shape curvature. Whilst this feature of the straight-frame ship was anathema to both the traditional shipbuilders and shipowners, it is suggested that, had the war lasted longer with the same level of ship losses, this novel method of construction would have met with acceptance. The angular, or hard chine, method of construction was probably less energy-efficient for propulsion purposes, but as its model was never tank-tested, there is no reliable data with which to make meaningful comparisons with similar ships of conventional shape.

The method of construction did, however, prove that it was cost-effective, as it demonstrated that serviceable ships could be built without the need for expensive plant to deal with shape. More importantly, it proved that significant elements of the structure could be prefabricated away from the building berth and, indeed, away from the shipyard.

With the shipbuilding 'boom' at the end of hostilities in 1918 and the subsequent recession, the straight-framed ship was quietly forgotten for some twenty years. With the start of the Second World War, Britain was again faced with the need to replace its merchant fleet, which was being sunk at a greater rate than the country's shipbuilding industry could replace it.

Once again, ships had to be produced as quickly and as cheaply as possible without any regard to conventional appearance or peacetime shipping economics. Conventional standard tramp steamers were selected which could be built in existing North American shipyards using conventional methods. However, it quickly became apparent that a different approach was needed if the requirements of both the British and, later, the American governments were to be met and so the 'Liberty' ship was born and Mr Henry J Kaiser arrived on the scene to play his major part. The first action in the Liberty project was to re-design the ship, initially for almost all-welded production, but latterly for all-welded construction. This revolutionary change was possible because in the 1930s the use of welding had been accepted in American manufacturing industries. As a natural corollary to this, welded construction became part of a production engineered and planning process that broke the ship down in to sub-assemblies that could be manufactured off-site by non-shipbuilding fabricators; shades of the National Standard Ships of the Great War.

Once the project started it quickly proved that by feeding in fabricated sub-assemblies from outside subcontractors, building berth occupancy could be much reduced. There was a limit to the reduction that could be economically achieved and, to speed up overall production of completed ships, additional building berths were required which, in turn, meant new 'green field' shipyards being created. This Henry Kaiser achieved using his construction industry expertise and ruthless business methods.

Although many called her an ugly duckling, the Liberty ship was responsible for a cultural change in world shipbuilding. It proved that an all-welded hull was both feasible and practical and, if its sub-assemblies were fabricated under cover rather than 'piece small' on the building berth, it could be constructed much quicker and cheaper than the then all-riveted ship.

As at the end of the First World War, there was another shipbuilding boom for Britain's shipbuilders. This lasted for the ten years immediately after 1945, when shipbuilders were busy replacing lost tonnage. With no competition from Germany and Japan, they were reluctant to prejudice their deliveries by making the highly disruptive changeover to all-welded construction. By the time that Britain did take all-welded prefabricated construction seriously, Germany and Japan had been helped back on to their industrial feet and the neutral and formerly occupied European countries' shipyards, with much leaner order books, had also adopted all-welded construction. So for a number of economic, governmental, financial and industrial relations reasons, British shipbuilding, alone of the world's shipbuilders, probably gained least, and that belatedly, from the all-welded Liberty project in which they had so whole- heartedly participated.

Ian Ramsay, CENG FRINA FIES
Formerly Secretary of the Institution of
Engineers and Shipbuilders in Scotland
February 2016

1 THE CONCEPT: AUSTERE, FUNCTIONAL AND LOTS OF THEM

A nation that is losing its merchant ships at a greater rate than it can replace them will inevitably lose the war. Britain found itself in this position in both the Great War and the Second World War, and Japan also realised the parlous state of its logistics in the Second World War. As island nations, both were solely dependent on sea transport to victual their people at home and both too were reliant on sea transport to take stores and munitions to their forces that were fighting away from home. So successful was the Allied destruction of German merchant ships in the Second World War that Germany also had a developing logistics problem in the Mediterranean and Black Sea by 1941 and later also in the Baltic and Atlantic.

In each case, the response to the attrition of merchant shipping was an emergency programme of building to standardised ship designs. The idea of standardisation was not new, but had previously been applied to ships of a particular trade, such as the Doxford Turret ships which were designed to minimise dues for transiting the Suez Canal. The standard engines-aft, bridge-amidships bulk tanker that emerged in the 1890s and evolved through to the 1960s was another example, with many standard types repeated over and over again to an identical design. Even in the fifteenth and sixteenth centuries, the standardisation technique was well advanced, as Filipe Castro reports:

… in England, as in Venice, predesigned frames were placed at regular intervals along the entire axis of the hull, while in Portugal and Spain the predesigned frames were clustered in the central portion of the ship's hull … Italian merchant cities such as Naples, Genoa, and Venice were home to highly developed shipbuilding industries, having highly organized shipyards where craftsmen were divided into specialized groups: woodcutters, sawyers, carpenters, and caulkers working within the enclosed shipyard complex. Organized shipyards with specialized sets of labor were able to construct the ships quickly in a reliable and repetitive fashion.

Savings were made in standardised construction as the design work had already been done. The shipyard workers worked efficiently, as they were familiar with the assembly procedure. Parts and, in due course, even engines could be ordered cost-effectively in bulk to arrive at the shipyard on set dates, ready to be installed in the new ship. In addition, the parts were interchangeable between ships and were generally available 'off the shelf'. Furthermore, crew that had worked on one standard-type ship could readily transfer to another of the same type without difficulty.

The wartime standard ships were built to straightforward designs, even to the extent that bent ribs were kept to a minimum. Some types of ships, indeed many of the Liberty ships, had no camber to the main deck to make construction even simpler. The ships were such that they could be assembled by semi-skilled workers, were utilitarian in that they were fit for purpose but no more, and optimised deadweight capacity for the size of ship. They ranged from concrete lighters and tugs to the most famous of them all, the Liberty ship. There were even wooden-hulled ships built in the Great War in response to the shortage of available steel. Wood was used whenever steel was in desperately short supply, and savings on steel were made with lightweight lattice derricks, absence of topmasts and other means. Not only were there fast cargo liners and troop transports, there were the tramp ship designs such as the American-built Oceans and the Canadian-built Forts and Parks, as well as the Liberty ships. The Oceans, Forts and Liberty ships were all based on a tried and tested design from work carried out in the late 1930s at Sunderland.

The ships were cut back to the bone: no frills, no luxuries. The Liberty ships of the Second World War were built to serve the Allied war effort with little prospect of commercial activity post-war. 'Built by the yard and cut off by

The austere surroundings of the crew's mess room aboard a British-built A- or B-type standard ship built in the Great War. The lack of creature comforts and basic lifesaving equipment was a feature of these vessels that seamen were only too well aware of. (AUTHOR COLLECTION)

the mile', the ships were built on rows of adjacent slipways, some in dry docks. Large sections were prefabricated, and widespread use was made of electric welding which brought construction times down to a record four days and fifteen hours from keel-laying to launching. The key to the speed was the supply chain, with parts arriving at the shipyard and held in stock until needed. In a report to Congress in 1941, the Liberty ship was described as having a five-year tenure:

It is slow and seaworthy and has the longevity of a modern steel ship, but for the demands of normal commerce in foreign trade it could not compete in speed, equipment and general serviceability with up-to-date cargo vessels. The design is the best that can be devised for an emergency product to be quickly, cheaply and simply built. They will be constructed for the emergency and whether they have any utility afterward will have to be determined then. The coastal trade may offer some possibilities in that direction.

As it was, the Liberty ship was to be the world's stock in trade well into the 1960s. It did have its problems: cracks developing in welded hulls, exacerbated, for example, by service in sub-zero temperatures in the Russian convoys, and propellers were prone to falling off the shaft. The latter was a corrosion problem between the two different metals caused by poorly fitting propeller bosses, a reflection of the speed at which the ships were put together.

The successor to the Liberty ship was the Victory ship, with its numerous improvements, including more expensive steam turbine en-

gines. These ships were intended both to serve the war effort and to get commerce back up on its feet after the war had been won. Although the ships were basic and lacked much of the innovation in ship design that had evolved by the late 1930s, they were functional and very much fit for purpose. Like all the other Allied standard ships they were built to classification so that they could carry war insurance. It also meant that the surviving ships could take up commercial work after the war. This was not the case with the Japanese emergency shipbuilding programme, in which several ship types were built out of class, none of which could be insured during the war, and most had to be rebuilt after the war to the satisfaction of the classification societies.

In both world wars, British yards were working to capacity to satisfy military and merchant demands. The shipyards were inevitably understaffed due to the migration of men into the armed forces. Consequently, Britain had to look overseas for help and turned principally to America and Canada.

The loss statistics for the Great War underline the need for an emergency shipbuilding programme. By December 1915 Britain had lost 1.6 million gross tons of merchant shipping, and it was obvious that a great effort would be needed to replace these ships in order to maintain the country's needs. Orders were, therefore, placed with British and later American and Canadian yards, and some even in China and Japan. The ships all had names prefixed by *War*. They comprised the A- to H-type tramp steamers and cargo liners and the N-type National prefabricated tramps, as well as coasters and tankers.

Orders were placed by Britain, through non-government agencies, with yards in neutral America for several hundred ships. The ships ranged in deadweight from the larger 12,500-ton ships built on the east coast to the small 3,000 tons deadweight (dwt) cargo capacity steamers built at yards on the Great Lakes. All were dry-cargo vessels. However, only a few were actually delivered to Britain, as the majority were requisitioned by America on its own engagement at war in 1917. This was the start of the 'bridge of ships', originally conceived to take American soldiers to war in Europe. Latterly, the building programme was intended to promote the United States Merchant Marine to a point where 50 per cent of that nation's trade could be carried in its own ships, and the United States Shipping Board continued to

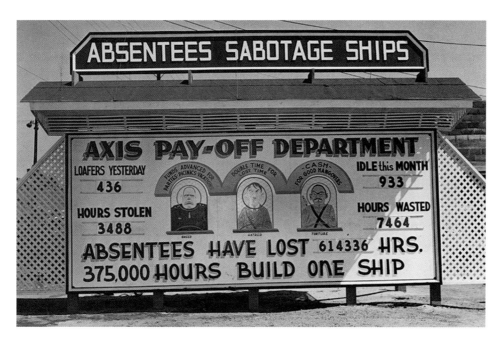

Repetitive, but skilled, single-task workers bored easily of their work and diversions were tempting. This information board posted at the entrance to one of the larger west-coast United States shipyards in the Second World War appeals to the latent patriots in the workforce. (AUTHOR COLLECTION)

sanction new building until 1921. Some 1,307 steel ships were built for the Emergency Fleet Corporation on behalf of the Shipping Board and a further 389 were requisitioned.

The Canadians built for a variety of nationalities and delivered some valuable tonnage, not least ships built at yards on the Great Lakes. As with the American yards on the Lakes, ships were limited in size by the canal locks connecting to the St Lawrence River. Canada, too, continued to build after the war, with government sponsorship for strengthening the Canadian Merchant Marine. Companies such as the MANZ Line were an outcome of this programme.

Only fourteen British-built ships with *War* names were lost in the Great War. The remainder looked for a commercial role when the government's interest in the ships ceased following the Armistice. The ships were sold at fixed prices, both to British shipowners and foreign-flag owners, the latter paying a premium price for their new tonnage. Post-war sell-off of low-priced surplus American ships and increasing regulatory control under United States registration encouraged owners to reflag in Panama, so creating the 'flag of convenience'. Between the wars, the ships fulfilled an important role, not only as tramp ships, but many were also adapted for a variety of liner trades. Most of the ships survived the Depression and traded throughout the 1930s. However, they suffered heavy losses in the Second World War.

By 1941 Britain was losing ships three times faster than the combined efforts of British and Commonwealth shipyards to replace them. The need for different ship types in the Second World War and optimisation of existing successful ship designs as a basis for standard ship construction led to a number of different designs. These, in turn, were followed by the highly successful Liberty ships that were constructed in great numbers in America. The British emergency shipbuilding programme essentially replaced the ordinary ad hoc scheme of commercial ship construction.

The ships with *Empire* names were those built in Britain. The Empire ships were principally tramp ships and tankers. Most of the standard ship designs evolved from successful vessels built before the war. However, they also included 15-knot cargo liners and refrigerated vessels, and there were also coastal cargo ships and coastal tankers, as well as a range of harbour craft and tugs. Other specific types were the Bel-type heavy-lift ships; the *Empire Malta* class, small, dry-cargo tramp ships; the general-purpose dry-cargo Scandinavian type; the Ocean 'Three Twelves' standard-type tanker (12,000dwt cargo capacity, 12 knots and an oil fuel consumption of 12 tons per day); the Norwegian-type tanker; and the Standard Fast-type tanker. Smaller tankers comprised the *Empire Pym* type and the Intermediate type as well as a range of coastal tankers, some designed for service in the Far East. Dry-cargo coasters com-

The construction sequence of the Liberty ship at Richmond, California, from a set of postcards issued by the Permanente Metals Corporation:
(i) Fourth day on the slipway following keel-laying.
(ii) Eighth day on the slipway.
(iii) Twelfth day on the slipway.
(iv) Sixteenth day on the slipway.
(v) Twentieth day on the slipway prior to launching four days later.

prised mainly the *Tudor Queen* type and the Empire F type. The programme placed increasing emphasis on tanker construction as the war progressed.

There were several reasons why Britain could not develop a single standard-type ship, as was the case with the American emergency shipbuilding programme. Peter Elphick explains in the introduction to his seminal book *Liberty: the ships that won the war*:

The general pattern [in America] was for these standard ships, as they were called, to be built on a one yard, one design basis, usually a design that the yard was used to building. But there was never a hard and fast rule and from time to time a yard could be ordered to switch to another type of ship. The overall guidelines were speed of construction and the cargo carrying capacity of the ship. There were several reasons why this tendency towards shipbuilding conformity was never carried through to its logical conclusion in Britain, ie that of getting all yards to build to only two or three basic designs, which as the Americans were to show, would have brought about the many benefits that accrue to near-complete standardisation. The reasons why this course was not

pursued in Britain include the historical layout of yards, the varying sizes of slipway, and the valuable and not to be lightly discarded local shipyard expertise that had been built up over many years.

It needs also to be remembered that most British shipyards that were not involved with Admiralty work had been unable to retool during the Depression. They were consequently ill-equipped for significant changes in construction methods. Nor could the British yards easily pursue a course of prefabrication, as both craneage and space were at a premium; there was insufficient factory area to construct large units, and inadequate lifting capacity when these units were taken to the ship that was being assembled. The rivet squads comprised skilled men and there was little experience of electric welding, so any move towards this instead of riveting was not an easy one to achieve, either. Peter Elphick again:

Perhaps the worst handicap of all to the industry in Britain, however, was the blackout, for to have worked the yards after dark under floodlights, especially during the long winter nights, would have been to invite the ministrations of the Luftwaffe, and German

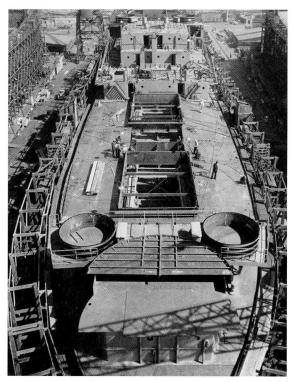

air attacks were quite bad enough without soliciting more.

Shipbuilding in America was in a very weak state in the 1930s. The American Merchant Marine was an ageing fleet, mostly built in and immediately after the Great War. America's shipbuilding capacity, therefore, was limited at the start of the Second World War. It had begun to rebuild its cargo ship fleet in the late 1930s, with the intention of building fifty powerful and fast C (cargo)-type ships and, in due course, T (tanker)-type ships per year. The first keel laid down in the new programme of rebuilding sponsored by the United States Maritime Commission took place in August 1938, but it was neither a C- nor a T-type ship. It was the transatlantic liner *America*, completed in 1940 for the United States Lines Company and converted for war use in 1941 as the troop ship *West Point*.

In order to satisfy wartime demand, the United States Maritime Commission was obliged to scale down the programme of building fast and well-constructed C1-, C2- and C3-type cargo ships (the suffix reflecting the length of the ship) and T2 tankers. It largely switched to simpler designs, the Liberty and, later, the Victory ships; it was also necessary to construct several new emergency shipyards and extend

The United States Lines Company's *American Shipper* (1946) was one of the last C2-type ships built under the auspices of the United States Maritime Commission. This later class of ship had a more streamlined profile than those built during the war. With a speed of 15½ knots and a deadweight capacity of 10,400 tons, they were valuable units in any commercial post-war fleet. (AUTHOR COLLECTION)

existing ones. Unskilled labour was recruited to work alongside existing skilled labour. Available skilled labour was also divided between the existing and new shipyards. One consequence was racial tension between the white workers imported to the Alabama shipyard and the black unskilled men who been recruited locally.

The precursor to the actual Liberty ship was the Ocean class, ordered from American yards by Britain in 1941. These were built to a standard tramp ship design originating from J L Thompson's shipyard at North Sands, Sunderland. The difficulties of mass production of the relatively sophisticated Ocean class led to the Liberty ship design, a design which came from the same source in Britain. The specifications stipulated tried and tested, old-fashioned, steam reciprocating engines. There was much debate before this was accepted by the Americans, but the engines could be readily constructed to a reasonable budget. The ships included the famous EC2-S-C1-type dry-cargo ship, the Z-ET1-S-C3 tankers and the EC2-S-AW1-type colliers. They were nearly all named after distinguished people who were no longer alive. Some 2,710 Liberty ships were built both at established yards and at new ones. Peter Elphick wrote:

> During the war by far the great majority of Liberty ships sailed under the Stars and Stripes, mostly as units of the American Merchant Marine, but some as ships of the United States Navy and Army. About 300 Liberty ships were handed over to other Allied nations under Lend-Lease arrangements

with the conditions that those that survived the war would then be handed back to the Americans. One hundred and eighty-seven of these were allocated to Britain (together with thirteen additional 'hybrids' of slightly shorter length). Forty-three were allocated to Russia and smaller numbers sailed under the Norwegian, French, Dutch, Greek, Belgian, and Chinese flags.

The incredible American shipbuilding programme, and the success of its standardised Liberty-type emergency standard ship, undoubtedly saved the Allies from losing the war. Dr Ronald Hope in his book *A new history of British shipping* noted that 'the Liberty played a large part in ensuring victory for the Allied forces'. Professor Sturmey in *British shipping and world competition* makes an interesting calculation that there were 11.9 million gross tons of British and Commonwealth shipping lost in the Second World War, plus a further 9.8 million gross tons of other Allied and neutral ship losses. He observes that the combined loss of 21.7 million gross tons was almost equalled by the total aggregate tonnage of the Liberty ships, which amounted to 19.4 million gross tons. His calculation is a reminder also of the appalling loss of life that destruction of such an immense amount of merchant shipping generated, many dying under awful circumstances concurrent with acts of immense bravery. Nevertheless, the Liberty ship was clearly the most important class of ship ever constructed, and almost of itself filled the wartime attrition gap.

Impressive broadside launch of the C1-B-type motor ship *American Packer* (1941) at the Western Pipe & Steel Company yard at San Francisco. She remained in the ownership of the United States Lines Company until 1945, when she was taken over by government; her registered owner then became the United States Department of Commerce. United States Lines bought the C2-type steamship *Titan* (1943) in 1948 and re-named her *American Packer*, so that two similar ships were both trading with the same name for the next twenty-two years. (WESTERN PIPE & STEEL COMPANY)

The Canadian Ocean and Park ships were built to the same North Sands shipyard design as the American-built Oceans. The Canadians used the title 'North Sands type', which was the same as the American Ocean-type dry-cargo ship. There was also the modified Canadian-type and Victory-type dry-cargo ship and the smaller Gray, Revised and Dominion types of dry-cargo ships. Tankers included the Dominion, North Sands and Victory types, and the smaller 3,600dwt cargo capacity type. There were also the B- and C-type coaster, and tugs built to a modified version of the tug *Warrior*. The 'Park' nomenclature denotes ships managed by the

Canadian government, owned by Park Steam-ships Company. A variety of other British de-signs were brought to Canadian yards, resulting in the construction of coasters, tankers and other specialised craft. The varied role of these ships and their contribution to the Allied war effort was equally important to the shipbuilding pro-grammes in both America and Britain.

The incredible rise and fall of the shipbuild-ing industries in both America and Canada in re-sponse to the emergency was a fabulous effort promoted by the respective governments. James Pritchard in his book *A bridge of ships: Canadian shipbuilding during the Second World War*, highlights the remarkably ephemeral nature of the wartime shipbuilding effort in Canada, a country which subsequently almost withdrew from the industry altogether:

The number of shipbuilding employees in full time employment in 1939 averaged just 3,500, but few actually built any ships. A year later the average annual number had grown to 9,707, which provides a more realistic base from which to measure the future growth of employment because we can be assured that most of these workers were building ships. Three years later when shipbuilding employment peaked in July 1943, approximately 85,000 workers were employed in the industry. This increase of 8.7 times compares quite favourably with the United States, where the increase was 8.9 times during the same period. Employment in Canadian shipyards subsequently declined owing to curtailment of war production programs and completion of defence projects that occurred during 1944, and numbers fell off rapidly afterward. By December 1945 they had dropped to just 22,000. The rapid expansion and equally swift contraction of the workforce reveal well the emergency nature of Canada's wartime shipbuilding programs.

The Victory ships were built to a higher specification than the Liberty ships, in order to satisfy a need for faster ships and to provide ships that would have a commercial value post-war. They all had names ending in *Victory*. There was much deliberation in the United States as to whether to continue the Liberty-ship programme, or proceed to the faster and better equipped Victory ship design. In the end sense prevailed, and the Victory ship became the natural successor to the Liberty ship. The Victory ships had steam turbine engines (the VC2-S-AP2 and AP3 types) and there was one experimental motor ship (the VC2-M-AP4 type). There was also the Attack Transport VC2-S-AP5 type and vessels completed to commercial specification after the war as the AP7 type.

The first Victory ship was delivered in February 1944. A later programme of Victory-type ocean tankers was also developed. Only a few of the Victory ships were lost in the war and they continued to be built after VJ Day, some adapted for commercial owners' requirements, although many contracts were cancelled. Postwar, many of the Victory ships were adapted for the commercial liner trades and they became familiar sights at ports around the world.

The C1, C2 and C3 class of dry-cargo ships and the T1, T2 and T3 tankers also continued to be built for the United States Maritime Commission throughout and immediately after the war. The C2 class evolved with time, so that post-war-built ships, such as, for example, *American Shipper*, bore little resemblance to the starker profile of the earlier ships. The dry-cargo ships were mostly equipped with turbine engines, but a few of the C1 and C2 ships had oil engines. For example, ten of the C1-B-type ships were motor ships; five were built at San Francisco and five at Seattle.

The German standard ships built in the Second World War were principally small dry-cargo tramp ships of the Hansa A class. Some fifty-two ships were delivered before the end of the war, while others remained on the stocks for considerable periods thereafter, before being bought by commercial companies and completed to their own specifications. The ships were not only constructed in German yards, but also in the shipyards of occupied countries. The Hansa A type was mainly of 3,200dwt cargo capacity and was equipped with the highly efficient, Lentz double-compound steam engine, which provided a speed of 10 knots. They were of similar design to the Hansa B-type 5,000dwt ships. There was also the C-type 9,000-ton ship, although only one of these was completed by the end of the war. Many of the ships were confiscated by the Allies after VE Day, with some of the A-type ships going to British owners, such as the United Baltic Corporation and General Steam Navigation Company, as well as to American owners.

Japan had built some standard ships for Britain in the Great War. However, Japan built standard design ships for her own account when she was an enemy of the Allies in the Second World War. These included 140 Type A, engines-aft, dry-cargo ships, although some were completed as tankers. The original hull design stemmed largely from the First World War British Type N National fabricated standard ship, two of which Japan still owned and operated, and these were used as models for construction. Japan had several other large standard types, but these mainly comprised only a few ships in each class. The differences between types were the angular hulls of the Great War design with bluff bows and transom sterns, and the more sophisticated hull designs of some of the other types. Many of the ships had their machinery aft, and all were steamships. The ships that survived the war eventually became a major part of the post-war Japanese merchant navy, but all built in 1943 and 1944 had to be substantially rebuilt to bring them into class. Most of the engines-aft ships were converted into three-island, engines-amidships vessels. Japan also built fast tankers and a vast coaster fleet.

During the war each ship was sold to a Japanese commercial company. The revenue so accumulated was put into a reserve fund to

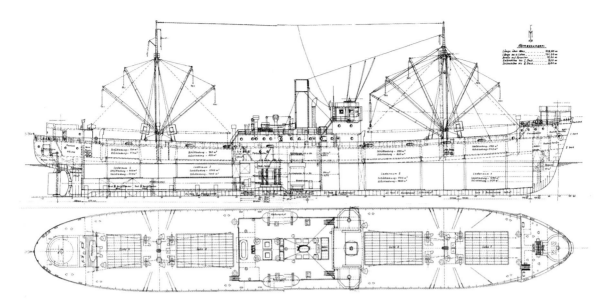

Das 5000 tonnen-Einheitsschiff, the 5,000-ton deadweight capacity Hansa-class cargo ship intended as a wartime class of fifty-five vessels, although only five had been commissioned by 7 May 1945. Bremer Vulkan at Bremen were the champions of this Hansa class and had the drawings completed and preparatory prefabrication work done ready for the first keel to be laid at their yard on 10 March 1943. This ship was completed as *Haussa* on 30 December 1943, having taken nine and a half months to build and fit out. (AUTHOR COLLECTION)

compensate owners for losses as an alternative to a conventional war insurance scheme. Payment for damage or losses was only to be made after winning the war. In the event, of course, compensation was not paid to owners, who were left to their own ends to get back to strength.

In complete contrast to the Japanese programme, in which numbers were more important than any degree of quality, was the Australian programme. Although small in numbers, the thirteen ships of the A-class, or River-class, dry-cargo tramps were all finished to a high standard and saw many years of commercial service after the war. Subsequent classes built to the order of the Australian Shipping Board were successively smaller in size.

Most of the Allied standard ships became surplus after the war. They were either laid up or scrapped, if at all structurally damaged, or sold for commercial use under a closed bidding process. The Canadian-built ships and the Liberty ships tended to be used in the tramping trades; although several were adapted for use in

the cargo liner trades, many later found their way into the Greek, Panamanian and Liberian registries. The faster Victory ships were ideally suited to cargo liner duties. The standard ships enabled companies to get their fleets up and running so that they formed an important component of the world's merchant shipping fleets throughout the 1950s and 1960s.

An important experience gained with the Allied emergency shipbuilding programmes was the application of the new technology of hull prefabrication, with the widespread use of electric welding. The use of arc welding has an advantage, in that the weight of steel in a welded ship is substantially less than in a riveted ship of similar dimensions and displacement. This is because of the absence of overlaps of plates and the connecting flanges of the steel sections. Initially, the labour cost was comparable to riveting, but with the gaining of experience it was quickly realised that prefabrication of large parts of a vessel's structure was ideally suited to mass production of standard-type ships. With experience of the new process and the increasing application of production line technology, building times were reduced and output per worker was considerably increased.

Properly welded joints are as strong, or even stronger, than the surrounding parent steel. In spite of these advantages, welding was slow to supplant riveting before the Second World War, mainly due to the capital cost in plant and equipment needed for the changeover, money being short in the depressed 1930s. However, in the post-war years automatic welding machines, that guaranteed weld quality, and the use of alloys for special applications, added greater speed to the shipbuilding process. As with every development, welded joints came with disadvantages such as unsightly distortion of the plating, and local fractures due to poor welding practice by individual operatives. Lax application and control of weld procedures could result in stress fractures, so that stories of welded ships breaking apart in heavy seas or of welded joints failing under mild stress, whilst infrequent, were not unknown in the early years of all-welded ship construction.

Prefabricated shipbuilding is now normal practice, but it is worth remembering that the first experience of its success in terms of speed and economy derived from the emergency wartime shipbuilding programmes. Analysis of weld failures, particularly of the Liberty ships, allowed considerable technical advancement with the spacing of frames and plate floors and welding procedures. Other advances included advanced steam turbine machinery and efficient oil-fired boilers.

In the 1960s the Austin & Pickersgill yard at Sunderland recognised a need for a cheap and functional ship to replace the ageing Liberty ships that were still in operation in the tramp trades, working under many different flags around the world. It developed its SD14 (Shelter Deck 14,000dwt cargo capacity) standard-type ship and later its 16,000- and 18,000dwt ships. The German yards also produced a similar ship, the GLR type, as did the Japanese. The Japanese ships took nine months from keel-laying to launch, whereas the first SD14-type ship took just fourteen weeks. Successful to an extent, the new standard types arrived just as the conventional tramp ship was being superseded by the bulk carrier and the cargo liner by the container ship. The commercial prospect of many of the new ships was, therefore, limited.

The scale of achievement of the various wartime standard shipbuilding programmes of the twentieth century is unparalleled. The huge success of all of these classes of ships within their own design roles demonstrates their highly significant contribution to the two world wars. This contribution was primarily to the benefit of the Allies but also, in a smaller way, to their enemies. The post-war commercial service that many of the ships subsequently gave demonstrates how advanced their designs actually were. Indeed, a small number of preserved but operational Liberty and Victory ships still exist, by way of a deserved tribute to these classes of standard ship.

2 FIT FOR PURPOSE: THE DESIGN CRITERIA

The main design criterion for the wartime standard ships was highest deadweight for lowest cost, coupled with ease of maintenance and efficiency of operation. The constraints were materials availability and the skills-base of the shipyard workforce. Most emergency standard-type ships had no tumblehome, little sheer and many had no camber to the main deck. They were mostly equipped with simple compound or triple-expansion steam engines which gave enough power to maintain station in convoy. There was no point in building lots of 'ugly ducklings' that would be too slow for the convoys and had to voyage independently as 'sitting ducks'.

In the Great War the British-built single-deck A-type and the spar-decked B-type tramp steamer standard ships had a design speed of 11 knots. Their pedigree stemmed from *Kalimba*, built by D & W Henderson at Partick in 1914, but the final drawings came from the design office at Harland & Wolff in Belfast. The ships were of the three-island type, but had a low profile and a single mast stepped just before the funnel. They were 400ft long and had a moulded breadth of 52ft. They were of 5,030 tons gross (grt) and just over 8,000dwt. The single masts were telescopic and could be let down to the height of the funnel to reduce the elevation of the profile; the derrick posts were hinged so they could be lowered out of sight to deck level. Measures such as these, coupled with dazzle camouflage, adopted in 1917, all helped confuse the enemy sightings through U-boat periscopes.

Later in the Great War, the A- and B-type hulls were adapted for the bulk tanker designs known as 'AO' and 'BO' oilers. The C type was a scaled-down version of the A and tramp ship types, being just 331ft long and built specifically to carry dense mineral cargoes. The D type evolved to suit yards with short slipways and were only 235ft in length, whereas the two-decked E types were suitable for larger slipways, although smaller than the 400ft-long A and B types.

The F class are of considerable interest, as the ships comprised shelter-deck vessels with two decks and, more importantly, they were conceived in the design loft of J L Thompson at Sunderland. The ships, twelve in number, were built by Thompson and at the Doxford yard as well, also located at Sunderland. The ships were 411½ft in length and 55½ft in breadth; they were of 6,440grt and had a deadweight capacity of 10,795 tons. They were equipped with a conventional triple-expansion steam engine (27in, 45in and 75in diameter cylinders and a stroke of 54in) which gave them an impressive service speed of 12 knots. Thompson was a name linked with excellence and innovation. It was this yard at North Sands that, unknowingly at the time in the late 1930s, carried out the preliminary designs and builds that would lead eventually to the Liberty ship design. There was also an F1 type that the Northumberland Shipbuilding Company was commissioned to build, the Admiralty being impressed with the economy of operation of this type of ship. The F1 type had an operational speed of 12 knots, coupled with sophisticated cargo-handling gear.

The G-type meat carriers built towards the end of the Great War were based on existing designs from Workman Clark at Belfast. Nearly all of this class of ship was completed after the Armistice and they became variations on a theme, depending on the requirements of whichever shipowner had purchased each partially completed ship.

The smaller H-type ship was a design product of S P Austin & Sons at Sunderland. They were commissioned as a single-deck steamer

An A- or B-type standard dry-cargo ship of the Great War following her launch into the River Wear, in full dazzle livery, preparatory to fitting out. The record for building and completing this type of ship was twenty-four weeks from keel-laying to delivery. (AUTHOR COLLECTION)

The N-type fabricated ship *War Music* (1918) was a product of Harland & Wolff at Belfast and managed by the Clyde Shipping Company during the war. This photo of her taken after the war as *King Bleddyn* in King Line colours clearly shows the cut-off transom stern of this class of ship, designed to avoid bent and twisted frames to simplify construction. Postwar modification included replacing the single pole mast with conventional fore- and mainmasts and lengthening the funnel. (AUTHOR COLLECTION)

with a deadweight capacity of 3,850 tons. Again, many were completed after the war to commercial requirements, some as two-deck ships for the Mediterranean fruit trade. They were of the well-deck type and the hull was divided into seven compartments: fore and aft peaks and four holds, two either side of the machinery compartment. There was a double bottom the entire length of the ship. They had two masts and an impressive array of cargo-handling gear, with each derrick served by its own steam winch. There were five derricks fore and aft, four were capable of lifting 5 tons and the fifth 9 tons, while additionally there were also two 2-ton derricks on the bridge deck.

Perhaps the most advanced standard ships of the Great War, the so called N type, or National 'fabricated ship', had additional constraints added to the design specification. For example, there were to be as few as possible bent frames incorporated in the hull and the ships were to include features that would confuse the enemy. The basic design was the work of Mr Graham at the Admiralty and Sir Tennyson D'Eyncourt, Director of Naval Construction. Their ideas were transcribed into working drawings by staff employed at Harland & Wolff in Belfast. As much as possible the ships were to be 'fabricated'. Bernard Leek wrote in *Sea Breezes*, July 1988:

The term 'fabricated' described a method of construction which utilised pre-formed and fully prepared material produced by bridge builders and other heavy steel fabricators and delivered by rail to a yard which, thereafter, would mainly be involved in simple assembly. Fully assembled standard engines were to be similarly delivered for direct installation and the limiting size of components, sections and plates was dictated by railway gauge and clearance …

The standard N type was conceived to take full advantage of the labour and material saving measures of multi-punching of plates, lack of bending and the shaping and alignment to template rather than having to depend upon mould loft and scrieve board. In this way, it was supposed, greater use could be made of unskilled labour and faster, less demanding building methods without conflicting with the requirements of the classification societies.

A number of special features were incorporated in the design of the so-called 'fabricated ships' in order to confuse the enemy. The hull had a pronounced sheer fore and aft, but was devoid of any sheer in the middle. This gave the ships a gondola-like profile, which, with a transom

stern, made it unclear from abeam which was the bow and which the stern of the ship. In order to disguise the course being steered, the mast and stern lights were offset to port and the derrick posts staggered. The overall profile was kept as low as possible, with a short, stumpy funnel and a single telescopic mast. The derrick posts could be lowered to deck level at sea, but in practice this was found to be too labour-demanding to actually happen on leaving most ports. The ships also had a 4.5in breech-loading naval gun mounted at the stern with an arc of fire up to 45 degrees forward of the beam.

They were otherwise built to a conventional three-island design. The hull was subdivided into five holds and 'tween decks with a cargo ballast/deep tank abaft the engine room. Cargo-handling gear was basically twelve 5-ton derricks with eleven steam winches. The triple-expansion steam engine (27in, 44in and 73in diameter cylinders) was supplied by single-ended Scotch boilers. The machinery was reliable and easy to maintain, and with 3,200 indicated horsepower it easily satisfied the design service speed of 11½ knots. However, coal consumption was excessive at 50 tons per day, the bunkers accommodating 913 tons of coal, with a reserve of 1,624 tons.

The basic dimensions of the N type were a hull of 428ft length overall, moulded breadth 55½ft, and a loaded draught of 28¼ft. They had a gross tonnage of 6,546, and 10,420dwt capacity. Steam and electric heating was provided in the accommodation areas. The crew quarters were aft below the poop – a safer place to be than amidships when U-boats were around. The

engineers' cabins were amidships and the officers had cabins in the bridge structure below a small wheelhouse and chartroom. The ships were acclaimed a great success, despite their odd appearance, and many of them served the commercial world between the wars, only to become vulnerable to attack at the start of the Second World War, when most were lost to torpedoes fired by U-boats.

Numerous ships were built in America during the Great War to British order, and later to American government account, as tramp ships. The ships were built to a variety of designs around a central theme. The original designs were based on successful existing ships, one group, for example, was based on *Hallbjorg*, an 8,800dwt steamer that had been built for Peder Kleppe of Bergen by J F Duthie & Company at Seattle in 1918. There were also the smaller Scandinavian-type ships, ordered by Norwegian owners from American and Canadian yards on the Great Lakes. In both cases, the actual design stemmed from the capability and experience of each shipyard, coupled with constraints laid down by the client, including agents acting on behalf of the British government when America was still neutral, or the American government thereafter. The tramp ships were powered such that they could maintain the required 11 knots for convoy duty, were equipped with simple, easily maintained machinery, and the minimum of cargo-handling equipment.

In the Second World War the story of standardisation of design quickly reverts to the yard of Joseph L Thompson at North Sands, Sunderland. Cyril Thompson, not yet thirty years old,

Hall Brothers' *Embassage* (1935), although not realised at the time of her launch, was the first prototype of the Liberty ship; her hull was designed by Cyril Thompson and her machinery was from Harry Hunter's North Eastern Marine Engineering Company. *Embassage* was sunk by torpedo in August 1941 in a position 100 miles west of Ireland. She was in convoy on passage from Leith to Sierra Leone in ballast to load iron ore. There were only three survivors. (AUTHOR COLLECTION)

Court Line's *Dorington Court* (1939) was the second prototype of the Liberty ship, being slightly longer and beamier than *Embassage* and equipped with a more powerful engine that gave her a service speed of 11 knots, an extra knot over her predecessor. She was sunk by torpedo in the Indian Ocean in November 1941. (AUTHOR COLLECTION)

led the design office in experiments to refine the hull form of the traditional tramp ship, such that it would offer optimum use of power applied to drive the ship, ie to design an energy-efficient hull shape. He used the experimental test tank at the National Physics Laboratory at Teddington to analyse his designs until he had what he considered to be the optimum shape. It had a sloping but full bow, and at the stern the lines were finer than normal in the shape of a 'V' rather than the traditional 'U'. Drag was reduced by developing a semi-balanced rudder. In addition, a new and efficient triple-expansion steam engine of the 'Reheat' type was commissioned from the North Eastern Marine Engineering Company, based also at Sunderland. The overall cost estimate for the new ship was just under the magic £100,000, then believed to be the price that tramp shipowners would be willing to pay for a new ship.

The new design attracted Hall Brothers of Newcastle, who ordered the first of the class at a contract price of £95,000. This was the 9,100dwt steamer *Embassage*, which was launched from Thompson's yard at the end of July 1935. On her maiden voyage she carried a full cargo of coal at 10 knots, using between 16 and 17 tons of coal to fire the boilers each day. This was a remarkably low daily coal consumption, the average for a similar-sized tramp steamer being nearer 25 tons per day. Seven further sister ships were built to the exact same design. The shipping community was excited by the efficiency of the class, and their economy of operation also caught the attention of My Lords Commissioners of the Admiralty.

Cyril Thompson was still not happy that the design was the optimum and the next refinement was *Dorington Court*, built for the London-based Court Line. She was a little longer and broader than *Embassage* and her sisters. *Dorington*

Court was powered by another, more powerful, new engine from the North Eastern Marine Engineering Company of the Reheat type, providing a service speed of 11 knots. In this design of engine, the HP (high pressure) and IP (intermediate pressure) cylinders were operated by cam-driven poppet valves, and for ease of valve maintenance, the HP cylinder was located at the forward end and the LP (low pressure) cylinder at the aft end of the engine, with the IP cylinder between them. In the Reheat engine, the superheated boiler steam on the way to the HP cylinder was used to reheat the steam exhausted from the HP cylinder via a tubular heater. This allowed the steam temperature to be higher than otherwise would be possible in a reciprocating steam engine, because the small quantity of heat taken from the superheated boiler steam was added to the input steam to the IP cylinder, and was not lost. The engine had been trialled in *Lowther Castle*, built in 1937 for J Chambers & Company. Three sister ships were then built – and again the Admiralty took note.

Cyril Thompson was asked to lead a delegation to the United States in the autumn of 1940 to try to procure sixty newly built tramp ships. He took with him the drawings of his latest design, *Empire Wave*, then on the stocks at Sunderland. Thompson was accompanied by Harry Hunter from the North Eastern Marine Engineering Company. On arrival in New York they met Admiral Land, head of the United States Maritime Commission. The commission had been set up in 1936 to upgrade the American merchant marine with the subsequent development of the C- and T-type standard ships. It agreed that Thompson could place orders with the Todd Corporation. But it was meetings with Henry J Kaiser, working in conjunction with Todd at Seattle, and with Bath Iron Works at Maine at which Thompson's shipbuilding challenge was finally accepted. With Admiral Land's consent, an agreement was reached with Todd–Kaiser to build sixty ships to the design of *Empire Wave* at Seattle, and at two other yards yet to be constructed under the agreement.

The plans of *Empire Wave* were modified in New York under Cyril Thompson's direction. The most important modification was the use of an all-welded hull, there being few rivet gangs in America, where welding was now commonplace, although the frames were to be riveted to the shell plating. The triple-expansion steam engine was no longer favoured by American ship-

yards, but it was agreed that it be used in the new ships to be built for the British. Again, drawings were modified for its construction under licence by selected engineering contractors. The engines were big and heavy, weighing 118 tons, but they were easy to manufacture and maintain.

In mid-November Cyril Thompson was instructed by the Admiralty to abandon plans to replicate *Empire Wave* and to concentrate on the slightly larger *Empire Liberty*, plans for which had just been released by J L Thompson to the Admiralty. The attraction of *Empire Liberty* over

The 140-ton, vertical triple-expansion compound steam engine was chosen for the Liberty ships. Eighteen different engineering companies built the engine. Parts manufactured by one company were interchangeable with those made by another, and the design allowed ready access to all moving components. The engine was 21ft long and 19ft tall, and was designed to operate at 76rpm to sustain a sea speed of about 11 knots. (AUTHOR COLLECTION)

Empire Wave was its slightly larger deadweight capacity, an important factor at any time, but particularly so in wartime.

Thus the third and last Thompson design favoured by the Admiralty was that incorporated into *Empire Liberty*. She was laid down at Sunderland in January 1941 and launched on 23 August 1941. She was smaller in beam than *Dorington Court* at 57ft and was 441ft long. The gross tonnage was 7,157 and deadweight capacity 10,170 tons. The first ship of the same design, *Ocean Vanguard*, had already been launched from the newly constructed shipyard of the Todd-California Shipbuilding Corporation at Richmond and others were under construction at the new Todd-Bath Iron Shipbuilding Corporation yard at Maine. Agreement was reached also with the Canadian government for ships to be built to the same design in Canada, where

The Liberty ship *Melville E Stone* (1943) was launched on 24 July 1943, just twenty-two days after her keel was laid. She is seen here being fitted out at the Kaiser yard in Richmond, and she was delivered on 4 August 1943. The ship was managed by Norton Lilly & Company, New York. On 11 November, just three months after she was commissioned, *Melville E Stone* was torpedoed and sunk about a hundred miles northwest of Cristobal. Twelve of the forty-two crew complement lost their lives, as did two of the twenty-three armed guard complement, and one of the twenty-three passengers who were on board. (The Permanente Metals Corporation)

they were known as the North Sands type after the Sunderland shipyard from which the plans had originated. The Canadian ships were named with the prefix *Fort*.

The Canadian ships were to be all riveted as was *Empire Liberty*. The Canadian ships later adopted a nomenclature with suffix *Park*; thus was born the Ocean standard ships and the Forts and Parks. Canada overcame its shortage of steel by using its abundant resources of wood. The Forts were fitted with wooden topmasts, wooden decks and wooden derricks.

America continued to build its sophisticated C1, C2 and C3 standard cargo liners, 400ft, 450ft and over 450ft length respectively, and T2 tankers. Admiral Land's team slowly realised that these ships could not be produced at a pace that would suit the emergency. It was eventually put to Congress that the Ocean-type hull be adopted with some modifications as the 'five-year ship', ie the Cs and T2s were twenty-five-year design-life ships, the five-year ship, later known as the Liberty ship, was for the emergency only. Peter Elphick describes the modifications:

The American versions were to be oil-burning instead of coal-burning and be fitted with water tube boilers instead of the Scotch type. There were other internal differences too, coal bunkers, for example, not being needed, but fuel oil tanks were. From the external aspect the most obvious differ-

The Russian Liberty ship *Kolkhoznik* (1943) was built as *Charles Wilkes* and transferred to Russia under the Lend-Lease scheme. She is seen in civilian guise showing off the lines of the Liberty ship to best advantage – not really that ugly a duckling at all. She served under the Russian flag until 1977, when she was broken up. (Author collection)

One of the prefabrication sheds at the Kaiser Permanente Shipyards at Richmond with an array of gun platforms in the foreground and the superstructure of two Liberty ships behind. (THE PERMANENTE METALS CORPORATION)

ence was that the Americans placed all the accommodation in one block amidships above the engine room, in contrast to the British (and Canadian) ships that had the original 'two island' layout, with bridge and machinery spaces being separated by No. 3 hold.

The ships were to be welded, but that statement needs some elaboration. Although Liberty ships are talked about as 'all-welded', there were in fact three variations, each of the shipyards involved keeping to one of them. Some were literally all-welded with not a rivet anywhere in the structure. In others rivets were used to connect the ship's side frames to the shell plating (the system used with the Oceans), all the other connections being welded. The third variation, used only at the Bethlehem-Fairfield yard at Baltimore, was one where all shell plate seams were riveted.

And so the Liberty ship was born, daughter of Cyril Thompson, and engines which were, indeed, the son of Harry Hunter; a British design modified to suit American shipyard mass-production techniques. Other improvements in

the Liberty ship over the Oceans were described by Stanley Bonnett in an article in *Sea Breezes*, December 1963:

> Other lesser alterations were: reinforced square hatch corners, no wooden decks, bulwarks instead of chain rails at the side of the weather deck, and ratproofing. There were after steering stations, 12 inch searchlights, more refrigerated storage space, running water in the officer's cabins, a new form of hawse-pipe ...

Stanley Bonnett continues by contrasting the Liberty ship to the high standards that the United States Maritime Commission aspired to:

> The high standards which the USMC had been trying to introduce were cut and cut, 35 times. The gyrocompass was one. Radio direction finders went, and radio equipment and searchlights in motor life-boats. Crew found their heads had cement instead of tiles. No fire detection system was installed. Seamen did not like this austerity. The ships worried the unions. They terrified the Germans.

The development of fabrication was led by Henry Kaiser. He saw that a continuous chain of properly ordered supplies and assembled sub-units would allow large prefabricated units to be constructed at the shipyard, which could later be assembled on the slipway once the keel had been laid.

The Victory ships that followed were designed for a minimum service speed of 15 knots and equipped to a higher standard. The hull lines were quite different from the Liberty, due to greater length and breadth and the ship's faster design speed. The bow was semi-'V'-shaped, the midships section was parallel and the after section was 'U'-shaped, with a cruiser-type stern. A long and high forecastle was built into the design to improve seaworthiness, but there was no sheer fore and aft. The three forward holds were fitted with 'tween decks, and much of the ancillary equipment was electrically powered rather than driven by steam. The biggest improvement of all was the survivability and stability of the ship itself, even with one compartment flooded. This contrasted with the Liberty ship, which was stiff and required permanent ballasting in the 'tween decks to raise her centre of gravity to make her more comfortable in bad weather.

The issue of hull fractures identified in some Liberty ships was overcome by allowing the hull of the Victory ships greater flexibility. This was achieved by spacing the frames 36in apart, whereas in the more rigid hull of the Liberty ships the frames were spaced just 30in apart. Subsequent operational experience proved this simple expedient to be successful, as hull fractures in the Victory ships were extremely rare.

A description of the standard Victory ship highlights some of the advantages they had over the Liberty type. The Victory ships were slightly over 455ft long and 62ft wide and, like the Liberty ships, had five cargo holds, three forward and two aft. The Victory ships had a deadweight capacity of 10,850 tons. They typically carried a crew of sixty-two plus twenty-eight naval personnel to operate defensive guns and communications equipment. They were different from the Liberty ships primarily in propulsion, the triple-expansion marine steam engine of the latter giving way to more modern, faster turbines. The AP1 Victory ship was powered by 5,500-horsepower (hp) steam-turbine machinery; the AP2 Victory by a 6,000hp steam-turbine unit; the AP3 by 8,500hp steam-turbine machinery; and the one AP4 by a diesel engine. The design service speed was 15 to 17 knots.

The Victory Ship had three masts, each with a mast-house. Cargo was discharged from the five hatchways by means of fourteen 5-ton derricks and two larger 50-ton and 30-ton derricks fitted on the mainmast and the mizzenmast respectively. The Victory ship had twelve electric motor-driven cargo winches, clustered in two groups of four around the mainmast and mizzenmast. They had an electrically driven, horizontal-shaft-type anchor windlass on the forecastle deck and an electric warping capstan on the after deck with its machinery below. There were four 24ft steel lifeboats stowed in gravity-type davits, two of the boats were motor-propelled, with a combined capacity of 124 persons. In addition, there were four twenty-person life rafts, mounted on skids fore and aft of the midships house, and two fifteen-person life floats, mounted aft on the deckhouse.

The captain's stateroom was on the boat deck, starboard side. The quarters for deck officers, engineers and radio operators were on the cabin and boat decks. The quarters for the crew

Beaverlodge (1943) was one of the 15-knot standard fast cargo liners equipped with two steam turbine engines and was completed as *Empire Regent*. She was one of six similar ships in the Canadian Pacific Steamships fleet when she was bought from the Shaw Savill Line in 1952. Four of the six were completed after the war to that company's own specification. (AUTHOR COLLECTION)

were on the main deck. The officers' mess and pantry were located at the after end of the deckhouse on the starboard side of the boat deck. The crew's mess and pantry were on the deck below the officers' mess. The galley was at the after end of the deckhouse on the main deck.

Each derrick kingpost also served as an exhaust vent trunk from the holds. Natural ventilation to below decks was supplied through four 36in cowl vents, two 24in cowl vents and two 18in cowl vents.

The main propulsion unit was housed amidships. In the AP2 type it was a cross-compound, double-reduction geared, impulse-reaction-type marine steam turbine unit rated at 6,000 shaft horsepower (shp). This drove a single screw at a speed of 100rpm via a shaft made of forged steel which was 16in in diameter. The propeller was made of manganese bronze, was four-bladed and right-hand screw. Steam was provided by two sectional-header, single-pass design water-tube boilers rated at 525lbs per square inch, with an operating pressure of 465lbs per square inch.

The bulk of the standard ships built in Britain during the Second World War, all with *Empire* names, were the PF-type tramp ship. The ships were 425ft long between perpendiculars and 56ft broad. The first type, the PF(B), had a split superstructure and the later PF(C) type had a single central island. The C type and the D type differed in having a full-sized poop, and both C and D ships had a transom stern. All the ships had a deadweight capacity of not less than 10,000 tons and a design convoy speed of 10 to 11 knots.

The remaining Second World War British-built standard-ship types were built to relatively small numbers. Almost without exception they were modelled on a successful pre-war design. A standard fast cargo ship was designed by the Furness Shipbuilding Company at Haverton Hill, to a remit provided to them by the Ministry of War Transport during 1942. Twelve were built, and others were constructed under licence for individual shipping companies, while those still on the stocks at the end of the war were completed to private account for whichever company bought them. Canadian Pacific Steamships of London, for example, was able to buy two of these, which became *Beaverburn* and *Beaverford*, and four incomplete ships, which they modified to their own needs before commissioning them in 1946. The subsequent purchase of *Beaverlodge* in 1952 brought the group of standard fast cargo ships owned by Canadian Pacific up to a total of seven ships. They were 16-knot ships with a deadweight capacity of 12,000 tons and fitted with an array of cargo-handling gear. The decks were clear of obstructions and were reinforced so that heavy military deck cargo could be carried. They were two-deck ships, except in No. 1 hold, where there was a third deck placed below the 'tween deck. As built, they were fitted with spartan accommodation for thirty-six passengers.

A small number of fast refrigerated motor ships were also built. The largest of them, of 12,300dwt, were modelled on a pre-war design commissioned from Harland & Wolff by the Shaw, Savill and Albion Line in 1934. The main difference from the original design was that the superstructure was one deck lower aft of the bridge in the wartime-built ships. Other ships were built to slightly different moulds, with a designed deadweight capacity nearer to 10,000 tons.

There was considerable demand in the Second World War for heavy-lift ships. The prototype came from the Danish fleet of Belships Skibs A/S, founded by Captain Christen Smith

There was considerable demand in the Second World War for heavy-lift ships. The prototype heavy-lift ships for those built in the Second World War were the sisters *Belpareil* (1926) and *Beljeanne* (1926), the latter pictured here. Both were built by Armstrong Whitworth for Belships Skibs A/S, founded in Oslo in 1921 by Captain Christen Smith. They were 11-knot motor ships, and cargo-handling gear included three 120-ton derricks. (AMBROSE GREENWAY COLLECTION)

in Oslo in 1921. His first heavy-lift ship, *Beldis*, was completed by Armstrong Whitworth in 1924. She had a single 40-ton derrick forward and a 100-ton derrick aft designed for loading and unloading railway locomotives. Two years later, Armstrong completed the engines aft and bridge forward of midships *Belpareil* and *Beljeanne*, which were 11-knot motor ships with three 120-ton derricks. In 1931 *Belpareil* carried three hopper barges, each 152ft long and weighing 185 tons, so providing the Bel ships with an enviable reputation. Richard Sayer wrote in *Sea Breezes*, February 1950:

> In 1940 the company's representatives in England were asked to advise the Ministry of Transport on the building of a class of heavy-lift ships for the British flag. Ten vessels were planned and built, of 10,000 deadweight tons, mounting three 120 ton derricks. Similar in design to the *Belpareil*, they were fitted with more modern methods of propulsion to give a speed of 14–16 knots.

The first two Bel-type heavy-lift ships were 12-knot ships equipped with oil engines. The other ships had steam turbine engines and could maintain 15 knots on a slightly smaller deadweight capacity of 9,750 tons.

There were three types of tankers built in the Second World War. The first was the 'Three-Twelves' tankers modelled on a pre-war Shell tanker design and was confusingly officially called the Ocean standard-type tanker. Some of these had a dummy funnel amidships and uptakes aft on the poop to confuse the enemy. A larger 14,500dwt cargo capacity tanker, the Norwegian type, was modelled on *Sandanger* and *Eidanger*, which were completed in 1938 for Westfal-Larsen & Company in Oslo by Sir J Laing & Sons at Sunderland. A small number of fast tankers were built towards the end of the war to a joint design put together by the Furness Shipbuilding Company at Sunderland and the Furness company at Haverton Hill.

A class of coastal cargo ships was based on Queenship's *Tudor Queen*, completed for them by the Burntisland Shipbuilding Company in Fife in 1941. These were stocky little ships of 1,360dwt, propelled either by a triple-expansion steam engine, or by an oil engine. The smaller Empire F ships were of hard chine design, in order to avoid shaped frames in their construction, and looked like floating boxes. They were dry-cargo ships, based on the earlier CHANT or Channel tankers that were built for support work after the D-Day landings.

There was also a coastal shelter-deck type of ship, for use in the Far East, built both in the UK and Canada. These were propelled by a triple-expansion steam engine, although those that were completed after the war for commercial owners had oil engines fitted. There was also the larger B-type coaster, modelled on the pre-war engines-aft, bridge-amidships, Coast Lines motor ships, although equipped with a triple-expansion steam engine.

The *Empire Cadet*-type of coastal tanker was a clone of Bulk Oil Steamship Company's *Pass of Balmaha*. She was completed for them in 1934 by the Blythswood Shipbuilding Company at Scotstoun. She was sunk in October 1941, while carrying petrol, by a torpedo fired from a U-boat. Her successor was the sister ship, *Empire Damsel*, which became the new *Pass of Balmaha* when she was purchased by Bulk Oil in 1947.

The other important clones were the colliers built to the design of the Gas, Light and Coke Company's *Icemaid*, which had been com-

FT Everard's coastal tanker *Alchemyst* (1945), seen at Plymouth in April 1968. She was built as *Empire Orkney*, a coastal tanker of the *Empire Cadet* type, based on the design of *Pass of Balmaha* (1933). (NICK ROBINS)

pleted in 1936 by S P Austin & Son at Sunderland. These ships had a deadweight capacity of 2,900 tons and were primarily used in the North Sea coastal convoys bringing coal to the Thames. A few colliers were also built to a larger 4,100dwt capacity.

There were numerous tugs that were given *Empire* names. These included the handsome deep-sea type, the smaller coastwise type and the estuary type of harbour tug. All of them were based on a variety of successful prototypes al-

ready in service. The smaller, prefabricated TID-type tugs were not given *Empire* names, but rather numerals after the prefix 'TID' (Tug Invasion Duty). They were primarily used as lighter handling tugs. Knight and Gaston wrote in their book *Tugs and Towing*:

> The tugs were built to a standard design developed to be assembled from prefabricated sections. The hull was a welded structure, designed to eliminate the need for complicated plate rolling or shaping. Each tug was made up of eight sections. Every section had to be capable of being transported by road. This enabled the various sections to be constructed by companies capable of welded steel fabrication work but not necessarily any shipbuilding experience. In the initial stages the design work and final assembly was carried out by a single company, the Humberside shipbuilder Richard Dunstan Ltd. The orders for this little tug were progressively increased from a dozen to the 182 vessels of the type that were actually completed.

There was also a large group of VIC-type Scottish 'puffers' built for the Ministry of War Transport, 'VIC' standing for Victualling Inshore Craft.

The importance of appropriate design, fitness for purpose, ease of construction and maintenance cannot be understated. As it was, the designs were, without doubt, optimised for the role the ships were intended for, especially the 'five-year' Liberty ship and the longer-term tenure of the Victory ship. Even the modest little TID tugs were perfect for their intended purpose, and easy to build and maintain. The adoption of successful commercial prototypes as the basis of emergency standards saved on design and drawing preparation time, and were, in any case, tried and tested. But the true heroes of the design story are undoubtedly Cyril Thompson and his North Sands-built prototype ships of the American and Canadian standard ships, and his engineering counterpart Harry Hunter. It was their work at Sunderland, and their emergency designs, that led to the Liberty ship, which allowed the Allies finally to beat the attrition of the U-boat and its dreaded torpedo.

Mr R Cyril Thompson: The Planning of Liberty Ships
From *The Times*, Saturday, 11 March 1967

Mr. R. Cyril Thompson, C.B.E., deputy chairman of the Doxford and Sunderland Shipbuilding and Engineering Company, died suddenly at his home at East Boldon, Sunderland, on Thursday. He was 59.

He was a former president of the Shipbuilding Employers Federation and of the North-East Coast Institution of Engineers and Shipbuilders, of which he was a Fellow. Until last year, when the Doxford and Sunderland Shipbuilding and Engineering Company was reorganised, he was also chairman and joint managing director of Joseph L. Thompson and Sons, the shipbuilders, and a member of the company.

In September, 1940, as joint managing director of Thompson's he went to the United States at the request of the Admiralty as head of a mission with the object of ordering 60 ships from American shipbuilders. He took plans and designs of his own company's standard ship and it was from these that the first Liberty Ships were built. On the way back to Britain he was torpedoed in mid-Atlantic in rough weather and spent nine hours at the oars of a lifeboat before he and others were rescued by another ship. Later he joined the Royal Air Force as an AC2 and became a Flight Engineer, serving in Liberator bombers in Italy. In June 1941, he was made CBE.

He became chairman of Joseph Thompson & Sons on the death of his father, Sir R. Norman Thompson in 1951, and in the years that followed was responsible for a modernisation scheme costing well over a million pounds.

He was a director of many companies both within and outside the Doxford group. He was chairman of the Wear Shipbuilders Association from 1950 to 1952, a member of the Council of the Institution of Naval Architects, and served on the technical committee of Lloyd's Register of Shipping. He was educated at Marlborough, and Pembroke College, Cambridge.

3 SHIPS BUILT IN BRITAIN DURING THE GREAT WAR

At the start of the Great War, the British merchant navy accounted for 52 per cent of the world's shipping. However, merchant seamen the world over had new and dangerous hazards to contend with, not least the magnetic mine and the submarine. Ship losses were high until the eventual introduction of the convoy system. Frustration ran high among the shipowners who were unable to replace ships lost to the enemy, as Sir William Forwood recounts in his book *Reminiscences of a Liverpool shipowner.*

> Between the 24th February and the 13th October 1916, she [Germany] sank 183 ships and 144 fishing vessels, the highest number in one week being 35; and the following year, between February 26th and November 18th (in nine months) the German submarine sank 661 vessels over 1,600 tons, 247 under 1,600 tons, and 161 fishing craft; the number of ships being unsuccessfully attacked being 550. During the War upwards of 8,000 British sailors lost their lives through submarine attacks.

An element of bitterness enters Forwood's reminiscences as he describes the frustration of the shipowner as the war continues:

> Probably the cause which has been most detrimental and disastrous to shipping was the obstinacy of the Admiralty in declining to recognise the urgent necessity for building more merchant ships. They filled all the yards with Admiralty work, and when the violence of the submarine attack aroused the nation to a sense of the danger before it, and the cry went up throughout the land 'Ships, ships and still more ships', the Government then – and only then – responded, and decided that further merchant ships must be built at once. There was great delay in giving effect to their decision to build 'standard' ships – plans had to be submitted and obtain the approval of so many officials

that many months elapsed before the keel of the first standard ship was laid, and in the meanwhile the losses through the submarine attack continued.

The situation had become so bad that in the summer of 1916 the shipowners took it upon themselves to develop the capacity to build their own ships. Lord Inchcape, in charge of P&O and British India, Sir James Caird of the Scottish Shire Line, and others invested £600,000 in a site at Chepstow on the River Wye at which they proposed to build their own ships. A further £300,000 of shares quickly sold to the shipowning community, including Federal and Furness. The site was adjacent to Edward Finch & Company's shipyard and this was incorporated into what became the Standard Shipbuilding & Engineering Company. Here it was planned to lay out eight large slipways; Lord Inchcape predicted that by autumn 1917 several 10,000dwt ships of standard design would be in frame. It was an attractive location, being close to the Welsh coal fields and the steel works in South Wales, and it was also out of range of attack by Zeppelin.

As it was, government intervention was to upset the plans. Norman Friedman, in his book *Fighting the Great War at sea: strategy, tactic and technology*, described how government addressed some of the developing issues:

> By December 1916 the British recognised that the shipping situation was becoming grim, so they appointed a Shipping Controller with wide powers. He began an emergency shipbuilding programme. The situation was exacerbated by the drastic decline in British merchant shipbuilding during the war, as the Admiralty took over most British shipbuilding capacity. That applied not only to new construction but also to repairs of existing ships. For example, it designed important combatants such as sloops to merchant standards specifically to make use of the large pre-war merchant

shipbuilding base. In April 1916 the Board of Trade, which was responsible for shipping, stated that naval orders had effectively crowded out merchant ship construction …

The new merchant shipbuilding programme emphasised foreign orders because they did not compete with the Admiralty for British shipbuilding capacity. After several false starts, the solution adopted in May 1917 was to make the Admiralty responsible for both naval and merchant shipbuilding, so that a single agency could decide how to balance the two. Trade-offs were not obvious, for example, was it better to build destroyers or other craft intended to neutralise the U-boats, or to build more merchant ships to replace those the U-boats sank? Some decisions had already been made. In March 1917 three of the four new *Hood* class battle-cruisers were suspended specifically to free capacity for merchant shipbuilding. In May Prime Minister Lloyd George took the unprecedented step of making a civilian, Sir Eric Geddes, Controller (in effect Third Sea Lord), with the new responsibility.

On 31 January 1917 Kaiser Wilhelm announced the reintroduction of unrestricted submarine warfare. All ships, British or neutral, became targets when entering the so called 'danger zone'. It was a calculated threat, made with the knowledge that it might intimidate America to join forces against Germany. The campaign was initially successful, so that between April and June one in four merchant ships leaving Britain never came home. Bernard Leek wrote in *Sea Breezes*, July 1988:

> The bitter experience of the Kaiser's action finally prompted a positive and effective series of responses. Prime Minister Lloyd George persuaded the Sea Lords to adopt the convoy system as a matter of policy; the decision was taken to arm vessels throughout the merchant fleet; and merchant shipbuilding was belatedly placed upon a war footing. Skilled men were recalled from the colours and formed into Shipyard Brigades and a series of Standard Merchant Ship designs were adopted for construction by both traditional builders and upon purpose built slips in newly created yards in the Bristol Channel.

The latter included the newly laid-out yard at Chepstow, which was taken under the Defence of the Realm Act, without compensation for its owners until after the war had ended. Two other yards were to be laid out, one at Beachley and the other at Portbury. These were the so-called National Shipyards, which had a planned function to build, among others, the innovative 'fabricated ship'. Government and military bureaucracy then took over and not one ship was completed before the end of the war. Ultimately, six N-type (N for National) fabricated ships were completed, the first in April 1920, as well as three H-type ships: a poor record for £6.4 million of government investment. The existing shipyards fared much better than the new yards at Chepstow and on the Bristol Channel, largely because of their pool of skilled labour and existing slipways and facilities. These yards were easily able to turn to conventional ship construction to standard designs, as well as production of the N-type fabricated ship.

In July 1917 Geddes announced an ambitious shipbuilding programme of 3.1 million tons, some six times that achieved in 1916. At the same time, attention was turned to standard-type ships, but the type and even size of ships was argued between Geddes and the Admiralty. The Admiralty wanted small 2,000-ton ships which would be small targets for submarines to attack and losses would occur only in small units. This argument was, of course, flawed, as it overlooked that the total cost of building five 2,000-ton ships would greatly exceed that of building one 10,000-ton vessel; the same argument also applied to manning the vessels. Friedman again:

> The first standardised ships were ordered some time early in 1917 … British policy was … to accept a trial or design speed of 11.5 knots (sea speed of about 10 knots) for most ships but to seek a sea speed of about 13.5 knots if ships of 450 feet length could be quickly and economically built …

In the event, the fast 13-knot refrigerated ships of the G class were, with one exception, completed after the war was over.

A variety of different ship lengths were adopted to suit the various sizes of slipways that were available. The most prolific British-built standard ship types were those of the 400ft-long A and B classes. The first of the single deck A-type, 8,175dwt, dry-cargo ships to be commis-

sioned was *War Shamrock*. She was ordered early in the year and completed in August 1917 by Harland & Wolff at Belfast. The first of the two-deck, B-type ships to go to sea was *War Cobra*, also a product of Harland & Wolff and delivered in December 1917. Harland & Wolff produced two more A-type ships in 1917 and five more B-type ships the following year, plus two more completed in 1920. Its Govan yard built five A-type ships and one B type, the latter completed after the war for the British & African Steam Navigation Company. D & W Henderson had built *Kalimba* in 1914 for the Glasgow Navigation Company, a ship which was adopted as the prototype for the A-type ship; Harland & Wolff acquired a controlling interest in the yard at Partick in 1916. Henderson built six A-type and three B-type steamers under Harland's control between 1917 and 1920.

War Crocus had the shortest career of all the A-type ships. She was allocated to the West Hartlepool Steam Navigation Company as managers and was taken over by them at 3.30pm on 17 July 1918 at the yard of William Gray & Company at West Hartlepool. That evening she left port on her maiden voyage, only to be torpedoed and sunk off Flamborough Head a few hours later. Her crew was all safely landed at Grimsby later the next day.

A very distinctive shipyard that built one A- and two B-type steamers between 1919 and 1921 was Lloyd Royal Belge (Great Britain) and situated at Whiteinch on the Clyde. The steamers were commissioned into the Belgian merchant navy, Britain having granted permission for Belgium to reopen and re-equip the defunct yard of Jordanvale Shipbuilding (John Reid & Company) in 1916. Belgium, of course, had been occupied by Germany since 1914. The yard built a

War Aconite (1918) was built by William Doxford & Son at Sunderland and was an A-type standard ship. She was sold to Hain Steamship Company in 1919 and renamed *Trefusis*; she was sunk by torpedo in the Second World War in March 1943 on passage from Pepel, in Sierra Leone, to London with a cargo of iron ore. (AUTHOR COLLECTION)

The first of the A and B types to be completed was the A-type *War Shamrock* (1917), seen fitting out at Harland & Wolff's yard at Belfast in the early summer of 1917. She was bought by Lloyd Royal Belge SA in 1919 and renamed *Belgier*, later renamed *Kabinda* by an associate company. She was wrecked in the Second Word War near the West Goodwin buoy in December 1939, having fulfilled a valuable twenty years in commercial service. (AUTHOR COLLECTION)

War Kestrel (1918) seen as Donaldson Lines' *Argalia*, was built as a B-type ship by Craig, Taylor & Company at Stockton-on-Tees. She is of interest for a number of reasons: note the lattice derricks designed to use less steel than tubular ones, and note also the use of timber rather than steel plate beneath the lifeboat. In 1929 she was resold to the Japanese, who renamed her *Myadono Maru*, under which name she was sunk by a torpedo fired by an American submarine in June 1943. (AUTHOR COLLECTION)

total of twenty-five ships (not all to standard designs) before it was taken over by Barclay, Curle & Company in 1924.

The prototype for the smaller C-type ships was *War Manor*, completed in May 1918 by the Tyne Iron Shipbuilding Company at Willington Quay. She was placed under the management of Steel, Young & Company. The outline design was based on similar ships that had previously been built at the yard, notably *Gardenia*, completed for the Stag Line in 1914. They were single-deck ships intended for heavy bulk mineral cargoes and grain, their smaller dimensions than the A and B type allowing their construction on shorter slipways.

The newly constructed yard of the Burntisland Shipbuilding Company in Fife had four slipways. By 1919 it had three C-type modified steamers under construction. The first, *War Bosnia*, was completed in August 1919, her construction being delayed by materials shortages. Unlike the National Shipyards, Burntisland went on to become a successful venture of the Ayre family, specialising in tramp steamers and colliers until the 1960s.

The smaller D-type colliers were designed by S P Austin and based again on earlier experience with collier construction at the yard.

Production of the four different-length types of standard dry-cargo ship (types A, B, C and D) for each year from 1917 onwards is shown in Figure 1. In 1917 just ten A and B types and two C-type ships were completed. Production peaked in 1918, with the largest number of ships being completed in the period between May and October. The momentum slowly declined through 1919, again with the majority of ships being completed from May

Launched as the Type A steamship *War Alyssum* (1919) at Caird & Company's yard at Greenock, she was completed as *Bathurst* for the British and African Steam Navigation Company to that owner's final specification. She was sold to Greek owners in 1933 and survived in service until she was wrecked in 1951. (AMBROSE GREENWAY COLLECTION)

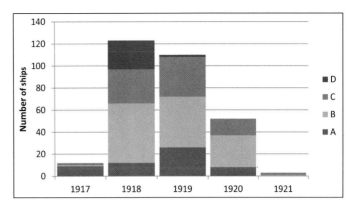

Figure 1. The production of the four different length types of standard dry-cargo ship (Types A, B, C and D) for each year from 1917 onwards. Production peaked as intended in 1918, with the largest number of ships being completed in the period from May through to October.

onwards. These seasonal peaks reflect both the weather and, more specifically, longer productive summer daylight hours.

The later classes of dry-cargo ships were built with a view to attracting purchases from commercial operators post-war; Friedman wrote:

> The main survivability feature was an added bulkhead, enabling a ship to survive the flooding of any single hold or compartment or two compartments amidships. In effect they were adding as many bulkheads as possible without losing cargo capacity. It proved impossible, however, to design a 450 feet ship to a two compartment standard. The bulkheads were also strengthened. Shaft tunnels were blocked at the engine room so that a ship could not flood through them and suction pipes to compartments were given non-return valves, so that the sea could not simply run up through them. In the 450 feet standard ship engine and boiler rooms were separated by a cross-bunker.

The ships of the class were just over 400ft long and only twelve of them were completed. Two Sunderland yards built the ships, William Doxford & Sons giving their ships cruiser sterns and J L Thompson, counter sterns. The ships had a deadweight capacity of 10,795 tons and a sea speed of 12 knots. However, a further thirteen F1-type ships were built by the Northumberland Shipbuilding Company to the same design as *Carlow Castle*, delivered by them to the Union-Castle Line in February 1917. These ships were slightly smaller than the F type, but were also good for 12 knots. The first of the class, *War Castle*, was delivered in October 1918 and the last, *War Bailey*, in June 1920. Only two of the F-type ships survived after the Second World War, and they were subsequently scrapped in the late 1950s, demonstrating the robust design and construction of the ships.

The crown of the Great War standard-ship classes was undoubtedly the larger and faster 450ft-long, G-type refrigerated ships. Twenty-two ships of this class were built, all but one of them completed after the Armistice. Many were sold to commercial operators before completion so that they could be fitted out to their new owner's specifications. They were all magnificent ships, some being twin-screw and others single-

War Beryl (1918) was a standard F-type ship from the Great War that was sold to the Canadian Pacific Steamship Company in 1919 and renamed *Bothwell*. Canadian Pacific sold her in 1934 and she eventually ended up under the German flag in 1939. The Germans used her as an auxiliary minesweeper in the Second World War and later as a target ship. She was sunk by torpedo in 1942 off the North Cape. (AUTHOR COLLECTION)

Barclay Curle at Whiteinch built two G-class, fast single-screw refrigerated ships in 1920; one of them, *Highland Warrior* (1920), was completed to the specification of the Nelson Steam Navigation Company. In 1933 she was transferred to parent Royal Mail Lines and renamed *Nogoya*; three years later she was sold to London owners for tramp duties and renamed *Marlene*. At this stage, the turbine unit that had provided a speed of 13 knots was replaced by a triple-expansion engine that enabled a more economical service speed of just over 10 knots. She was sunk by torpedo in April 1941. (AUTHOR COLLECTION)

screw ships, but all capable of a service speed of 13 knots. The lead ship in the class was *War Argus*, completed by Workman, Clark & Company in December 1918, and sold the following year to the White Star Line to become *Gallic*. Other vessels of the class were bought by British companies such as British India, although their four ships, *Nuddea*, *Nardana*, *Nowshera* and *Nerbudda*, were not completed as refrigerated ships, and by Houlder Brothers, New Zealand Shipping Company, Union Cold Storage Company, Royal Mail Steam Packet Company and Nelson Line. One ship, *Salland*, was completed for Dutch owners Koninklijke Hollandsche Lloyd.

Impressive ships though the G class were, the most innovative class was the fabricated, or N-type, ships. The first N type, *War Climax*, was launched into the Tyne from Swan Hunter & Wigham Richardson's yard on 8 August 1918; her keel had been laid on 25 February. On completion, she sailed on 7 October from Newcastle to take up duty for the Government Shipping Controller. The class was distinctive and easy to recognise as the ships had a shapeless hull and a triangular transom, both features designed for ease of construction. The last of the fabricated ships was laid down at Caird & Company's shipyard at Greenock in 1920, but work was later

suspended on the incomplete hull. The ship was eventually completed as *Grantleyhall* for the West Hartlepool Steam Navigation Company and commissioned only in August 1927. She was sold after just four years of service to Russia and given the name *Angarstroi*. The National Shipyards, however, were singularly unproductive, delivering only six N-type ships between April 1920 and August 1921, long after the war was over.

Like the fast G-type ships, many of the N-type vessels were bought by British liner companies. Although their service speed was only 11 knots, they were attractive units to operate in the 1920s when fuel consumption was not an issue. The British & African Steam Navigation Company, later Elder Dempster, for example, bought a group of eight of the Harland & Wolff-built ships and gave them the distinctive *New* nomenclature: *New Brunswick*, *New Columbia*, *New Mexico* and so on, with the final purchase being given the strangely more parochial name *New Brighton*. *New Brooklyn* was only sold in 1954 and *New Texas* in 1955, demonstrating the suitability of the ships for their owner's West African trade. The Glen Line also bought four N-type ships, although two were sold on quite quickly.

War Courage (1918) was one of the first of the N-type prefabricated ships characterised by straight frames and transom stern. They were designed to allow labour from other industries to construct the hulls. *War Courage* was built at Armstrong Whitworth's yard at Newcastle with labour from nearby steel fabricators. She was bought by Glen Line in 1919 and renamed *Glensanda*, and sold again in 1929 to Essex Line as their *Essex Lance* and sunk by torpedo in October 1943 in the Second World War. (AUTHOR COLLECTION)

As the war progressed, the demand for oil far outstripped delivery. This was compounded by the ever-present risk of submarine attack to the existing tanker fleets, and a number of A- and B-class hulls were completed as tankers, the so-called AO and BO types. Because of this need for oil, new bulk tankers became an increasingly important part of the emergency building programme, and in 1917 the

War Melody (1918) was built by Harland & Wolff and was also one of the first N-type ships to be completed. After the war she was bought by the Dollar Steamship Company of London and renamed *Grace Dollar*, later re-registered at Vancouver and then Hong Kong. She was acquired by the Japanese in 1924, and became first *Hakatatsu Maru* and then *Ryuun Maru* under the ownership of Tatsuuma Kissen KK and Ryuun Kisen KK, respectively. She was one of two N-class ships owned in Japan at the start of the Second World War. (AUTHOR COLLECTION)

construction of tankers was given priority over dry-cargo shipbuilding. A total of forty-two tanker conversions were planned with cylindrical tanks built into the single-deck A-type ships, while the two-deck B-type ships were less easy to convert and incorporated tanks in the main holds and in the 'tween decks. In addition, forty Z types were ordered – similar in dimensions and profile to the A- and B-type ships save that the expansion tank, or trunk, was placed centrally over the main deck. This gave the ships a raised outline with a harbour deck, akin to the pre-war Doxford Turret ships. The design of the tanks incorporated a single bottom hull.

Only six Z-type tankers were completed by the end of the war, and six additional contracts were then cancelled. Many of the ships became fleet oilers thereafter, and a tranche of them was sold to the Anglo-Saxon Petroleum Company in the early 1920s for commercial use. Others went mostly to British owners, including the British Molasses Company, later the Athel Line,

while one became an oiler for the Imperial Japanese Navy. Most survived into the Second World War when they became vulnerable to submarine attack.

The wartime shortage of steel led inevitably towards a small programme of shipbuilding with concrete. The technology was not new, the Norwegians having already constructed a 200grt, concrete-hulled coaster by 1917, while the French and Italians were busy using concrete for lighters. Interested parties in concrete hull construction formed the Ferro-Concrete Ship Construction Company at Barrow in conjunction with the Vickers group of companies. Although the new company planned to build a series of 1,100dwt dry-cargo ships, it was instead instructed to build lighters as part of the government's concrete shipbuilding programme announced at the end of 1917. This programme comprised both lighters and tugs, as the traditional tug building slipways were now largely taken up by Admiralty work. Orders for the concrete vessels came too late in the day and

only one barge was delivered before the Armistice. Where work was advanced, it was decided to fulfil the contracts, but wherever it was cheaper to scrap the order, then work was stopped. Two partially complete concrete lighters lay on the banks of the River Ribble at the former yard of Hughes & Stirling for many years, a monument to the concrete shipbuilding programme that took place in the Great War. Eventually, fifty-two lighters and twelve tugs were delivered.

Building work was carried out either at existing yards that were adapted for the work, or at new yards. The first vessel built at each yard took the most time, as timberwork for shuttering had to be procured and constructed, whereas each subsequent build used the same shuttering. The Board of Trade insisted that each lighter be registered and as such they had a steel plate bolted appropriately to the hull carrying the load line. Each lighter had two bulkheads, providing three separate cargo compartments. It was hoped that unskilled labour could be employed on construction and that costs would be cheaper than steel construction. In the event neither intention was fulfilled, as supervision of the unskilled workers required additional skilled workers to be employed. Total costs of a like-for-like concrete lighter was some 62 per cent

higher than its steel counterpart. All the concrete lighters and tugs were given names beginning *Crete-*.

The concrete tugs were powerful sea-going vessels with a triple-expansion steam engine placed aft of midships. They were heavier than their steel equivalent, and tended to remain stable in adverse conditions, even when the tow was girted. Special bolts and fixings were emplaced into the concrete during construction of the hull. These were used to fix the girders ready for the engine and boilers to be attached, and for attaching fenders and other equipment. Each tug required a crew of twelve, and there was a small dining saloon on the lower deck. None of the tugs survived the Depression, most being sold for recovery of engines and steel frames in the mid-1920s and early 1930s. One, *Creterope*, sank at her moorings in Hull docks in February 1920 and was later raised and broken up. The lighters, for the most part, also had short lives, many being hulked or used as breakwaters during the 1920s. The British concrete shipbuilding programme did save a commitment of about 70,000 tons of steel and, as such, could be deemed a success.

Conventional coasters and coastal colliers were also built to a variety of designs ranging from 400–3,000dwt. Many hulls were still building at the Armistice. Three of the larger type

The coastal steamer *Western Coast* (1919) was laid down to the order of the Ministry of Transport, but was completed to Coast Lines' specification. Note the lattice derricks alongside conventional pole derricks. Sister ship *British Coast* (1919) was launched as *War Shannon* but completed also to Coast Lines' requirements. (AUTHOR COLLECTION)

vessels building at H & C Grayson's yard at Garston were purchased by MacAndrews & Sons and completed as *Cervantes*, *Colon* and *Ciscar*, and used on their services to the Mediterranean. Two more, building at Swan Hunter & Wigham Richardson's yard at Wallsend, were completed as *British Coast* and *Western Coast* for Coast Lines Limited.

A few ships were also ordered by the British Shipping Controller from yards in South Asia. Nine B-type vessels and one C type were built by the Hong Kong & Whampoa Dock Company and the Taikoo Dockyard in Hong Kong, and three more C-type ships were delivered by the Shanghai Docks & Engineering Company in China. Twenty ships were also bought from Japanese shipbuilders through agents for the government, including the Federal Steam Navigation Company and Furness Withy. These comprised four different standard designs, including the Japanese T class (see Chapter 13) and the shelter-deck version of the T class. The shipbuilding industry in Japan was a new innovation for a proud nation that had hitherto looked inwards, shunning all contact with overseas traders. This was also the beginning of a modern and innovative outlook on the industry that would eventually allow Japan to overshadow the traditional shipbuilding nations of Europe.

The concerns and frustrations shown by the shipowners in the early stages of the war continued to be voiced throughout 1917. Shipowners remained disparaging about the government shipbuilding policy as reported in the *Glasgow Herald* on 28 December 1917:

> From the shipowners' point of view, there are several reasons for apprehension in the present shipbuilding policy of the country. One is inherent in the principle of standardisation. On that principle handy cargo steamers will be, it is hoped, turned out very rapidly, but they will not be specialised vessels, and so will not be suitable for specialised services after the war is over. They will be tramps pure and simple, of the most ordinary kind, in all probability incapable of competing effectively on definite routes with vessels built either before or after the war for trade on these routes. The majority of them may be fast enough, seeing that a fair speed is necessary for avoiding sub-marines, but internally they will be suitable only for bulk or general cargoes. But as a standardised programme was considered necessary for war purposes, and is now a part of the national policy, standard ships will have to be accepted as a part of the British post-war merchant service …

Of the National Shipyards and the proposed N-class fabricated ships, the article is even more downbeat:

> As to the simplification of the design, this is being carried so far that the term 'scientific shipbuilding' will almost be a misnomer if it is associated with the National Shipyards. The vessels built will be the plainest of plain structures, in shape they will dispense almost wholly with the bending of frames and plates, they will be composed of a remarkably small number of sections, and all the frames, plates, angles and bars will be manufactured to size at specified steel works, and 'assembled' at the yards by 'unskilled' labour (composed largely of prisoners of war), working under the direction of leading hands and foremen drawn from private establishments and the national dockyards. What effect will all this have on future progress in shipbuilding is a very difficult question, but the 'improvement' can hardly be called of a 'scientific character'.

Eventually, the fears were allayed by government amid cries of 'too little too late'. Although it took two years before the Emergency Shipbuilding Programme was put into action in Britain, the tonnage that was eventually produced enabled the country to sustain its supply lines in order to feed its people and victual its forces, at home and overseas. Many ships ordered by government from British shipyards during the war were not delivered until after the Armistice and thus did not contribute to the war effort. They did, however, enable Britain to get back on its feet again during the immediate post-war years, although post-war boom was soon followed by a serious decline in trading conditions. Despite all this, the A types and B types, and even the N types, found favour both in the tramp trades and the liner trades, and were the backbone of Britain's international maritime trade throughout the interwar years.

4 THE AMERICAN AND CANADIAN GREAT WAR 'BRIDGE OF SHIPS'

Neither the United States nor Canada had any significant merchant shipbuilding capability at the start of the Great War. What they did have was targeted at the coastal and Great Lakes trades rather than at deep-sea shipping. This was to change dramatically during the war, with the United States becoming the leading shipbuilding nation by 1918, both in terms of technology and output.

With the appointment of the British Shipping Controller in December 1916, orders were placed in the United States for a variety of ship types built to agreed standard designs. These orders were principally with west-coast shipyards that were best placed to develop new slipways for the size of ships required. A number of new yards were also planned or were already under construction to satisfy this new demand. Demand was increased by Scandinavian owners, who would normally place orders with British shipyards, but were now crowded out by the war effort. They turned to yards on the eastern seaboard and Great Lakes to build the so-called 3,500dwt Frederikstad-type ship. By March 1917 Britain alone had orders for an aggregate 700,000 tons of shipping placed with yards in the United States, almost all ordered at the behest of the Cunard Steamship Company. As America was at that time a neutral state, the orders were placed on behalf of the Shipping Controller by a variety of agents, Cunard being the main one, while other shipowners such as Lamport & Holt and Furness Withy were also contracted to act on behalf of the British government.

Each shipyard had its own version of the 'standard design'. On the west coast, the Union Iron Works at San Francisco built 440ft-long single-deck and shelter-deck ships of 11,800dwt, and a smaller version of 10,000 tons which was 410ft long. Both were equipped with single-screw turbine machinery and had a sea speed of 11 knots. Slightly smaller versions came from west-coast yards at Oakland, California, while others were built at Seattle and Portland, Oregon. The smallest of all, a 380ft long version,

came from the Todd Drydock & Construction Corporation at Tacoma, Washington, and was equipped with a triple-expansion steam engine. For the most part the ships had two holds forward and two aft, with a fifth hold splitting the midships superstructure between the bridge and the funnel. Each hold was served by two derricks mounted either on the mainmast or foremast, while Nos 3 and 4 holds were served by derricks mounted on twin king/derrick posts. Smaller versions had just two holds forward and a single large hold aft. The officers and engineers were accommodated amidships, and the crew, as tradition had it, were berthed in the poop.

The ships ordered from yards on the western seaboard were much more varied in size, though of similar basic design, to those building on the east coast. The largest from the east coast were the 12,500dwt capacity ships, with a length of 450ft, built by the Pennsylvania Shipbuilding Corporation. There were also 10,000dwt ships ordered from both the Bethlehem Steel Corporation at Sparrows Point in Maryland and the Sun Shipbuilding Company in Pennsylvania. Smaller units included 8,800dwt and 8,500dwt ships of 400ft and 390ft length respectively, and an even smaller 7,500dwt version from the Bethlehem Steel Corporation. Smaller ships were built to suit smaller slipways in New York State and Baltimore with even smaller 4,350dwt, 4,000dwt and 3,500dwt vessels ordered from yards at Wilmington, Staten Island, and Tampa in Florida. Numerous ships of less than 3,500dwt were also on order with American yards in the Great Lakes.

In addition, Cunard ordered two wooden-hulled ships from the National Shipbuilding Company in Texas. They had a deadweight capacity of 4,850 tons, a length of 305ft and a breadth of 48ft. They were powered by a steam reciprocating engine placed three-quarters aft and had water-tube boilers. They were built to a robust design with the hull built up of three diagonal strappings of 9in by 1¼in dense southern yellow pine, placed at right angles to each

War Penguin (1917) undergoing completion at Cleveland, Ohio. She was ordered by Cunard and was one of the many ships requisitioned by the United States and completed as *Lakeport*. She was one of thirty-five Laker Type A ships and was in commission in the United States Navy as USS *Lakeport* between January 1918 and July 1919. She was sold to Lloyd Royal Belge SA in 1920 and renamed *Danubier*. She ended her days under the Japanese flag as *Kosin Maru* and was wrecked off Nagasaki in a storm during December 1945. (US NAVAL HISTORICAL CENTER)

other. There was an additional 4¾in of planking on the outside. Completed in 1918, neither lasted more than a year. One was gutted by fire at Oran, having just arrived from Nantes with a cargo of grain, and the other sprang a leak and sank in mid-Atlantic. Despite these mishaps, a number of wooden ships to a similar design were built by the same company in Texas for the United States Shipping Board as the 'Daugherty-type' steamer, or emergency Design 1056.

Britain was satisfied with its order book and looked forward to commissioning its new American-built ships. As it happened, events were to upset this idyll. America declared war on Germany on 6 April 1917. The natural desire of America to isolate itself from the European war was understandable and Democrat President Woodrow Wilson wanted America to remain at peace. However, America had already become the 'arsenal of democracy', and its flagging economy was revived as Wall Street raised giant financial loans for the Allies to pay for numerous orders for ships and a whole range of military equipment. Many held the view that it was better to prosper on these terms, rather than push the nation's young men into the conflict. Neutral rights were important to the country and its people. However, the unrestricted offensive by U-boats on Allied and neutral shipping now extended to the waters around Britain and several hundred miles west into the Atlantic Ocean. The sinking of the Cunard liner *Lusita-* *nia* off Ireland in May 1915 with the loss of 1,198 lives, including American adults and children, led to outrage in America. It was this unrelenting German U-boat offensive that finally led America to war.

On 17 April, less than two weeks after it formally joined forces with the Allies, America created the Emergency Fleet Corporation. The new corporation was to work alongside the United States Shipping Board, established in 1916, to encourage the building of larger and faster ships in order to strengthen the United States merchant fleet in peace and war. The board declared that it could not fulfil its task, as all shipbuilding capacity was taken up either by the United States Navy, or by the merchant shipbuilding programme now established for Britain and elsewhere. The obvious decision was made to requisition all the new ships being built which were over 2,500dwt, and as a consequence on 3 August 1917 some four hundred partially completed vessels became US government-owned. But all was not well, as Roger Chickering and Stig Förster wrote in their book *Great War, total war*:

A shortage of shipping space and America's inability to provide the necessary tonnage gave further evidence of the country's unpreparedness for war. Ample shipping space was essential for transporting material and troops to France, where a German offensive threatened in the spring of 1918. Although the German submarine menace had diminished after the British had adopted the convoy system, the U-boat war had caused severe losses and left the Allies in a critical situation. Accordingly, the rapid enlargement of the American merchant marine was an urgent issue. Together with the newly founded Emergency Fleet Corporation (EFC), the US Shipping Board was the government agency responsible for this undertaking. Bureaucratic infighting of the manager of the EFC, General George Goethals, and the Shipping Board's pro-German Chairman, William Denman, delayed decision making. [President] Wilson fired both men in July 1917 and appointed Edward N Hurley to direct the two agencies. In May 1918, however, Wilson selected Charles Schwab of the Bethlehem Steel Corporation to be president of the EFC. Schwab moved the operation of the EFC from Washington to Philadelphia, the center of the American shipbuilding industry, and he instituted numerous measures to expand production. These bore fruit in the second half of 1918. In 1914 only 10 per cent of America's foreign commerce had been carried in American ships. By the end of the war America's commercial fleet was nearly half the size of the British merchant marine. Nonetheless, German sabotage, initial mismanagement, and labor disputes delayed the shipbuilding campaign, so a large part of the American troops and supplies were transported to Europe on British and neutral ships.

So what did all this mean for Britain? At the time of the requisition of partially completed and undelivered ships, Britain had on order nearly 950,000dwt of shipping. This ranged from units as small as 2,930 tons building on the Great Lakes to 12,500-ton steam turbine ships. The British Shipping Controller actually took delivery of just twelve ships comprising a total aggregate 73,200dwt: three at 10,000 tons, *War Knight*, *War Monarch* and *War Sword*; two 8,800-ton ships, *War Baron* and *War Viceroy*; *War Captain* of 3,500 tons; four 3,100-ton ships from the Great Lakes, *War Cross*, *War Patrol*, *War Major* and *War Tune*; and two 4,850-ton wooden-hulled dry-cargo ships, *War Mystery* and *War Marvel*. The United States government took the remaining 150 ships with an aggregate deadweight of 869,000 tons. In addition, it acquired

ships building for Scandinavian owners and elsewhere, as well as the American domestic building programme.

Not only did this cause huge headaches at the British Shipping Controller's offices in London, it also created massive problems for the US Emergency Fleet Corporation. Britain did not get its ships and America now had insurmountable management and staffing issues to face, not least manning the ships under the Stars and Stripes, both at sea and with appropriate numbers of shore-based support staff. It was not long before British officers and seamen who had lost their own ships to enemy action were dispatched to American shipyards to take delivery of American-registered ships for service under the management of the Emergency Fleet Corporation – a wholly unsatisfactory outcome in the eyes of the officers and men concerned. But, nevertheless, the ships were delivered and they did contribute to the Allied war effort, no matter which flag was flying at the stern.

The United States Shipping Board continued to sanction new building, with emphasis on 'fabrication' to standard designs until 1921. This was the so called 'bridge of ships' project, which enabled America to build up its merchant navy to a point where it could begin to satisfy its stated aim of transporting half the nation's commerce in its own ships. In all, 1,307 steel ships were built for the Emergency Fleet Corporation, and a further 389 were requisitioned. Many were slow, cumbersome, partly prefabricated tramp steamers that were ideal for the wartime conditions, but on the way to obsolescence in the post-war era. There was a small number of troop transports built under the programme, but the majority of orders for these vessels were cancelled after the war.

The largest yard in which fabricated ships were assembled was Hog Island. It was built specially for the construction of fabricated ships by the American International Shipbuilding Corporation, with the United States Shipping Board Emergency Fleet Corporation responsible for the yard and its operation. In addition to Hog Island in Philadelphia, which had an incredible fifty slipways for 7,500-ton vessels, the Submarine Boat Corporation, at Newark Bay, had twenty-eight slipways on which it built 5,000-ton ships, the Bristol yard had twelve for building 9,000-ton ships; the Federal Yards also twelve for 9,600-ton cargo ships, and the Southwestern Shipbuilding Company, six slipways for 8,800-ton ships.

Conehatta (1920) was a Hog Island Type A freighter (Emergency Fleet Corporation Design 1022). She was transferred from the United States government in 1929 to the American Scantic Line, trading to Scandinavia and the Baltic as the ownership suggests. She was wrecked later that same year near Holmsund, Sweden, carrying a cargo largely comprising wood pulp. (AUTHOR COLLECTION)

Two basic designs were fabricated at Hog Island: the Hog Island Standard Fabricated Type A freighter, which was designated Emergency Fleet Corporation Design 1022, and the Hog Island Standard Fabricated Type B passenger cargo troop ship which was Emergency Fleet Corporation Design 1024. Both designs focused on mass production, with hulls that were totally without sheer. The first ship was ready to be launched on 8 August 1918, but none of the ships were ready for use until after the Armistice. In all, 110 Type A and twelve Type B ships were completed (many more were ordered, but later cancelled); the last keel was laid on 8 December 1919.

The Hog Island Standard Fabricated Type A freighters were 401ft long, 54ft breadth and a depth of 24ft, and had a sea speed of 11 knots. They were mainly equipped with triple-expansion steam engines, although some had turbine machinery. The larger 436ft long by 58ft breadth Type B transports had steam turbine machinery and a service speed of 15 knots. They were equipped as troop transports, although some of them were converted for commercial use in the 1920s.

In addition, there were the smaller Design 1013 freighters, built on slipways of limited length. A total of fifty-five of this type of ship

Saccarappa (1918) was a Design 1022 Hog Islander, seen here post-war in the colours of the South Atlantic Steamship Company of Philadelphia, which acquired her from government in 1929. In 1941 she became *Alcoa Clipper* for the Alcoa Steamship Company of New York and was sold to Panamanian flag owners in 1947. Note the differences in the central island to those of *Conehatta*. (B & A FEILDEN)

were completed. The ships built on the Great Lakes to fit the confines of the Welland Canal were Design 1020. There were several other types, such as Design 1015, of which only a few ships were completed. Large army transports with four sets of Samson posts were designated Design 1029, and had two shafts and turbine units to provide a fast speed of 18 knots. A small 520ft-long version was designated Design 1095.

The Emergency Fleet Corporation set up the Department of Concrete Ship Construction in December 1917. Three small concrete-hulled motor ships had been completed that year in Norway, and Lloyd's Register recognised this type of construction in September 1917. Eight concrete tankers were built, as Colin Turner reported in *Sea Breezes*, December 1996:

> The four yards in which the tankers were built, were created on land which was

One of many small steamers built for the Emergency Fleet Corporation during and after the Great War was *Chautauqua* (1919). She was one of the Design 1020-type ships that would fit the Welland Canal and was built by McDougall-Company (which ceased shipbuilding in 1920). Her triple-expansion engine gave a service speed of 10 knots; note the steam exhaust pipe forward of the funnel. (B & A FEILDEN)

leased, cost free, to the Emergency Fleet Corporation by the localities in which they lay. Agency contracts were then let by the Corporation to four shipbuilding companies, in which each received a contract to construct a four way shipyard and eight ships of the 7,500 deadweight types. In the event, each yard was to produce only two tankers. The ships and their builders were as follows:

Fred T Ley & Company, Mobile, Alabama: *Selma* and *Latham*.

San Francisco Shipbuilding Company, Oakland, California: *Palo Alto* and *Peralta*.

Pacific Marine and Construction Company, San Diego, California: *Cuyamaca* and *San Pasqual*.

A Bentley & Sons Company, Jacksonville, Florida: *Moffitt* and *Dinsmore*.

The heavy weight of the hull reduced the actual deadweight capacity from 7,500 tons to just 6,400 tons. However, a lighter-weight aggregate incorporating expanded clay-grade material was used for the construction of a 3,000dwt dry-cargo ship, *Atlantus*. Three 3,500dwt dry-cargo ships were also built: *Cape Fear*, *Sapona* and *Polias*. As none of the ships were completed during the war, and all had an inherent deadweight ca-

West Galoc (1918) was one of a class of fifty-five cargo ships of the Emergency Fleet Corporation's Design 1013, also called the Robert Dollar type, or variations of that design. *West Galoc* was acquired by the United States Navy and placed in commission on 21 August 1918 as USS *West Galoc*. She was returned to the United States Shipping Board on 29 April 1919 and was broken up in Baltimore in 1930. (US NAVAL HISTORY AND HERITAGE COMMAND)

The Type 1015 cargo ship *Alloway* (1918) seen on trials on 5 July 1918. She was built by Moore Shipbuilding Company at Oakland, California. She was 402ft long and 53ft beam and her single steam turbine engine sustained a sea speed of 11 knots. (MOORE SHIPBUILDING COMPANY)

pacity problem, they were not economic to operate in peacetime.

The Emergency Fleet Corporation announced in October 1919 that 1,468 vessels had been built under its auspices, with a total aggregate deadweight of 8.1 million tons. These included a variety of wooden-hulled ships, as Fred Hopkins noted in a paper in *The Northern Mirror* in October 1994:

In 1917 Theodore E. Ferris, the chief naval architect, designed a 3,500 deadweight ton (dwt) wooden steamship that became the EFC's model. Soon others entered the field and eventually nine other designs – Hough, Allen, Dougherty, Grays Harbor, McClelland, Pacific American Fisheries, Peninsula, Seattle, and Supple and Ballin – were built. It should be noted that some Supples and Ballins, and all the McClellands, were composites with iron or steel frames and wood planking. The cost of a wooden cargo ship averaged $676,703. The contract value was $533,786 plus $74,981 for overhead and administration, $6,100 for a wireless, $7,500

for finishing lumber, $25,000 for the installation of machinery; and $29,336 for miscellaneous materials. Using the same cost factors, a steel cargo vessel's average cost was $1,287,547.

The magnitude of the United States Shipping Board in its wooden-hulled shipbuilding programme is demonstrated by an advertisement placed in the press on 1 May 1919 for the sale of over 350 partially completed wooden-hulled ships:

The building programme of the United States Shipping Board, Emergency Fleet Corporation, was so gigantic in proportion and so successful in accomplishment, that with the sudden ending of the war, it was found more keels had been laid and ships completed than will now be required by the Government. In consequence at the yards enumerated below wood ships in various stages of completion including those already launched are offered for sale, to the highest bidder. The Corporation is in a position to

One of the American Ferris-type, wooden-hulled ships built for the Emergency Fleet Corporation. They were 282ft length overall and offered a deadweight capacity of 3,588 tons. The triple-expansion steam engine sustained a speed of 10 knots. They were cumbersome ships and had steering problems. In all, 703 Ferris and other types of wooden ships were ordered in America, 214 orders cancelled and some 323 delivered, the balance scrapped. (AUTHOR COLLECTION)

supply ship fittings such as engines, boilers, winches, capstans, anchors, cables, etc. In the majority of cases materials for the completion of the vessels has been accumulated, and is in the yards, which permits of arrangements being made for their quick and accurate completion.

Wood ships have proved themselves, and offer excellent opportunities for conversion to sailing vessels, barges, coal or ore carriers, or for the installation of Diesel Engines if considered more desirable.

British orders, which were placed with Canadian shipbuilders through the Imperial Munitions Board (IMB), fared better than those placed within the original shopping spree in America. The British War Cabinet established the IMB in Canada under Joseph Wesley Flavelle in 1915, specifically to procure manufactured materials in Canada. These included a total of eighty-seven ships, forty-eight of them with wooden hulls, ordered with an aggregate deadweight of 300,000 tons. They were to be powered by standard-type turbine or reciprocating marine engines, generally built outside the shipyard so that specialist engineering companies could focus on their construction. The Canadian effort is all the more remarkable con-

sidering it came from almost nowhere, with precious little shipbuilding capability, certainly of anything bigger than a 'Laker', before the war started. The large proportion of wooden-hulled ships reflected both the availability of raw materials and the existing skills base in the timber industry, both in ship construction and in other applications.

Johnston and others wrote in the history of the Royal Canadian Navy:

An initial order for wooden steamships was explored in the summer of 1917, but it was not until later in the year that the IMB was asked by London to place contracts for the construction of steel-hulled merchant ships. In December 1917, the British government proposed a program for building up to 4,000 tons of steel and 300,000 tons of wooden merchant ships in Canada at a cost of some $150,000,000, the vessels to be delivered before the end of 1919.

Although the Canadian-built merchant ships would be the property of the British government, the British treasury had no means of financing payments while the fighting continued. As a result, Ottawa was asked to fund the scheme and be reimbursed by Britain sometime after the war. The mer-

Launch of one of the Canadian 3,300-ton deadweight capacity, wooden-hulled ships, *War Sumas* (1918), at the Pacific Construction Company yard at Coquitlam, British Columbia. The yard was formerly the Coquitlam Shipbuilding Company and was taken over by Pacific Construction specifically to build the sisters *War Tyee* and *War Sumas* in 1918. They were both of a number of such ships that were bought by Italian companies after the war; both were scrapped at Trieste in 1923. (AUTHOR COLLECTION)

chant ship construction program was to be supplied with steel plate purchased from recently expanded steel plants, and a contract for rolled steel plate was awarded to the Dominion Steel Corporation of Sydney, Nova Scotia. Because contracts for the Canadian-built merchant ships were not awarded until 1918 – and delivery was not expected until sometime in 1919 – most of the vessels were not completed until after the Armistice.

The larger steel-hulled ships were each clones of existing ships building at three separate yards, two yards in Vancouver and one in Montreal. J Coughlan & Sons at Vancouver delivered ten 8,800dwt ships to the design of an initial order placed by Damps A/S Alaska Haugesund. This initial ship of the ten was launched as *Alaska* and she retained her name, even though she was requisitioned by the IMB and placed under the management of Furness Withy & Company. The other nine ships all carried *War* names. Before the war, Coughlan was dedicated to fabricating steel parts for structures such as bridges and buildings, and only turned to shipbuilding when orders eased at the onset of war and ships became in demand.

Six 7,200dwt ships were completed by Canadian Vickers at Montreal. The initial pair was ordered by Westfel Larsen & Company A/S and retained that company's names as *Porsanger* and *Samnanger* when delivered and requisitioned for the Shipping Controller, again under the

management of Furness Withy & Company. The remaining four clones were given the names *War Earl*, *War Duchess*, *War Faith* and *War Joy*; all six were completed during 1918. The Wallace Shipyard at Vancouver produced three 4,600dwt ships, the first being ordered by the Kishimoto Steamship Company of Osaka and requisitioned before she was completed and launched as *War Dog* in May 1917. Her sisters *War Power* and *War Storm* were completed in 1918.

The remaining steel-hulled ships were all built on the Great Lakes, and dimensions were accordingly limited by the confines of the locks on the Welland Canal, which has a depth of just 14ft. Twenty-two 3,500dwt ships were built for the IMB, the largest group of twelve ships shared equally between the Port Arthur Shipbuilding Company on Lake Ontario and the Polsen Ironworks in downtown Toronto. The *Toronto World*, 24 July 1919, carried the headline 'Vessel ordered by Imperial Munitions Board will leave slipway at noon' (anyone who has been to Toronto will immediately picture what is meant by 'at the bottom of Sherbourne Street'):

The *War Algoma* which will be launched today at noon at the bottom of Sherbourne Street and is the one hundred and forty ninth vessel constructed by the Polson Company; the one hundred and fiftieth is now on the ways and will be launched two or three weeks later. The principle dimensions are: length overall 261 feet; breadth moulded 43

War Fish (1917), seen ready for launching at Port Arthur Shipbuilding Company, Ontario, on 4 August 1917. She was a 4,300-ton deadweight capacity cargo ship with a triple-expansion engine and fit for 10 knots. She was bought by French owners in Le Havre in 1920 and ten years later passed into Finnish ownership as *Malve*. *Malve* was wrecked at Tiree in February 1931. (AUTHOR COLLECTION)

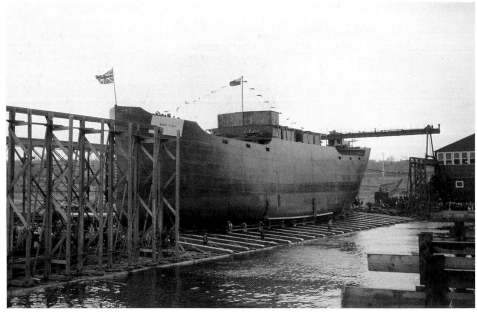

feet 6 inches; depth moulded 23 feet. The propelling machinery consists of a triple expansion surface condensing engine, cylinders 20½ and 33 and 54 inches in diameter by 36 inches stroke, developing 1,150 horsepower. Boilers (two), Scotch marine type, each 14 feet diameter by 12 feet long, equipped with Howden forced draught, are designed for 180 pounds working pressure, designed and equipped throughout for ocean service, with electric plant cargo winches, steam and hand steering gear, steam windlass, evaporator outfit, etc …

This class of 3,500dwt ship had two holds forward and one aft of the central island. There were four hatches with two over the aft hold, and served by two 5-ton derricks each with its own winch. The crew accommodation was steam-heated with electric lighting.

In addition, the Nova Scotia Steel & Coal Company produced two smaller ships at their yard at New Glasgow. *War Bee* was of 2,400dwt and *War Wasp*, 1,800dwt. The smaller ship was equipped with a turbine engine, there being a chronic shortage of large castings, including crankshafts, in late 1917 and early 1918.

The construction of the steel-hulled ships was a remarkable effort. It was paralleled by a separate major shipbuilding programme initiated by the Canadian government. In mid-November 1918 the first two Canadian ships were launched by Canadian Vickers, but neither managed to escape the river before it froze over for the winter. The first was the 4,300-ton *Canadian Voyageur*, delivered to Canadian Voyageur Limited, and a smaller 8,100-ton cargo vessel, *Canadian Pioneer*, which was managed by Canadian Pioneer Limited. In all, a total of sixty-three ships with an aggregate deadweight of 380,435 tons, all prefixed by the name *Canadian*, were completed in Canadian shipyards between 1919 and 1922, for what effectively was the Canadian government merchant marine. There were six different types of ships and they varied in size up to 10,100dwt. They were both of the single-deck and shelter-deck type, with design speeds of between 10 and 12 knots. The programme was similar in aim to the American 'bridge of ships' programme, providing Canada with its own merchant fleet capable of sustaining its own needs.

Ownership and management of the ships was quite unique, as described in *The Monetary Times*, 9 June 1922:

As each ship was completed it was incorporated as a limited liability company. From the company the Government received in payment demand notes at 5½ per cent secured by a mortgage on the vessel, and also, all the issued capital stock of the company; this stock was exchanged for an equivalent amount of stock of the Canadian Government Merchant Marine and was held by the Minister of Finance and the Receiver General.

War Hathor (1918) was typical of the 3,500-ton deadweight capacity ships constructed in Canadian yards between 1917 and 1919. She is seen here on Lake Superior loading grain. In 1920 she was bought by the British India Steam Navigation Company and renamed *Warla*, and resold to Chinese owners in 1934. As *Yuan Chan* she was scuttled three years later in the Yangtze River as a blockship. (AUTHOR COLLECTION)

The initial order from the IMB for wooden-hulled ships was placed with the American-owned Foundation Company, whose yard was at Victoria in British Colombia. Fred Hopkins again:

> While the EFC was being organized, officers of the Foundation Company of New York were called to Washington to discuss the feasibility of having engineering and construction firms build wooden vessels. As a result, the company was commissioned to build a shipyard in New Jersey. It also acquired an order from the United Kingdom's Imperial Munitions Board to construct the hulls for five 2,800-ton wooden cargo steamers. The Foundation Company selected Victoria, BC, as the site for a yard to supply these hulls. Four ways were laid, with enough property purchased for an additional seven. On 27 July 1917, the first keel was laid and the initial hull was launched exactly five months later. Although the IMB had contracted with other west coast yards, the launching of the *War Songhee* occurred a month ahead of the nearest competitor. A French contract for forty 3,000 ton wooden auxiliary schooners to be delivered by December 1918 was also received in July 1917.

The British wooden-hulled ships were all of the same design. They had a deadweight capacity of 3,300 tons, a length of 250ft and a moulded breadth of 43ft 6in. The triple-expansion steam engine was aft of midships, along with a pair of water-tube boilers. The design speed of the ships was 10 knots. The ships were constructed with Douglas fir or Oregon pine, materials long favoured by the traditional builders of wooden schooners in Canada. They had a well deck forward of the bridge, which offered two hatches and two holds, and were of the single-deck type. Some ships had cargo-handling equipment, others had none. The bridge was placed amidships, and the space aft of the bridge was devoted to machinery spaces, and also housed the officers and crew, bunkers and stores – unlike the numerous American Ferris-type ships, which had the engine and accommodation amidships. The coal bunkers in both types of ships were a particular problem, as any spontaneous ignition of the coal would inevitably cause the loss of the entire ship to fire.

The IMB had its own yard at Ogden's Point on the west coast to match ship to engine, the engines mainly being sourced from eastern Canada. Vessels built in the Great Lakes, St Lawrence and Nova Scotia were completed by their own builders. For the wooden ship programme, the IMB acquired two existing yards, and constructed four new ones on the Pacific coast and arranged for the enlargement of eight other yards.

The wooden hull was heavier than its steel counterpart and required a larger displacement, like for like. As a consequence, the ships tended to lie deeper in the water. Seamanship was an essential prerequisite for any man who stepped onto the bridge of these ships. By the same token, the engineers had to be wary of the fire hazard that the wooden structure posed. The one and only benefit, it seems, was that they conserved steel stocks during their construction. That they were expensive to maintain and to operate had not been part of the equation when they were designed and ordered. Despite the claims of the United States Shipping Board in its advertisements for hundreds of partly completed wooden ships in 1919, the ships were generally not successful in post-war trading and few of them survived into the mid-1920s (see Chapter 5).

The massive investment that Britain made in shipbuilding in North America contributed only marginally to the war effort. The steel ships completed before 1918 were valuable and did contribute to maintaining supply lines, but few of the many wooden-hulled ships were available in time to help the Allies. With hindsight, it is questionable if the wooden-hulled shipbuilding programme was a sound and worthwhile investment, the design of vessel being described by the Ottawa government at the time as an 'experimental ship'. Similarly, the loss of the majority of orders for steel ships placed with the American shipyards before that country joined forces with the Allies, albeit placed through commercial agencies acting for the British Shipping Controller, also questions the value of that investment. Nonetheless, the American orders were fulfilled for the Allies, although flying the Stars and Stripes rather than the Red Ensign, but at the expense of the post-war British mercantile marine.

Both the United States and Canada were worried about their own capability to transport men and equipment to fight in Europe. The consequence was that both countries started to build in earnest a merchant marine that would make them independent from foreign-flag ships to provide their wartime logistics, and thereafter in peace to be able to sustain a significant proportion of their own commerce. These massive shipbuilding programmes depended on standard types of ships built to generalised specifications that suited most trades, principally in the Pacific and Atlantic, as well as to the West Indies and elsewhere. The post-war outcome of all this was increased competition for the British shipowner (see Chapter 5).

Ocean-going concrete ship construction
From an article in *Sea Breezes*, December 1966, by Colin Turner

In a paper read to the Society of Naval Architects and Marine Engineers in November 1919 Rudolph Wig [Principal of the Department of Concrete Ship Construction] described the steps which were involved in the construction of a concrete ship.

1. The blocking, or underpinning for supporting the floor forms was placed on the ways, and the scaffolding for holding the outside forms was set in position.
2. The outside bottom and floor forms were erected complete, thus providing means for supporting the steel reinforcing bars. These forms were constructed of wood. Cypress was used at the eastern yards and Oregon pine at those on the west coast.
3. All steel inserts such as the stern frame, stern plate and hawse pipes were secured in place on the inside of the outside forms.
4. The bottom and side shell steel reinforcement was placed within the outside forms. The steel rods used for the reinforcement were round with a diameter ranging from 1⅜in to ⅜in.
5. The bottom and side frame steel and the keelson reinforcing steel were erected. Splice bars between the bulkheads and the shell were placed in position.
6. The inside frame, keelson and side shell forms were erected to a height of 5ft.
7. Concrete was placed in the keelsons and in the bottom and sides of the shell and frames up to the 4ft and 5ft draught line. The thickness of the concrete was 5in for the bottom and 4in for the sides.
8. Bottom inside forms were removed and the concrete was pointed up where necessary. The top surface of the concrete, where it would join the succeeding pour of concrete, was thoroughly cleaned and roughened.

The same process was then employed for the next three pourings, with which the hull was completed up to the weather deck. Finally concrete was placed in the forms for deck erections, hatch coamings and bulwarks. The hull was painted with either two coats of magnesium fluorosilicate, followed by two coats of spar varnish, or three coats of bituminous paint.

5 THE COMMERCIAL ROLE OF THE STANDARD SHIPS OF THE GREAT WAR

The Union-Castle Line's cargo liner *Dundrum Castle* (1919) was a modified B-type Great War standard ship built by Caird & Company at Greenock (Harland & Wolff). She was launched as *Dundrum Castle* and completed to Union-Castle's specifications with three extra pairs of kingposts; she had a 'tween deck in No. 1 hold. *Dundrum Castle* was lost in the Second World War on fire in the Red Sea on 2 April 1943. (A DUNCAN)

Peace at the end of the Great War was followed by a brief period of high freight rates, the so-called post-war boom. Shipowners were left with depleted fleets, but cash was in the bank, as compensation for losses had been received and handsome fees had been paid on behalf of the Admiralty for ships that were requisitioned. At the same time, the British and American governments were holding extremely large stocks of shipping, including ex-German tonnage, and both were keen to relieve themselves of this burden once ships came off wartime duties.

Although contracts for new ships still being built in Britain were cancelled if construction was at an early stage, many other ships were committed to completion at government expense. Initial attempts by the British Shipping Controller to sell the ships piecemeal by auction proved unsatisfactory, with two identical vessels selling at £100,000 one week and just £41,000 ten days later. It was, therefore, decided that ships of similar type and condition be sold at a fixed price. Sale proceeded on this basis, but obviously as more ships were sold, so demand for even more of them declined, and the price shipowners were willing to pay also went down. Eighty-eight ships were actually sold in this way, but

thereafter it was realised that an alternative method of disposal would need to be found.

The answer lay at the hands of Lord Inchcape, chairman of the merged P&O and British India interests, who stepped in as agent for government to take over and sell selected ships under construction at cost price. The attraction to shipowners was that they could buy a partially built vessel and complete it to their own specification. This arrangement was welcomed by the government, which was under pressure within its ranks to retain the ships as a nationalised fleet, a prospect anathema to the shipowners. Inchcape proposed offering the ships initially only to shipowners that had lost ships during the war. In February 1919 a total of seventy-seven ships with an aggregate deadweight 682,000 tons were sold for £16 million. These included forty-eight Type A and B cargo ships. Three months later fifty-five Type A, C, D and H steamers and twenty-three coasters were sold, totalling a further aggregate deadweight of 375,000 tons for a total sum of £8.5 million.

Inchcape also undertook to sell ships operated by the Shipping Controller. These included forty ships, twenty-six built in Britain, and the remainder, more expensive, ships built in Japan

and North America. While the cheaper British ships were sold at a profit, the overseas-built ships balanced this excess, as they attracted a considerable financial loss.

The outcome of all this activity was a sudden slump in the value of shipping throughout 1920. For example, one A-type steamer was bought for commercial use in 1919 at £235,000 and resold in 1920 for just £165,000. The market was effectively dead. There were other reasons for the slump in prices, not least the decline in cargo rates that occurred at the same time, a trade depression that lasted throughout 1920 and the first half of 1921. While the United States recovered to enjoy the Roaring Twenties, Britain was hard pressed to pay its war debts and was struggling to provide its labour force a fair wage. Notwithstanding, the British merchant marine was back on its feet and operating many of the surviving standard *War* ships, both on the tramp market and on liner services. For the latter, many of the ships were adapted or restyled on the stocks for owners' requirements, while others were operated as they were.

Many of the liner companies bought groups of similar ships. The African Steamship Company (later Elder Dempster) and the Glen Line, for example, bought several N-type fabricated ships. However, there were problems with these ships, as described by Bernard Leek in *Sea Breezes*, July 1988:

The propulsion machinery was somewhat disappointing in that although the standard 3,000 ihp triple expansion engine proved to be reliable and easily maintained, consumption of 50 tons of coal per day at a service speed of 11½ knots fell far short of the hoped for economy.

Joinery in the cabins was seen to be shoddy and the use of steel screws led to rust marks on accommodation bulkheads. The crew deplored the absence of awning spars and lack of shade in tropical waters and the unsupported wooden deckheads in the accommodation spaces amidships released globules of pitch in hot climates.

Various liner companies bought into the sale. The Prince Line bought three B-type two-deck ships and three smaller C-type ships to replenish its fleet, the latter for its Mediterranean service. The Strick Line bought the B-type steamers *War Magpie* and *War Lark*, which became their *Arabistan* and *Turkistan*, respectively, and the C-type steamers *War Beacon* and *War Surf*, which became *Sharistan* and *Serbistan*, and a third C-type ship launched as *Muristan*. Two of the five 7,020dwt cargo ships that formed the E type were bought by the Anchor Line in June 1919. The ships, *War Pintail* and *War Wagtail*, were renamed *Vitellia* and *Vindelia*. These sales were conducted through the Cunard Steamship Company as agents for the Shipping Controller; the two ships were used as stopgaps by the Anchor Line and they were both resold to the newly formed Scindia Steam Navigation Company of India three and a half years later.

War Magpie (1918) was a typical B-type standard ship; she was built by Earles Shipbuilding & Engineering Company at Hull. She became the Strick Line's *Arabistan* in 1919, before coming under Japanese ownership in 1926 as *Kohryu Maru*, owned by Kobe Sanbashi KK of Kobe. She was wrecked two years later on the Japanese coast, inbound for Yokohama with a cargo of timber from Everett, Washington. (AUTHOR COLLECTION)

Other liner companies that bought standard ships included Canadian Pacific Steamships and Union-Castle.

Twenty tankers were bought by Anglo-Saxon Petroleum Company to form its A and C class, denoted by the first letter of the ship's name. The A-class ships were all of the AO and BO type and the C class of the Z type. For example, *War African* and *War Begum* became *Absia* and *Anomia*, while *War Jemadar* and *War Rajput* became *Cliona* and *Conia*. A number of Z-type tankers had long careers: *War Sikh*, which worked commercially as *British Soldier*, was sold by the British Tanker Company in 1952 and scrapped only in 1959; *War Rajah* worked for the same company as *British Sailor* until 1951, but was wrecked three years later under her new ownership; and *War Kookri* worked for Eagle Oil & Shipping Company, formerly Eagle Oil Transport Company, as *San Zotico* until 1950, when she was scrapped.

Many of the dry-cargo ships went to tramp shipowners, while others were sold to overseas owners. Prices for overseas owners were a little lower than those offered to British owners, reflecting the operating conditions then in force for British-flagged vessels. A group of twelve A- and B-type ships were acquired by the Hain Steamship Company, of which nine were still in service at the start of the Second World War, each with its characteristic Cornish name: *Trecarrell*, *Tregenna*, *Trekieve*, *Trelissick*, *Trelyon*, *Trematon*, *Tremorvah*, *Trevarrick* and *Treverbyn*. Two of the twelve had been sold in the late 1930s, and one had been lost. That Hain should keep these standard ships in service throughout the Depres-

sion demonstrates the versatility of both the two-deck A-type ships and the B-type single-deckers working in the break bulk and bulk trades. One British tramp ship, *Barrgrove*, owned by Barr Crombie of Glasgow, and built as the A-type *War Anemone*, even retained her single pole mast rig between the wars.

Further evidence of the value of the A- and B-type ships was that many of them were still in service in the liner trades at the outbreak of the Second World War. British India still maintained thirteen A- and B-type ships in 1939, each with a name beginning with 'G', for example, *Gairsoppa*, *Gamaria*, etc. In addition, it still owned two Japanese-built standard ships, the former *War Sailor* and *War Lance*, as *Hatarana* and *Hatipara*, respectively. Other ships of this type still in service in 1939 were *Sabor*, *Sambre*, *Sarthe*, *Siris* and *Somme*, which had served the Royal Mail company since 1919, most still with their original lattice derricks in place. C-type ships were also still much in evidence, the Union Steamship Company of New Zealand still operating three of them in 1939: *Kaikorai*, *Kaiwarra* and *Kekerangu*. Elder Dempster even had five remaining N-type fabricated ships in service, each with deep tanks arranged to carry vegetable oil. Most of these N-type ships were laid up for protracted periods in the early 1930s, but they were retained and put back into service once business recovered.

Though not strictly standard wartime ships, the three roll-on roll-off train ferries built for the British Army in 1917 by Armstrong Whitworth and Fairfield were of landmark design. *Train Ferry No I*, *Train Ferry No II* and *Train Ferry*

Tremeadow (1918), seen in the colours of the Hain Steamship Company, was built as *War Picotee*, a typical Type A standard ship. After giving Hain twenty years' reliable service in the tramp trades, she was sold to Italian owners who renamed her *Sagitta*. She was sunk by Allied gunfire in the Second World War off the Italian coast. (AUTHOR COLLECTION)

No III, along with former Canadian ferry, *Train Ferry No IV*, ran between the military terminal at Richborough in Kent and the continent, with four parallel tracks carrying fifty-four 10-ton army wagons. *Train Ferry No IV* was converted into a tanker post-war. The other three were sold first to the Port of Queenborough Development Company, and in 1924 served between Harwich and Zeebrugge as commercial train ferries operated by the Great Eastern Train Ferry Company, and later the London & North Eastern Railway. As such, they were the first commercial roll-on roll-off ferries operated from Britain to the continent.

A number of classes of tugs had been built to standard designs in British yards. They were all managed by commercial firms and were not given *War* names. The Saint class was the largest in number, forty-six tugs in all, designed as rescue tugs. They were the first sea-going tugs to have a raised forecastle carried back to the after end of the boat deck. The Saints are reputed to have assisted in the salvage of 140 vessels and helped a further 500 ships during the Great War. After the war they were surplus and sold off largely to overseas owners, three, for example, going to sawmill owners in British Columbia to tow log rafts, while fifteen of them were re-

London & North Eastern Railway's *Train Ferry II* (1917) at anchor at Harwich. She was built for the British Amy to run between Richborough in Kent and various Continental destinations. She and her sisters paved the way for roll-on roll-off commercial traffic between Britain and the Continent. *Train Ferry II* was beached at St Valery-en-Caux in June 1940 after being damaged by shells. (AUTHOR COLLECTION)

Tyne-Tees Steam Shipping Company's collier *Persian Coast* (1919) was a typical three-island type, coastal standard (CS) ship launched as *War Colne*. She was a single-decker with a deadweight capacity of 900 tons, a useful size, which gave her a commercial service for a variety of owners before she was eventually sold for scrap in 1956. (AUTHOR COLLECTION)

tained in Admiralty service. Smaller harbour tugs of the so-called West class were sold for port duties, mainly in Britain, and again some were retained by the Admiralty. The army also had the HS class of small sea-going tugs suitable for inland navigation along rivers and canals in France. These too were sold, four of them, *HS15*, *HS16*, *HS17* and *HS18*, for towage duties with the Manchester Ship Canal Company. The twelve concrete-hulled tugs remained in service until the mid-1920s. They were used for towing barges across the North Sea to German and Baltic ports, and one, *Cretegaff*, towed the steamship *Flour* from Petrograd to Bremen in 1922. Thereafter, the heavy displacement of these tugs rendered them uneconomic and unserviceable.

Coasters and colliers were also put on the market, finding a variety of new owners mostly, but not all, under the Red Ensign. For example, Coast Lines Tyne-Tees Steam Shipping Company and the Moss Steamship Company were among those to gain new tonnage.

The American sell-off was even more dramatic. In February 1922 the Emergency Fleet Corporation placed an advertisement in the press:

The United States Shipping Board through the United States Shipping Board Emergency Fleet Corporation, invites offers for the purchase of any or all of its steel cargo vessels, steel passenger and cargo vessels, steel tankers, steel refrigerators, ex-German cargo vessels, ex-German passenger and cargo vessels, ex-German sailers, concrete cargo and tankers, steel and wood ocean-going and harbor tugs, which have been duly appraised and are to be sold at private competitive sale.

The sale included numerous three-island-type cargo ships:

21 ships of 2,875 tons deadweight capacity single deck coal-burning cargo ships and 21 more at 3,300 tons;
104 at 3,500 and 3,550 tons deadweight capacity single deck coal-burners;
138 at 1,050 tons deadweight capacity single deck oil-burners, 57 at 4,200 tons and a further 112 at 5,075 ton;
36 at 7,500 tons deadweight capacity two decked oil-burning cargo ships, 97 at 7825 tons, 227 at 8,800 tons, 91 at 9,000 tons deadweight capacity, 76 at 9,400 tons deadweight capacity, 89 at 9,500 tons deadweight capacity; and
23 at 13,000 tons deadweight capacity, these being passenger and cargo ships with four decks, twin screws and oil-burning.

Five of the Hog Island Type B transports (Design 1024), *Aisne*, *Cantigny*, *Ourcq*, *Tours* and *Marne* were adapted for commercial use in 1924 and placed on the New York to London service for the United States Shipping Board's American Merchant Line. They were renamed, respectively, *American Merchant*, *American Banker*, *American Farmer*, *American Shipper* and *American Trader*. Each ship had cheap tourist-class accommodation for seventy-eight passengers, offering a single transatlantic trip for just £20 10s. They became part of the United States Lines Company at its formation in 1931 and were joined by two more Hog Island Transports, *Somme* and *Cambrai*. This pair became *American Importer* and *American Traveler*, and served the London route until 1934, when they inaugurated the New York to Cobh and Liverpool service, returning via Glasgow and Belfast.

American Farmer (1920) was one of five Type 1024 ships adapted for passenger use on the New York to London service under the flag of the American Merchant Line. (AMBROSE GREENWAY COLLECTION)

Two fast Design 1029 army troop transports were also put into commercial use with the American Merchant Line, *President Harding* and *President Roosevelt*. Commander Vernon Gibbs in his book on Western Ocean passenger lines described them:

Laid down as army transports but redesigned as commercial vessels on the stocks. They were completed for the United States Shipping Board early in 1922 as *Peninsula State* and *Lone Star State* respectively, renamed *President Pierce* and *President Taft* in May and again renamed *President Roosevelt* and *Presi-*

dent Harding after three months. They looked essentially freighters with four 'goalpost' masts for working cargo and their masts proper were signal poles mounted on the second and third. Passenger accommodation was altered to 320 cabin class and 324 third class in 1924.

President Roosevelt was transferred to the Antwerp Navigation Company in 1940, but was sunk in the Scheldt in May that year. *President Harding* was taken back by the United States government in the Second World War and converted into the troopship *Joseph T Duckman*. As such she was broken up by the Kaiser Company at Oakland in 1948.

Other Design 1029 troop ships were adopted for commercial use for the Admiral Oriental Line, which in 1926 became the

American Trader (1920) was a sister ship to *American Farmer*, this image showing the distinctive lines of this class of vessel after adaptation for the carriage of passengers after the war. (AMBROSE GREENWAY COLLECTION)

The Hog Island-built transport *Somme* (1920), launched as *Siskowit*, was acquired by the United States Lines Company in 1931 and renamed *American Importer*. Her accommodation was reconfigured to provide seventy-eight tourist-class passenger berths for the New York to London service and she later inaugurated the New York to Liverpool, Glasgow and Belfast service in 1934 along with her sister, *American Traveler*. (AUTHOR COLLECTION)

American Oriental Mail Line. They all had *President* names: *Pine Tree State* became *President Grant*; *Silver State*, *President Jackson*; *Wenatchee*, *President Jefferson*; *Bay State*, *President Madison*; and *Keystone State*, *President McKinley*. Each ship offered tourist-class berths for about ninety passengers.

Captain Robert Dollar inaugurated his round-the-world service with the former *Wolverine State*, renamed *President Harrison*. She was a Design 1095-type, 502ft-long transport, and was rebuilt to offer just over a hundred passenger berths. A further group of Design 1029- and smaller 1095-type ships were acquired; E Mowbray Tate wrote in his book on Pacific liners:

> *President Hayes* followed *Harrison* on 2 February [1924] and *President Adams* (ex-*Centennial State*) sailed on 1 March. After that time the around-the-world departure schedule was maintained at every other

week, 26 a year, even though the government in its mail contract required only ten trips a year. The additional four vessels were *President Garfield* (ex-*Blue Hen State*), *President Polk* (ex-*Granite State*), *President Monroe*, (ex-*Panhandle State*) and *President van Buren* (ex-*Old North State*), each with tourist class accommodation for 103 passengers. Major ports of call announced by the Shipping

The United States Mail Steamship Company's *Old North State* (1920) was a Design 1095 transport converted for passenger cargo duties. She carried seventy-eight first-class passengers. On the failure of the company, she became the Dollar Lines' *President van Buren* in 1924 and was downgraded to tourist class with 103 berths. She was renamed *President Filmore* in 1940. She was requisitioned in 1944 as the troop transport *Marigold* and broken up in 1948, after reverting to the name *President Filmore* in 1946 as a troop ship under United States government ownership. (AUTHOR COLLECTION)

Board on the occasion of the sale were Honolulu, Kobe, Shanghai, Hong Kong, Manila, Singapore, Penang, Colombo, Suez, Port Said, Alexandria, Naples, Genoa, Marseilles, Boston, New York, Havana, Colon, Panama, Los Angeles and San Francisco. Later Yokohama, Bombay and Barcelona were added.

Captain Dollar also successfully bid for four Design 1029 troop transports; Mowbray again:

Their beam was 72 feet, their gross tonnage over 14,100 tons, and their speed 17 knots. They could carry 260 passengers in first class, and 200 in third class. R Stanley Dollar, vice-president of the Dollar Line, began negotiations with the Emergency Fleet Corporation as far back as 1923, but it was not until March 1925 that the sale was consummated.

The Dollar Line eventually operated six Design 1029 and six smaller Design 1095 passenger cargo ships. The company went on to become American President Lines following its near-collapse in 1938. The ships were then used for a direct Pacific service to Manila: *President Lincoln*, ex-*Hoosier State*; *President Pierce*, ex-*Hawkeye State*; *President Taft*, ex-*Buckeye State*; and *President Wilson*, ex-*Empire State*.

The United States Shipping Board was able to sell its American Scantic Line to Moore McCormack in 1927. With it came a group of Emergency Fleet Corporation Design 1013 and Design 1022 Type A Hog Islanders. Four of the Type A freighters, albeit with turbine machinery and a sea speed of 13 knots, were restructured to provide ninety tourist-class passenger berths in 1932. They provided a circuit from New York to Gothenburg, Copenhagen, Gdynia, Stockholm, Helsinki, and back to Copenhagen and New York. The ships were *Chickasaw*, *Bird City*, *Schenectady* and *Saguache*, and they were renamed as the passenger cargo ships, respectively, *Scanmail*, *Scanpenn*, *Scanyork* and *Scanstates*. *Scanpenn* was operated by the American Caribbean Line for a while in the mid-1930s. They were all sold to Brazilian Lloyd in 1940.

The American West African Line was another company set up by the United States Shipping Board using Design 1013 and 1022 cargo ships. It was operated by Barber Steamship Lines, with each ship offering up to twelve passenger berths. Several other companies were floated and sold by the shipping board using surplus tonnage. Lykes Brothers Steamship Company (later Lykes Line) managed a number of ships for the shipping board during the Great War and later bought a number of them. The Submarine Boat Corporation (Transmarine) took the last thirty-two ships built at its shipyard at Newark when the orders were cancelled by the shipping board, and operated them on the Atlantic routes. Sperling Steamship & Trading Company of New York also bought tonnage from the shipping board.

Other ships were bought by single-ship operators and other small companies registered in the United States to work the tramp trades. This

Scanpenn (1919) was built as the Design 1022 Type A Hog Islander *Bird City* and converted to carry ninety passengers for the American Scantic Line in 1932. She is seen here in a press photo in September 1939 with the caption 'American flags painted on her sides, the *Scanpenn*, an US ship, sails from her pier at Jersey City, NJ, September 2, so marked that in the event of a general European war, enemy planes and battleships will make no mistakes'. (ACME NEWSPICTURES)

West Nohno (1919) was an Emergency Fleet Corporation Design 1013 vessel, and is seen here in the Manchester Ship Canal under the ownership of the American West African Line. She was repossessed by government and eventually scuttled as a blockship as part of Gooseberry No. 2 at Normandy in June 1944. (AUTHOR COLLECTION)

glut of cheap shipping soon impacted on freight rates which, coupled with an influx of new regulations from the United States Shipping Board, forced many operators to register their ships and the owning companies in Panama. Here cheaper taxes were available, and less stringent safety and operational rules prevailed. So started the notorious flag of convenience.

A singular career of one of the freighters, a Design 1023-type tramp steamer that was finally broken up in 1952, was described by Frank Bowen in *Sea Breezes*, March 1952:

One of the enormous number of standardised steamers laid down by the Submarine Boat Corporation of Newark, New Jersey, for the US Shipping Board during the First World War, the *Admiral Chase* was originally the *Sutransco* and, not being completed until 1920, she was operated by her builders. With a gross tonnage of 3,545, her single screw was driven by a double reduction geared turbine supplied by two water tube boilers, giving her a speed of 11 knots. Her builders planned to operate over 30 of these ships but they were overtaken by the slump and after a short spell the *Sutransco* was laid up, spending a very large part of her time out of commission until 1930, when she was sold to the Admiral Line of Seattle and renamed *Admiral Chase*. They employed her on their services on the North Pacific coast until 1940, when she was sold to Carpenter's of Sydney

and ran between the Pacific Islands and Sydney. In 1951 she was sold to Wallem & Company of Hong Kong ...

A great deal of tonnage was scrapped, while some was also put into reserve. A large group of over two hundred of the smaller ships built on the Great Lakes for the Emergency Fleet Corporation was sold as one lot to shipbreakers in Detroit. Other ships with known deficiencies that would cost too much to repair were also sold for scrap. The concrete-hulled ships tended to suffer cracks caused by oxidation of the steel reinforcement struts, and few lasted more than a handful of years in service. The wooden-hulled ships fared even worse, being obsolete before they were even launched. Fred Hopkins wrote in *The Northern Mariner*:

In September 1922 George D Perry, a California lawyer representing the Western Marine and Salvage Company, purchased 233 wooden vessels of the World War I emergency fleet for $750,000, or approximately $3,300 per craft. Lying idle in the James River, the ships were taken to Alexandria, Virginia, stripped of their engines, and towed downriver to be burned so that the iron and steel could be salvaged. Eventually 152 wood and composite vessels were hauled into Mallow's Bay on the Maryland side of the Potomac, about six miles downstream from Quantico, Virginia, until the poor scrap market in the late 1920s halted the process. Thereafter the hulks remained beached in the shoal waters of Mallow's Bay until early in World War II, when there was a renewed demand for steel and iron scrap. Once again they became important, but the cost of salvage soon ended the project.

Some of the eight concrete tankers and the four small, concrete, dry-cargo ships saw brief service as intended. Two of the tankers were managed by the American Fuel Oil & Transportation Company, but after three trips to Mexico, *Selma* struck rocks off the oil jetty at Tampico and fractured her hull over a length of 60ft. *Latham* did exactly the same thing a few weeks later, but neither ship was repaired. *Cuyamaca* and *San Pasqual* saw a few months service with the France and Canada Oil Transport Company and were then withdrawn, while the other four tankers saw no service at all. Of the dry-cargo ships, *Polias* was wrecked in a storm in 1920, *Sapona* was hulked on completion, in October 1920 *Cape Fear* collided with *City of Atlanta*, the concrete hull described as 'shattering as if a teacup was hit', and sank in three minutes, taking nineteen of her crew with her. *Atlantus* did make one trip across the Atlantic, but was laid up in 1920. The problem with all the concrete-hulled ships was their poor deadweight and poor resistance to impact damage.

Many of the Canadian wooden ships built for the Imperial Munitions Board went to Italian owners for use in the eastern Mediterranean. However, all but one was scrapped by 1925, although nine had earlier been lost to fire, and a

further four foundered or wrecked. *War Yukon* was the exception. She was owned and registered in Norway until sold in 1926 to owners in Ecuador. She traded until 1933, finally under the Panamanian registry, when she was converted to a hulk for use as a fish processing plant at San Pedro, California, but sank the same year while at anchor.

The eight 11,800dwt ships laid down for the British government at the Union Iron Works in San Francisco were used after the war for experiments with turbo-electric and diesel-electric propulsion. The experiments resulted in an increase in speed, but were not a complete success, as significant wash problems gave rise to damage claims from a number of harbour authorities. Nevertheless, five of the ships, laid down as *War Harbour*, *War Haven*, *War Surf* and *War Wave*, along with *Steadfast*, all requisitioned by the United States Shipping Board, were converted for passenger use in 1931. They were each re-engined with steam turbine units, lengthened by 53ft with a new streamlined bow fitted, and equipped with eighty tourist-class berths. The wash from the stern continued to cause problems, but the ships maintained a service for the newly formed Baltimore Mail Steamship Company, complete with a large operational subsidy from the United States government.

In March 1930 the United States postmaster-general had awarded the Roosevelt Steamship Company a subsidised mail contract for a weekly service from Baltimore and Norfolk to Hamburg. The Roosevelt Steamship Company, and its parent company, the International Mercantile Marine Company, founded

Another Type 1023 with a spectacularly long career was *Valles* (1920), built by the Submarine Boat Corporation at Newark as *Surico. Valles* survived in commercial service in Far Eastern waters under the Panamanian flag until she was finally broken up in 1967.
(AMBROSE GREENWAY COLLECTION)

the Baltimore Mail Steamship Company, which operated from Baltimore to Southampton, Bremen, Hamburg and Havre. The service was closed in 1938 when the government subsidy was withdrawn, the ships later being converted into Second World War attack transports.

Most of the ships in the Canadian single-ship companies were sold out of the Canadian Merchant Marine mortgaging arrangement within two or three years. The only stipulation was that the buyer needed to be a Canadian-registered company. Some, however, were retained into the 1930s, *Canadian Freighter*, for example, passing to Canadian Pathfinder Limited in 1927 as *Canadian Pathfinder* and renamed *Chomedy* in 1932, only being sold foreign after the Second World War. The Merchant Marine was originally run at a profit, but soon ran into financial difficulties as trade declined. Nevertheless, Ottawa was keen for its merchant navy to continue, not least in promoting Canadian exports. Batches of ships were put up for sale as their trade ceased to be aided: for example, *Canadian Observer*, *Canadian Rover* and *Canadian Coaster* were sold in 1929. Numerous services were promoted, some alongside existing commercial services already aided by government.

Some of the Canadian Merchant Marine's activity did develop into commercial enterprise, proving the success of the original post-war concept to develop trade. For example, the Merchant Marine's interests in services from Canadian west-coast ports to the Antipodes were bought by the Montreal Australia–New Zealand Line in 1936. The so-called MANZ Line was a venture between the Commonwealth and Dominion Line (later Port Line), the Ellerman and Bucknall Steamship Company and the New Zealand Shipping Company. In 1936 it operated the 10,400dwt, oil-fuelled, triple-expansion steamships *Canadian Constructor* and *Canadian Cruiser* with accommodation for nine passengers, and the 8,400dwt, coal-fired, triple-expansion engine ships *Canadian Challenger*, *Canadian Conqueror*, *Canadian Highlander* and *Canadian Scottish*, each with accommodation for six passengers. All these ships were built between 1920 and 1921 for the Canadian Merchant Marine.

The wartime standard ships were thus used on a variety of services post-war. The American and Canadian ships were built specifically to bolster their respective national merchant navies, while the British ships were designed as much to help the Allied war effort, as to provide a merchant navy that could still maintain Britain's empire trade routes after the Armistice.

The Canadian Merchant Marine's *Canadian Scottish* (1921) was built by the Prince Rupert Dry Docks & Engineering Company, She was originally registered under the ownership of Canadian Scottish Ltd. In 1936 she joined the Montreal Australia New Zealand Line, but the following year was sold to Greek owners as *Mount Parnassus*, before becoming the German-owned *Johann Schulte* in 1939. She foundered with a full cargo of iron ore in 1940. (AUTHOR COLLECTION)

6 AT WAR AGAIN — REBUILDING, LESSONS LEARNT AND LEND-LEASE

In 1936 Britain interpreted the increasingly tense political atmosphere in Europe as an appropriate time to re-arm. This had the knock-on effect of increasing the price of new ships, as the merchant navy now had to compete with the Admiralty, the military organisation responsible for procuring the Royal Navy's warships. The recession was finally but slowly ending, and new ships were being ordered once again, albeit at a slow rate. Across the Atlantic, the United States Merchant Marine Act of 1936 heralded the modernisation of the American merchant navy by providing a capital outlay subsidy. This was intended to reduce American shipbuilding costs to the price of equivalent ships built in Britain and elsewhere (see Chapter 7). This meant an increase in American shipbuilding capacity, as well as an upgrade in the American commercial fleets, which were largely comprised of the Great War and post-war emergency ships. In addition, the United States Maritime Commission led the way towards the development of a new standard-type cargo ship, the fast C2 freighter, which was to be the mainstay of the United States fleet-rebuilding programme. The C2 freighters were followed by the smaller C1 and larger C3, and eventually also C4, types.

Britain was also aware that its shipowners were not building enough new ships to modernise its commercial fleets. A similar shipbuilding incentive to that in America was put in place in the years leading up to the Second World War, although the British incentive programme did not lead to classes of standard ships. The vehicle to do this was the British Shipping (Assistance) Act 1935, which was in two parts. The first offered a subsidy in the form of a voyage grant that could be applied for by tramp shipowners. This was a response from a government that was conscious of the strategic importance of these ships and their operating companies in times of war. However, the subsidy was only eligible to ships with an all-British crew, and discriminated against ships that were part-crewed by Lascars and other foreign seamen. There was considerable disquiet over this part of the Act, much of it led by the National Union of Seamen. The second part of the Act introduced the 'scrap and build' scheme of subsidised loans to shipowners. Many fleets had been reduced in size during the Depression and

Aquarius (1943) was one of the many C2 standard ships built by America in the 1940s. She had a turbine engine that drove her at 15½ knots and had an impressive array of cargo-handling and ancillary equipment. She was sold to the United States Lines Company in 1947 and renamed *Pioneer Lake* and later *American Trapper*, as seen here. She reverted to government ownership in 1962 and was sold for demolition in 1967. (ANDREW DUNCAN)

American Scout (1946), seen at Manchester in the early 1950s with most of her funnel removed to decrease her air draught for the fixed bridges on the Manchester Ship Canal. She was a typical C2 fast freighter built to the order of the United States Shipping Commission, many also for individual American shipping companies. (THE MANCHESTER SHIP CANAL COMPANY)

few shipowners could, as a result, afford to up-grade their surviving vessels. The *Glasgow Herald* expanded on the Act on 12 March 1935:

> … there will be available to British shipowners a fund of £10,000,000 from which they may receive loans to assist them either in the building of new tonnage or in the modernising of their existing fleets. It is part of the Government's larger scheme designed to aid home shipowners to compete against subsidised foreign shipping, the first section of the Act having provided £2,000,000 to assist tramp vessels to secure freights.

This second portion of the Act embodies the governments 'scrap and build' policy, the main conditions of it being that the vessels to be built must be of the same general type as those demolished, and that, in the case of building and modernising, the ships must be of the general cargo carrying type … In other words for every new ship he constructs with the aid of Government money,

Ben Line Steamers' *Bennevis* (1943) was completed as an American C3-type cargo steamer and rebuilt as the escort aircraft carrier *Puncher* in 1944, for use by Britain as part of the Lend-Lease agreement. She was converted back for commercial civilian duties in 1946, when she was renamed *Muncaster Castle* under the ownership of the Lancashire Shipping Company, of London, passing to Shaw, Savill & Albion in 1954, for whom she became *Bardic*, and finally to Ben Line in 1959. She is seen as *Bennevis* at Southampton in August 1964; she was eventually sold for scrap in 1973. (NICK ROBINS)

a shipowner must demolish two, and for every one he brings up to date he must scrap one.

The case of the Prince Line was typical, as reported in the book *Ships that came to Manchester*:

By 1936 the Prince Line fleet had been reduced to only 19 ships but in October of that year the first of four new 2,090 gross ton sisters were completed for the Mediterranean service: three by W. Hamilton & Company of Port Glasgow, the *Arabian Prince*, *Palestinian Prince* and *Syrian Prince*, and one, a new *Cyprian Prince*, by the Furness Shipbuilding Company at Haverton Hill. The company was given a 100 per cent Government loan of £130,000 for the construction of the *Arabian Prince* and the *Syrian Prince* on the condition that [four] ships were scrapped under the 'Scrap and Build' Bill.

Thus from the mid-1930s impetus was both to rebuild British military capacity and, in Britain and America, to encourage the rebuilding and modernisation of their respective merchant marine services. It also meant much needed modernisation and re-equipping of some of the shipyards, but by no means was enough done to meet the demands that were to follow in the 1940s. Had these government initiatives not been taken at the time that they were, both Britain and the United States would have been sorely unprepared for the war that would shortly overtake them. Indeed, the Tramp Shipping Administrative Committee repeatedly stated that without the grants in place from 1935, the industry would have collapsed.

The inevitability of war grew as time went on, and in September 1939 Britain again declared war against Germany. As before, America was initially neutral. At the start of the war, the British merchant fleet, and more so the American and Canadian fleets, consisted largely of ships dating from the Great War and the immediate post-war shipbuilding initiatives. Indeed, the first American C2-type freighter was only commissioned in 1939.

America had commissioned few new ships in the interwar years. This resulted in shipyards closing, with a consequent decline in the pool of skilled shipyard workers. Britain, however, had continued to build merchant ships, although very few during the recession years, and its shipyards had neither been re-equipped, nor had

new ship production methods been introduced; little had changed since the Great War. Indeed, the surplus of British shipyards was being reduced from the early 1930s by a government-funded purchase and closure scheme of those yards whose owners were prepared to offer them for total closure. Ship design, however, had continued to advance, with investigations into modern energy-efficient hulls, like that incorporated in Thompson's *Embassage* of 1935, in conjunction with fuel-efficient propulsion systems. If Britain was to survive this second war, it would need to look carefully at how it could nurture its merchant navy, and how it could collaborate better with the United States with its wartime resources potential.

Many technical lessons had been learned from the emergency shipbuilding programmes during and since the Great War. It was established that welded and part-welded hulls could be constructed which had a lighter weight of steel, but had the same or greater strength as an equivalent riveted ship. When the building of the ship was done in a shipyard specially set up for wartime production, and having no historical labour demarcations and attitudes, it soon became apparent that a welded ship could be completed in less time, and with far fewer skilled workers, than a riveted ship.

Prefabrication was a method of ship construction where the overall structure was subdivided into a number of pre-constructed units, or sub-assemblies. The physical size of the units was determined by the capacity of the craneage in both the fabrication workshops and at the shipyard slipways. This method also allowed for off-site construction of these units, often complete with their fittings, which would be brought to the shipyard within a precise assembly programme for the rapid final assembly of the ship on the slipway. This technique also made use of the skilled labour to be found in the bridge-building and other steel construction industries which could be readily adapted for ship construction work. It was early recognised that in planning and introducing all of the foregoing, ships and their machinery had to be designed and constructed to be both efficient and easily maintained.

While the philosophy of standardisation was widely understood and appreciated, its limitations were also recognised. Standard ship-type construction was easily applied to shipyards that specialised in one type of ship such as dry-cargo, shelter-deck or tank ships. It did not suit

Emilia (1918) was one of the ships ordered in the Great War by the British Shipping Controller as *War Mercury* and requisitioned by the United States and completed as *Cape Romain*. She was bought from government in 1929 by A H Bull Steamship Company Inc of New York and renamed *Emilia*. She survived the Second World War and was sold out of the US registry only in 1951. She foundered in the eastern Mediterranean in 1956 having given nearly forty years' continuous service. (ACME NEWSPICTURES)

shipyards that built a mix of different types of passenger, passenger-cargo, general cargo and tank ships, with an occasional major warship included in the construction mix.

The issues surrounding a neutral nation building ships for another nation which was at war, and the subsequent ownership of those ships were complex and about to become more so. The United States was too well aware that the British Empire closed ranks in times of need. It had done so in the early 1930s, when Canada gave special cheap cargo rates to goods imported in British or Canadian ships through its west-coast ports, especially from Australia and New Zealand. The same goods shipped via an American port would have incurred larger dues. A similar situation had arisen with shipbuilding in the Great War, with Britain paying premium rates per ton for ships built in the United States, and significantly reduced rates in Canada, albeit still more expensive than the costs per ton for the equivalent ship types in the UK. Ownership was even more complicated, with American ships either sold or mortgaged to the British Ministry of Shipping in the Great War, with many more ordered by Britain, but never delivered once America had entered the war.

The Canadian ships were built largely on the promise of post-war repayment as part of the British war debt. Many were registered in Britain while, post-war, others were retained under Canadian government ownership. The issues were difficult and needed a wholly different and transparent approach in the Second World War. Besides, Canada was at Britain's bidding in the Great War, but as an independent Dominion within the empire in the Second War. Besides, by 1939 Canada had already signed up to various trade and economic agreements with the United States.

President Roosevelt declared in September 1939 that the United States would remain neutral. American public opinion generally supported the victims of Hitler's aggression rather than Nazi Germany. As early as 15 May 1940, Prime Minister Winston Churchill telegraphed the president: 'If necessary we shall continue the war alone, and we are not afraid of that. But I trust you will realise, Mr President, that the voice and force of the United States may count for nothing if they are withheld too long,' and two days later, Churchill sent the message, 'Nothing that America could do would be of greater help than to send fifty destroyers – except sending a hundred.' However, the Neutrality Act of 1939 banned both victims and aggressors from procuring war materials from the United States unless they could pay cash; credit could not be extended to countries, such as the United Kingdom, that had not completely paid off their debts from the Great War. Nevertheless, Britain was able to buy some essential and timely military goods with its available but scarce dollars, and was able to start negotiations for shipbuilding.

There was a succession of American Neutrality Acts. The first in 1935, prohibited the export of 'arms, ammunition, and implements of war' from the United States to foreign nations at war and required arms manufacturers in the United States to apply for export licences. The outbreak of the Spanish Civil War in 1936 and continued unrest in Europe increased support for extending and expanding the restrictions in the Neutrality Act of 1937. This Act of 1937 did contain one important concession: belligerent nations were allowed, at the discretion of the president, to acquire any items except arms from the United States, so long as they immediately paid for such items and carried them on non-American ships – the so-called 'cash-and-carry' provision. Roosevelt had engineered its inclusion as a deliberate way to assist Great Britain and France in any war against the Axis powers.

Eight American C2 freighters were transferred to Britain in 1941 under the Lend-Lease agreement. *Exemplar* (1940) became *Empire Widgeon*, but all the ships were returned to the United States Registry in 1942 with their original names. *Exemplar* was later operated by the American Export Lines and was eventually scrapped in 1968. (AUTHOR COLLECTION)

Design 1013 ship *West Cressey* (1918), seen in the peacetime colours of the United American Line was the kind of ship that Britain acquired early in the Second World War. The upper part of the fidded central communication mast has been taken down to reduce air draught in the Manchester Ship Canal; she is seen here passing the Barton Road Bridge. This ship was loaned to Russia in 1943, but she was wrecked shortly after the war ended.

(Author collection)

Following Germany's occupation of Czechoslovakia in March 1939, Congress rebuffed Roosevelt's attempt to renew 'cash-and-carry', but President Roosevelt persisted, and in November 1939 a final Neutrality Act was passed. This lifted the arms embargo, and put all trade with belligerent nations under the terms of 'cash-and-carry'. The ban on loans remained in effect, and American ships were barred from transporting goods to belligerent ports.

During the 'cash-and-carry' phase, Britain managed to obtain four, newly built, premium C2 cargo ships in 1941 (see Chapter 7): *Nightingale*, *Robin Doncaster*, *China Mail* and *Extavia*, which were renamed by the Ministry of Shipping (Ministry of War Transport from May 1941 onwards), respectively, *Empire Egret*, *Empire Curlew*, *Empire Peregrine* and *Empire Oriole*. No money was paid for them and the transaction was described as 'transferred to London registry'. They were all returned to the United States in 1942. The C3 freighters, *Howell Lykes*, *Almeria Lykes*, *Exemplar* and *Hawaiian Shipper* were also obtained, and renamed *Empire Pintail*, *Empire Condor*, *Empire Widgeon* and *Empire Fulmar*. These too were taken back by the United States in 1942. Shortly after *Empire Condor* reverted to the American registry as *Almeria Lykes*, she was attacked by E-boats and sunk off Cape Bon, in Tunisia (see Chapter 16). While under

'British ownership', the ships were managed by British shipowners, *Almeria Lykes*, for example by Donaldson Brothers & Black of Glasgow, and *Empire Egret* by the Royal Mail Lines.

The cash-and-carry phase allowed Britain to buy seventy-six old American ships built towards the end of, and immediately after, the Great War (America's 'bridge of ships' project). Most of them had been laid up for the previous twenty years and were barely seaworthy. Because of American ship-repair costs, it was decided after their first voyage to Britain that the expenditure required to repair them should be incurred in Britain, where shipyard costs were considerably cheaper. Some of these ships had been made idle by the Neutrality Act, as they were no longer allowed to trade with belligerent nations. They included fifteen of the former West-class Design 1013 ships and numerous Hog Island Type A Design 1022 vessels. However, fuel oil that had been stagnant for so long in the bunkers became thick and unusable, making that first voyage to Britain hazardously slow; one ship reported being overtaken by *Queen Mary* three times!

However, Britain needed much more help with replacement shipping to overcome the dramatic losses suffered in the Atlantic during 1941. Britain's dollar reserves were running low, and could no longer pay for such services even though there was a series of fire-sales of British assets in America to make good the payments. Hancock and Gowing wrote in their book *British war economy*:

By the end of 1940, the British had committed nearly all their available dollars. By reason of their own circumspection or the delays and obstacles that had beset them in America, the curve of their demands had been slow in rising; but by now it had reached a respectable height. The Kaiser shipbuilding enterprise had been launched by Admiralty orders; Lord Beaverbrook's expansive visions were embodying themselves in specific aircraft contracts ...

... He [Churchill] reminded the President that the British Commonwealth in defending itself, was buying time for the United States to prepare their own defences: the future of both democracies depended upon successful British resistance during the coming year. The decision in the coming year would lie on the seas; Britain, having survived direct enemy assault in 1940, might be overwhelmed in 1941 by the less spectacular but no less deadly attack upon her shipping. Should she fall under this attack, the United States might not find time to complete their own preparations. The Prime Minister reiterated the urgent need for American help at sea — strategic help, through the transfer of American warships or the reassertion of the American policy of freedom of the seas, and industrial help, in the form of a shipbuilding drive comparable with the Hog Island programme of the last war. Industrial help was hardly less indispensable in the sphere of air and army production. This brought Mr Churchill to the question of finance: 'The moment approaches [he said] when we shall no longer be able to pay cash for shipping and other supplies. While we will do our utmost, and shrink from no proper sacrifice to make payments across the Exchange, I believe you will agree that it would be wrong in principle and mutually disadvantageous in effect, if at the height of this struggle, Great Britain were to be divested of all saleable assets, so that after the victory was won with our blood, civilisation saved, and the time gained for the United States to be fully armed against all eventualities, we should stand stripped to the bone. Such a course would not be in the moral or the economic interests of either of our countries.'

Roosevelt was aware that the fall of Europe would threaten American security. He looked for an instrument that would bypass the constraints and would enable the United States to provide Great Britain with supplies necessary to resist Germany. One way of doing this was through a temporary 'lease' of resources which, in theory, would need to be returned or repaid after the war.

Both American law, and public fears that the United States would be drawn into the European war, blocked Roosevelt's plans to aid Britain directly. The Johnson Act of 1934, for example, prohibited the extension of credit to countries like Britain that had not repaid war loans from the First War. In addition, the American military opposed sending military hardware to the United Kingdom since the chief of staff of the army, General George C Marshall, believed that Britain would surrender following the collapse of France, and any American supplies would then fall into German hands. Marshall argued that national security would be better served by keeping the military supplies for the defence of the western hemisphere. Besides, many Americans opposed the United States becoming involved in another war, even though most Americans supported the British defenders, rather than the German aggressors. President Roosevelt, therefore, needed to develop an initiative that was consistent with the law preventing the granting of credit, was satisfactory to the military, and was acceptable to American public opinion.

In September 1940 President Roosevelt signed the 'destroyers for bases' agreement. The United States gave the British more than fifty obsolete destroyers in exchange for ninety-nine-year leases to territory in Newfoundland and the Caribbean that would be used as American air and naval bases. Roosevelt was not keen to suggest the destroyers be made a gift to Britain, as he knew that a deal that gave the United States long-term access to the British bases was a significant contribution to the security of the western hemisphere. In this way, he satisfied the concerns both of the public and the military leaders.

The Lend-Lease Act was passed by Congress on 11 March 1941, after a partisan debate and protests by those who wanted true neutrality. The Act authorised the president to 'sell, transfer

A product of the Bethlehem-Fairfield Shipyard at Baltimore, the Shaw Savill Line's *Tropic* (1943) was launched as the Liberty ship *J Whitridge Williams*, and completed as *Samsylvan* as part of the Lend-Lease programme. Shaw, Savill & Albion managed the ship during the war for the Ministry of War Transport and bought her in 1947. She was resold in 1952 to Italian owners who renamed her *San Francesco*. She was broken up in 1960 following grounding damage. (NICK ROBINS)

title to, or otherwise dispose of military supplies', including merchant ships, to any foreign government whose defence was considered vital to the security of the United States. Thus the neutral United States once again became, in Roosevelt's own words, the 'arsenal of democracy' in the war against Nazi Germany. Materials were not just confined to hardware, but included food and fuel as well. When Hitler declared war on the United States on 11 December 1941, he cited the Lend-Lease Act as an aggressive enemy action. Of course, the United States then had to hastily repeal its Neutrality Act.

Under the Lend-Lease Act, the United States could provide Britain with the supplies it needed to fight Germany. However, it would not insist upon being paid immediately and the United States would 'lend' supplies to the British against deferred payment. When repayment could eventually take place, it was decided it need not necessarily be in cash dollar payments. The tensions and instability engendered by inter-Allied war debts in the 1920s and 1930s had demonstrated that it was unreasonable to expect cash-strapped European nations to pay for every item they had purchased from the United States. In Britain's case, payment would primarily take the form of a 'consideration' granted by Britain to the United States, which

was described in Article 7 of the agreement. The consideration was to be in the form of joint action directed towards 'the creation of a liberalised international economic order in the post-war world'.

In due course, the Lend-Lease agreement was rolled out to a number of other Allied nations, including countries such as China and, of course, Russia. All had to sign Article 7 in their agreement with the United States. None of the signatories realised the significance of this article until long after the war had ended. In effect, Article 7 Lend-Lease agreements signed by the United States and the recipient nations laid the foundation for the creation of 'the new international economic order of the world'.

Under the various agreements between Allied nations and the United States, a total of $50.1 billion of supplies were shipped to the Allies between 1941 and 1945: $31.4 billion to Britain, $11.3 billion to Russia, $3.2 billion to France and $1.6 billion to China. The United States was also a recipient of foreign aid. The system of 'reverse Lend-Lease' partly offset the costs of Lend-Lease, and usually took the form of supplies and services for American troops stationed overseas, and repair and maintenance of equipment. A key outcome for Churchill was that the Act guaranteed Britain access to new merchant ships – enough it was hoped, to stem the losses that were being inflicted, particularly on the North Atlantic. Without this aid, the aspirations of Britain and the Allies would have become untenable. A flow of new Liberty ships did eventually cross the Atlantic, all with names with the prefix *Sam-* (Superstructure Aft of Midships); perhaps also an intended reference to 'Uncle Sam', being a fondly applied title for the United States government, in use since the nineteenth century.

The United States paid for the Liberty ships and Victory ships. It also paid for all but two of the Canadian-built North Sands-type 'Fort' ships (see Chapter 10), these being *Fort Ville Marie* and *Fort St James*, which had already been delivered prior to the Lend-Lease Act being passed. America ordered additional ships over the original Canadian contract for twenty-four, and paid for these too. Britain leased them on a bareboat charter, at a rate of $1.00 per month per ship, a monthly cash payment made in Washington that reached as high as the princely sum of $90! In addition, a further sixteen more old,

Great War-vintage, American freighters were transferred to the Ministry of War Transport in 1942, also under the Lend-Lease scheme. In due course, the Allies also had access to the faster Victory-type ships.

Lend-Lease, clearly, was a lifeline, and a timely one at that. At the end of 1941 Britain finally had the prospect of new ships from the United States. Apart from a lack of ships, there were other problems that included slow voyage turnaround times in the Mersey and the Clyde; east- and south-coast ports were effectively closed to the North Atlantic trades. The congestion in the ports did slowly ease as a number of port clearance measures were put in place, although turnaround times were nowhere near those achieved in peacetime. The non-availability of merchant ships for prolonged periods to shipyards for repair was another issue, but not one that could be easily rectified, as manpower and materials for upkeep were in short supply. Another issue was the maintenance of international trade with British-flagged ships, rather

Built at the Bethlehem-Fairfield Shipyard as *Samglory* (1944), as part of the Lend-Lease scheme, and managed on behalf of the British Ministry of War Transport by the King Line (Dodd Tomson). She became *Serbistan* when she was bought in 1947 by the Strick Line. She was resold in 1962 and renamed *Calypso* for Monrovian owners, for whom she gave a further seven years of service before going to the scrapyard. (AUTHOR COLLECTION)

than diverting them to the North Atlantic or using chartered neutral tonnage. Again, little could be done to affect this, as chartered neutral tonnage was expensive, and neutral states were not keen to engage in belligerent trade.

The lease of goods by the United States was intended to cease at the end of the war, with some form of repayment requiring to be made. The mode of repayment was deliberately left unspecified, but had to be negotiated separately with each recipient country. Part of the repayment was covered through reverse Lend-Lease, and with equipment lost or destroyed due to enemy action being considered a common loss. At the end of the war, large quantities of Lend-Lease goods were sold to Great Britain at about 10 per cent of their cost value. This generated a loan of $1,075 million, to be paid off over sixty years at 2 per cent interest; the last British payment on the loan was made on 29 December 2006. In 1972 the United States accepted an offer from the Soviet Union to pay $722 million in instalments to settle its war debts, including the costs of a number of Liberty ships. Large parts of the Lend-Lease debts were written off, as both President Roosevelt and his successor, President Truman, considered the fighting and sacrifice of the Allies to have been sufficient repayment.

The United States was able to recoup some of its investment by the sale of wartime assets considered surplus to requirements. A comprehensive inventory of these assets was prepared and published as a supplement to *The Code of Federal Regulations of the United States of America* in 1947. It provided 'unadjusted statutory sales prices', and included a basic Liberty ship priced at $639,000, a Victory ship at $979,000, a standard T2 tanker at $2,026,500, and even included the passenger liner *America*, formerly the troopship *West Point*, with accommodation for 1,802 passengers, at $9,250,000. Nevertheless, a large number of Liberty and Victory ships were laid up in the Reserve Fleet, many never to see service again.

All signatories of a Lend-Lease agreement remained bound, whether they liked it or not, to the Article 7 agreement whereby they contributed towards what was, in effect, a new global economic model. And this they did, not all intentionally, but eventually the fall of Communism in the Soviet Union brought Russia into the global economy, and the industrialisation of China did the same for her, even though the Communist model is retained to this day in China as the best means of managing such a vast and diverse nation. That apart, the Lend-Lease Act was an essential cornerstone of the Allied defeat of the Axis powers, without which an Allied defeat would have been inevitable, and Britain might well have been forced to surrender after the fall of France.

7 UNITED STATES MARITIME COMMISSION – C, T AND N CLASSES

The United States Merchant Marine Act of 1936 provided for the modernisation of the American Merchant Marine. It proposed to do this through a building subsidy that would reduce construction costs to equivalent costs in Britain and elsewhere. Costs were higher in the United States than in Europe due to higher wage bills and costs of materials. Part-payment for new ships could also be arranged by selling back the Great War-era ships to the United States Maritime Commission. The 1936 Act, section 101, states:

It is necessary for the national defense and development of its foreign and domestic commerce that the United States shall have a merchant marine (a) sufficient to carry its domestic water-borne commerce and a substantial portion of the water-

borne export and import foreign commerce of the United States and to provide shipping service on all routes essential for maintaining the flow of such domestic and foreign water-borne commerce at all times, (b) capable of serving as a naval and military auxiliary in time of war or national emergency, (c) owned and operated

The C1-B-type three-deck motor ship *American Press* (1941), following her launch on 20 May 1941 at the Western Pipe & Steel Company yard at San Francisco. She is attended by the tugs *Sea Queen*, on the left, and *Reliance*. *American Press* was owned by the United States Lines and was one of only ten C1-B-type ships equipped with an oil engine, which provided a service speed of 14 knots. She remained in private ownership until 1945, when she was taken over by the United States government and later renamed *Cape Lookout*. (WESTERN PIPE & STEEL COMPANY)

under the United States flag by citizens of the United States insofar as may be practicable, and (d) composed of the best equipped, safest, and most suitable types of vessels, constructed in the United States and manned with a trained and efficient citizen personnel. It is declared to be the policy of the United States to foster the development and encourage the maintenance of such a merchant marine.

A significant outcome of the Act was the C2 standard freighter, the smaller C1 and larger C3 cargo ships, and the T2 tanker and its variants. Although not at this stage classed as wartime standard ships, they soon would be. The 'C' number of the three standard designs of cargo ship indicated the waterline length of each class of ship, C1 being less than 400ft; C2, 400–450ft; and C3, greater than 450ft. The same numbering applied also to the 'T' for tanker classes.

Successful commercial shipping companies were encouraged to buy into the C2 shipbuilding plan – Lykes Lines, for example, as described in an article in *Sea Breezes*, October 1976:

After the passing of the 1936 Merchant Marine Act, the company [Lykes Brothers] came to an agreement with the United States Maritime Commission to build 28 new C Type vessels, and at the same time, to dispose of the older ships, dating from the First World War. As the new ships came along, so the old ones were sold, many of them going to Britain to join the Ministry of War Transport's 'Empire' fleet ... The momentous events of December 1941, which brought the United States of America into the war, completely altered Lykes' plans and caused the shipbuilding programme to be shelved. On December 7, 1941, when Pearl Harbor was attacked by the Japanese, the Lykes fleet consisted of 26 old vessels and 12 new C type ships ... Four other new ships were under construction but only one of these, the *Adabelle Lykes* was delivered to the company in 1942, the Government requisitioning the other three for war service.

Lykes had grown since its inception in 1922. It bought Tampa Interocean Steamship Company and its government-owned ships in 1925, the Lone Star Company two years later, and the fifty-two-ship fleet of the government-owned Dixie and Southern States Lines in 1933. How-

ever, not all companies were as co-operative as Lykes: others unsuccessfully determined that they be allowed to charter the ships from government; government insisted that the commercial operators pay their share of the costs of new ship construction.

The C2-type, shelter-deck cargo ships were designed by the United States Maritime Commission in 1937/38. An initial design based on a five-hold general-purpose cargo ship was drawn up and put out for consultation with shipowners and others. The design that was finally agreed upon was believed to be an ideal balance of speed, cargo capacity and economy of operation. It was planned to build fifty ships per year, but a total of only 173 ships were built between 1940 and 1945 because the emergency shipbuilding programme intervened (see Chapter 9). The first group of fast freighters were 459ft long, 63ft broad, 40ft depth, with a draught of 25ft. The sea speed was 15½ knots.

The basic specification comprised a five-hold, steel cargo ship with raked stem and cruiser stern, with shelter decks, and a third deck in Nos 1 to 4 holds. There were four deep tanks in No. 4 hold. Dimensions of the hatches were 20ft by 30ft, except for No. 2 hatch which was 20ft by 50ft to allow carriage of large items, including military hardware. Ventilation to the holds was provided via the kingposts which supported the cargo-handling gear: fourteen 5-ton derricks, and two 30-ton derricks plumbing Nos 3 and 4 holds.

Crew accommodation was amidships, officers' quarters on the boat deck, and the captain's suite on the bridge deck, along with the wheelhouse, chart room, gyro and radio room. Hot and cold running water was provided throughout. There were four two-berth cabins for passengers.

Ships varied in size and configuration as the design evolved; ultimately the various configurations were:

C2 (19 ships built 6,100grt)
C2-F (7 ships built 6,440grt) pre-war modification of Lykes Line design
C2-G (2 ships built 8,380grt)
C2-S (5 ships built 7,101grt)
C2-S-A1 (4 ships built 6,555grt)
C2-S1-A1 (3 ships built 7,486grt, sea speed 20 knots)
C2-S-AJ1 (64 ships built 8,335grt) a 460ft-long wartime modification
C2-S-AJ2 (5 ships built 8,290grt)

C2-S-AJ3 (32 ships built 8,160grt) US
  Navy's *Tolland*-class attack cargo ships
C2-S-AJ4 (6 ships built 8,328grt)
C2-S-AJ5 (10 ships built 8,295grt)
C2-S-E1 (30 ships built 6,190grt) a 469ft-
  long modification of the C2
C2-SU (3 ships built 7,780grt)
C2-S-B1 (R) (6 built 7,989grt) turbine re-
  frigerated ships
C2-S-B1 (123 ships built 6,230grt) 460ft-
  long cargo and passenger ship
C2-S1-DG2 (3 ships built 8,610grt)
C2-T (3 ships built)

The United States Maritime Commission had
a similar complicated and detailed code system
for all the different types of standard ship built
in the Second World War. The key types, nevertheless, were C1, C2, C3 and C4 cargo, and
cargo and passenger, ships; T1, T2 and T3
tankers; and N3 dry-cargo coastal ships. Each
variant in each of these eight types was given a
separate identifying code, steam or motor ships,
different power engines, different cargo-handling gear, modified for the military, and so on.
Thus, although the C2 list looks daunting, the
standard C2-type cargo ship is the steam turbine
freighter so often associated with the mainline
American shipping companies in the 1950s and
1960s.

The first C2-type ships were the motor vessel *Donald McKay*, launched in June 1939 at the

Sun shipyard in Chester, Pennsylvania, for
Moore McCormack Lines, and the steam turbine *Challenge* launched the following month
by the Federal Shipbuilding and Drydock Company at New Jersey. *Challenge* remained in government ownership and, like other ships not
bought commercially, was given a name after
one of the former fast American 'clipper' sailing
ships. Only seven ships had been delivered by
the start of the Second World War, four of them
to Moore McCormack; all seven were taken
into the service of the US Navy before the year
was out. Oil engines were offered as an option
for the C2, but only twenty-two C2s were
equipped as motor ships; most owners preferred
the steam turbine option.

The American C2-class ships continued to
be delivered after the war. Typical of these was
the C2-S-AJ5-type *American Scout*, delivered to
the United States Lines in February 1946. She
is described here by James Pearce in an article
in *Sea Breezes*, December 1950, alongside an in-
terview with her master Captain Archie Horka:

A welded ship of 8,228 gross tons on dimensions 441.1 feet by 63.1 feet by 38.3
feet, the *American Scout* was built by the
North Carolina Shipbuilding Company at
Wilmington. She has a cargo capacity of
about 8,200 tons and refrigerated space totalling about 36,000 cubic feet. She has accommodation for twelve passengers, and her

The C2-S-B1-type
ship converted into
the attack transport
USS *Oglethorpe*
(1945) was ordered
by the United States
Maritime Commis-
sion from the Fed-
eral Shipbuilding &
Drydock Company,
New Jersey, as a pas-
senger cargo ship.
She was bought by
the navy on the
stocks and com-
pleted for military
use. She was eventu-
ally decommissioned
in 1968. (OFFICIAL US
NAVY PHOTOGRAPH)

normal sea speed is 16 knots. Her propulsion machinery, built by the General Electric Company at Lynn, Mass., consists of two double-reduction steam turbines geared to a single screw. Navigation equipment includes radar, wireless, direction finder, gyro-compass, and echo sounding device.

The C2 freighter was designed for one purpose. Its role was long-haul, general cargo runs that required large capacity and fast ships to maintain a competitive service. This suited many companies that were capable of filling a 9,200dwt ship on each run, there and back, to an extent that the voyage was profitable. The ships suited many of the transatlantic trades and transpacific trades, but did not suit the services to the West Indies, and elsewhere, that required smaller vessels. For these trades, the C1 type was developed, and these ships were to be found on the Atlantic runs where smaller capacity was required than, say, to the UK, France or Germany, and the Pacific runs, where smaller ships were needed to supply some of the smaller island ports. There was also a need for large, fast passenger and cargo ships, and this need was satisfied, but at a later date, by the engines-aft C4-type ships.

There were a number of reasons why the rebuilding initiative was led by the state, and not by the shipping companies themselves. Between the wars, the American shipbuilding industry had withered to only a few companies capable of designing and building ocean-going ships. The shipowners themselves had returned little dividend to their shareholders since the Wall Street Crash, and had no appetite for employing naval architects to redesign and update their fleets. There was, therefore, no ongoing dialogue between shipowner, shipbuilder and ship designer as there was, and always has been, in the United Kingdom and elsewhere in Europe. Indeed, without the state intervention created by the 1936 Merchant Marine Act, America would have been in a parlous state when Germany declared war on her in December 1941.

The C1 type was the smallest. The seventy-eight Type C1-A shelter-deck ships were 412ft long with a deadweight capacity of 6,440 tons; the ninety-five full scantling C1-B-type ships were 418ft long, with a deadweight capacity of 8,015 tons; and the 239 shallow-draught C1-M-A-V1 (known as the 'Cimarvy') full scantling type were 339ft long, with a deadweight capacity of 5,032 tons. The A and B types were equipped with an oil engine and had a speed of 14 knots, although some A types had steam turbines. The Cimarvy ships were good for only 11 knots, again motor ships although one, *Coastal Liberator*, was diesel electric; the engines were aft, along with the bridge and all accommodation. There was a deep tank situated at the forward end of No. 1 hold. Like the other C-class ships, they had a raked bow and a cruiser stern.

The C1 types were not as well known in the UK as the C2 types, the latter calling regularly on business for Lykes Line and United States Lines. However, the C1 is remembered when it is associated with the name *Flying Enterprise*. This was a C1 ship that ran into trouble on a voyage from Hamburg to New York, being hove-to in a storm on Christmas Eve 1951 until it finally foundered two weeks later. The saga very much caught the attention of the media on both sides of the Atlantic.

Some thirty-five of the B type were delivered prior to the attack on Pearl Harbor; the

One of only very few Cimarvy-type ships to be acquired by European shipowners after the war was Booth Steamship Company's *Dominic* (1945). She was completed as *Hickory Stream* by Consolidated Steel Corporation at Wilmington, California, and transferred to the Ministry of War Transport without change of name. She worked the Booth Steamship Company's service from UK to Amazon ports from 1947 to 1962, when she was sold to owners in the Far East and foundered nine years later. (AUTHOR COLLECTION)

first B type were laid down in 1939. The first of the A type was only delivered in May 1941. But many C1-A and C1-B ships were already on the stocks and were delivered during 1942. Some were converted to military purposes including troop transports during the war. The Type C1-M-A-V1 ship (the Cimarvy) was a separate design, for a significantly smaller and shallower draught vessel. This design evolved as an answer for the projected needs for military transport and supply of the Pacific Island campaigns and was often referred to in the American press as the 'pint-sized freighter'. The ships had 9,800cu ft of refrigerated space as standard for perishable goods. The first Cimarvy was delivered in August 1944; she was also the first in the *Alamosa* class of attack cargo ship.

Thirteen C1-A-type ships with *Cape* names (*Cape St Vincent*, etc) were chartered by the British government in 1943 and 1944. They had all been completed as infantry attack ships for the United States government under the classification C1-S-AY1. They were managed by commercial ship operators on behalf of the Ministry of War Transport, some later transferring to the Royal Navy, designated as Landing Ships, Infantry (LSI). They were each given an *Empire* name within the theme of tools of war: *Empire Broadsword*, *Empire Rapier*, *Empire Spearhead*, etc. One, *Empire Javelin*, was sunk by torpedo in December 1944. Another C1-A type, *Cape Farewell*, was taken by the US Navy and converted for use as the torpedo-boat tender, USS *Cyrene*.

The larger ships, the C3 class, comprised a number of variants. The standard C3-S-A2 class of shelter-deck ships was 492ft long and had a deadweight capacity of 12,595 tons. Their turbine machinery maintained a sea speed of 16½ knots, and they could accommodate twelve passengers in twin-berth 'staterooms'. The first standard C3 was *Sea Fox*, delivered in March 1940 to the Maritime Commission, but quickly transferred into the ownership of Moore McCormack lines as *Mormacport*. Some 465 ships of this class were built.

The C3-P&C was the pre-war design, 492ft-long, standard C3 with passenger accommodation, and equipped either with steam-turbine machinery or oil engines. The C3-A P&C prototype was a 492ft-long passenger and cargo steam-turbine ship built for American President Lines, eventually becoming a six-ship class of the *President Jackson* type. C3-E was a 473ft-long, cargo-only version built for the American Export Lines. The first, in fact the first C3 to be commissioned, *Exporter*, was launched on 18 July 1939 and delivered to American Export Lines in September. She was requisitioned by the United States Navy in 1941 as USS *Hercules*. The C3-M was a 492ft-long cargo version built for Moore McCormack Lines. The C3-S-A1, C3-S-A2 and C3-cargo were 492ft-long cargo ships, and these formed the majority of the class, most being built between 1942 and 1945. The C3-S-A3 was a 473ft-long version built for American Export Lines in 1945 and 1946. Post-war modifications of ships still building included the C3-S-BH ships, five built for Lykes Brothers (C3-S-BH1) and six for Farrell Lines of New York (C3-S-BH2). There were also three passenger and refrigerated cargo ships designated C3-S1-BR1, *Del Norte*, *Del Mar* and *Del Sud*, built for the Mississippi Shipping Company of New Orleans.

The last of the C3 type were delivered in 1946. In addition, seventy-five ships were built

The C3-S-A1-type *Mendocino* (1944) was completed with accommodation for a limited number of passengers. She was transferred in 1947 to the Pacific Argentine Brazil Line, later coming under Moore McCormack Lines ownership in 1957 as *Mormacwind*. (AMBROSE GREENWAY COLLECTION)

HMS *Searcher* (1942) was a Ruler-class escort carrier of the C3-S-A1 standard type received by Britain under the Lend-Lease scheme. She was laid down at Seattle as a naval ship and completed as an escort carrier, rather than converted from a completed C3-type cargo ship. She could carry up to twenty-four aircraft. Decommissioned in 1945, she was returned to the United States, converted into a conventional C3-type cargo ship and renamed *Captain Theo* under the Greek flag. (AUTHOR COLLECTION)

to other designs. The C3 was larger and faster than the C1 and C2 types (the C2 was just 459ft long) and designed to make 16½ knots (one knot faster than the C2). Like the C2, it had five cargo holds. The first ships of the class were delivered in 1940. They differed from pre-war designs principally in their widespread use of high-pressure, high-temperature turbine machinery with double-reduction gearing, which allowed the ships to combine fuel efficiency with reasonable speed. One ship of this class is reputed to have attained a trials speed of 19.5 knots, with a fuel consumption rate of 0.563lbs of fuel oil per shaft horsepower (shp) per hour. Building times were in the order of 190 days.

A small number of the C3 ships were of all-welded construction, and as a consequence had about 600 tons less steel in their construction than the riveted ships. Some were fitted out as C3-C&P ships with accommodation for between ninety-five and 192 passengers. Others were completed for the United States Navy, and some C3-type ships came to Britain, reconfigured as escort aircraft carriers. The only real failing of the C3 type was that it was built to a high standard that could not be produced fast enough under emergency wartime conditions.

The C4 type was a large, full scantling vessel of 15,570dwt. They were based on a design originally developed for the American-Hawaiian Lines in 1941. Some seventy-five ships were built as cargo and troop ships, thirty-five by Kaiser at Richmond in California, twenty by Kaiser Vancouver, and twenty at the Sun Shipbuilding & Dry Dock Company in Chester, Pennsylvania. They were equipped with steam turbine machinery situated aft, generating 9,900shp, and they had a sea speed of 17 knots.

The C4-S-B5 cargo ship *Marine Fiddler* (1945) was one of a number of ships especially designed as a cargo and troop transport. She was built at the Sun Yard at Chester; the keel was laid on 15 December 1944 and she was launched on 15 May 1945. She is seen here after conversion to a heavy-lift cargo ship in 1954, when her troop decks were cleared out of the 'tween deck spaces. She was only demolished in 2004 after a protracted period in the Reserve Fleet. (AUTHOR COLLECTION)

Among the variations of the design was the *Haven*-class hospital ship. The various sub-types were:

C4-S-A1 troop transport, 30 ships with names beginning *General-*
C4-S-A3 troop transport, 15 ships
C4-S-A4 cargo, 10 ships
C4-S-B1 tank carrier, 1 only, *Marine Eagle*
C4-S-B 2 troop transport/hospital, 14 ships
C4-S-B5 cargo/troop transport, 5 ships.

The ships other than the C4-S-A1 troop transports mostly had names beginning with *Marine*: *Marine Fiddler*, *Marine Raven*, etc; five had names beginning *Mount*. The exceptions were one C4-S-A4 ship which was named *Ernie Pyle*, and three C4-S-A4 ships, *Louis McH Howe*, *Scott E Land* and *Willis Vickery*. The six *Haven*-class hospital ships converted from troop transports were

USS *Consolation* (1944) was one of the C4-S-B2 *Haven*-class hospital ships. She was launched as *Marine Walrus* at the Sun Shipbuilding & Dry Dock Company Yard in Chester and immediately taken in hand for conversion to a hospital ship. She had a crew complement of 564 and could accommodate 800 hospital patients. Her first duty was to assist repatriation of American prisoners of war from Japan, and after lay-up in the late 1940s she was sent to assist in the Korean War. (AUTHOR COLLECTION)

given passive names: *Benevolence*, *Consolation*, *Haven*, *Repose*, *Sanctuary* and *Tranquillity*.

The wartime C4 ships were followed post-war by thirty-seven of the larger C4-S-1 class, also known as the Mariner class. These were modern 20-knot cargo ships with four holds, that were built in the early 1950s.

The standard N3-type Baltic coaster was a single-deck vessel with a cruiser stern. It had a triple-expansion steam engine amidships con-

The N3-S-A1-type 'Yankee Jeep' *Samuel V Shreve* (1943) was built by the Pacific Bridge Company at Alameda, California. She served the Ministry of War Transport until 1949, when she was bought by Clydesdale Shipowners Company, managed by Glen & Company, Glasgow, and renamed *Jura* as seen here. She was resold in 1957 to become *Barcelona*, but in January 1963 she sprang a leak and sank off Matapalo Head, Costa Rica. (AUTHOR COLLECTION)

nected to a single shaft, and had two hatches forward and two aft. Designed as small general-
purpose ships, they soon attracted the sobriquet
'Yankee Jeep'. Some 109 of these ships were
built, many on the Great Lakes, the first being
delivered in December 1942, the last in 1946.
The original design was the fifty-nine ships of
the N3-S-A2 class, which had oil-fired boilers,
but at the request of the British Ministry of War
Transport, thirty-one ships of the N3-S-A1 type
were built with coal-fired boilers and chartered
to Britain. They all retained their American-style
names of well-known people, and were managed by a variety of British companies including
Elder Dempster, Glen & Company and the
Currie Line. They were full scantling ships with
a length of 260ft and a deadweight capacity of
2,900 tons. The oil-fired version had a slightly
smaller deadweight capacity. The coal-burners
could make 10 knots and the oil burners 11
knots. The crew complement was twenty-three.

A third variant, the N3-M-A1, was a very
limited design of only fourteen motor ships
with superstructure and machinery aft instead
of amidships, and all built by Penn-Jersey Shipbuilding Company, New Jersey. They were constructed both for the United States Navy and
British use. Four of the fourteen ships of this
type retained the original configuration and
were transferred to Britain in the winter of
1943/44 in preparation for the liberation of
France. They were managed by Currie Line,
Leith, for the Admiralty as *BAK-1*, *BAK-2*,

BAK-3 and *BAK-4*, and were originally named
Asa Lothrop, *Lauchlan McKay*, *John L Mason* and
Nathaniel Mathews.

Several of the major oil companies and
tanker operators, which normally used relatively
slow speed tankers, were approached by the
United States Maritime Commission in 1939.
They were asked what the cost would be if they
ordered a fast 16-knot tanker that could be used
as a naval oiler in times of emergency. The Maritime Commission offered to pay the difference
between that price and the cost for a similar 12-
knot tanker. The lowest bid came from Standard
Oil, who in conjunction with the Sun Shipbuilding & Drydock Company at Chester, came
up with a design costing $3.13 million, of which
$2.25million would be paid by the oil company,
and the rest by government. Twelve ships were
built and delivered in 1939 and 1940, and designated as the T3-S2-A1 type. The ships were
able to steam at 18 knots with a deadweight capacity of 18,300 tons. They had four steam turbines geared to two shafts. Only five of the ships
were delivered to Standard Oil, three of the
twelve being bought on the stocks by the
United States Navy and four converted into escort aircraft carriers. Of the seven received by
Standard Oil, *Esso Albany* spent only seven
months in Civvy Street before becoming a fleet
auxiliary; her sisters soon followed.

The standard T2 tanker followed as a
wartime defensive measure. The T2 was based
on two ships built in 1938 and 1939 by Bethle-

hem Steel for Socony-Vacuum Oil Company, *Mobilfuel* and *Mobilube*. The T2 differed from the Mobil ships principally in the installation of more powerful machinery for higher speed. The first ships were delivered in 1940. The standard T2s were 501ft long, and 68ft in beam and were measured as 9,900grt and 15,850 tons cargo deadweight capacity. A steam turbine of 12,000hp drove a single propeller to provide a sea speed of up to 14 knots. The Type T2-A consisted of five ships built in 1940 for Keystone Tankers, and all of them were converted during the war to naval oilers of the *Mattaponi* class. Type T2-SE-A1 was the standard design and 481 were built, seventy days being allowed from laying of the keel to completion of fitting out. Type T2-SE-A2 was a more powerful version of the A1 type, whilst the A3 was an A2 type reconfigured as a naval oiler. Some twenty-five Type T3-S-A1 ships were built as standard-design ships with lower-powered machinery. The last of the T2 tankers were delivered in 1946.

The United States Maritime Commission's type T2-SE-A1 was initially built by the Sun Shipbuilding Company for Standard Oil Company of New Jersey. Expanded wartime production brought the Alabama Drydock & Shipbuilding Company of Mobile; Kaiser Company's Swan Island Yard at Portland, Oregon; Marinship Corporation at Sausalito, California;

and Sun Shipbuilding & Drydock Company at Chester, Pennsylvania, also into the T2 building programme. The record for the fastest build was by Marinship Corporation which completed *Huntington Hills* in just thirty-three days; twenty-eight days on the slipway and five days fitting out.

The T2-SE-A1 ships were 523ft long overall, with a beam of 68ft. They displaced about 21,880 tons, with a gross rated tonnage of 10,448 tons and 16,613 tons cargo deadweight capacity. The propulsion machinery was of the turbo-electric type, where a steam turbine drove an electrical generator which, in turn, produced the electrical power to drive the main propulsion motor. This 'electrical gearing' eliminated the need for the conventional reduction gearing associated with steam turbine propulsion machinery, allowing it to be diverted as a priority to the extensive United States Navy's warship building programme. The propulsion system delivered 6,000shp, and a sea speed of 15 knots. The ships had nine sets of tanks with a small dry cargo space of about 15,200cu ft located forward of tank No. 1. There were two pump rooms located forward, with two pumps each, and one pump room aft with six pumps. A number of these ships found their way into the British registry after the war, despite claims, rightly or wrongly, that their structure was

Esso Albany (1939), fresh from the builder's yard, became a fleet auxiliary only seven months after Standard Oil took delivery of her. She was one of twelve ships paid for by her owners and upgraded to 18 knots with funds from the Maritime Commission, conditional on her owners releasing her to government at a time of emergency. These twelve ships were the precursor to the later T3-type fast tanker. (AUTHOR COLLECTION)

weakened in freezing conditions. The Esso Petroleum Company fleet (formerly Anglo-American Oil Company), for example, still owned four T2 tankers in 1963: *Esso Purfleet*, *Esso Glasgow* (which was lengthened in 1957), *Esso Birmingham* and *Esso Manchester*, albeit with the three smaller ships laid up by the year end.

Some 481 of the 525 tankers ordered on behalf of the Maritime Commission were of the T2-SE-A1 type. The machinery was located aft, with the accommodation both amidships and aft. The midships superstructure was situated above Nos 4 and 5 tanks, and accommodated the master, deck officers and radio officers and radio room, with the engineer officers and all other crew accommodated aft. There was also the T2-SE-A2 type which had more powerful machinery and was capable of 16 knots. The T2-SE-A3 were tankers that had been converted for naval duties, notably refuelling at sea.

Eighteen of the Type T2-SE-A1 tankers were lost in enemy action or broken up after the war, 244 were either sold off or returned to their United States owners, and the United States Navy acquired a further eighteen existing vessels. The remaining 203 T2-SE-A1 tankers were sold post-war to overseas owners, the biggest

total (seventy-one) going to Panama-flag companies, and Britain acquiring a total of fifty-two of the vessels.

The T3-S-A1 type tankers were of 16,000 tons cargo deadweight capacity. They were essentially a shorter version of the T2 tanker, being 502ft long overall, whereas the T2 was 623ft long overall, but both had the same breadth of 60ft. The T3 type had steam turbine engines and a service speed of 15½ knots.

A smaller class of motor tanker (T1-M-A) was developed in two variants. The twenty-six ships of the type T1-M-A1 had a deadweight of 1,600 tons and the thirty-two ships of the T1-M-A2 design a deadweight of 1,453 tons. They were commissioned between 1943 and 1945. Both types had a service speed of 10 knots and were of the standard engines-aft configuration with the bridge amidships over Nos 2 and 3 tanks, there being nine tanks in total. The ships were all named after places relating to the American-based oil industry. Some twenty-four of the A1-type ships were bareboat chartered to the British Ministry of War Transport and managed, six each, by F T Everard & Sons, Rowbotham & Sons, J Cook & Sons and Immingham Agency. Later in the war, the surviving ships were all managed by the Anglo-Saxon Oil Company, as the sphere of operation had become international rather than domestic.

A later version was the larger T1-M-B2-type, 4,205 tons cargo deadweight tanker commissioned in 1945, which had a sea speed of 10 knots. The first three, *Tancred*, *Tarascon* and *Tarantella*, completed in July 1945, were transferred to the Ministry of War Transport on bareboat charter. *Tancred* was managed by the Anglo-Saxon Petroleum Company and the other two by the Anglo-American Oil Company, and all three ships were returned to the United States by 1948. Two ships went to the Military Sea Transportation Service and three more were laid up in the Reserve Fleet. The remaining ships were surplus.

The T1-MT-M1 type was even smaller, with engines and accommodation aft, a long forecastle and a long central trunk topped by a catwalk. They were designed by the navy to carry fuel and lubricating oils to the various outstations in the Pacific, to service the needs of aircraft, motor torpedo boats and other small craft. They had ten tanks for the carriage of petrol and other light fuels, and two small 2,200-gallon tanks forward that were used for lubricating oils. The ships were all completed between 1943 and 1944. The tankers were known as the *Patapsco* class after the lead ship.

Numerous harbour tugs were built for the United States Maritime Commission. A few of the so-called 'TUSA' type were sent to Britain as deck cargo. They all had names beginning with *Port*, as in *Port Sewall*, and were originally designed as propulsion units for United States Maritime Commission with a crew complement of eight men. They had oil engines providing 240 brake horsepower (bhp) and were just 80grt. Some forty-seven were ordered by the Ministry of War Transport, but twelve were cancelled at the end of the war. Many of them were later used in the Mediterranean by Greece, Italy, Yugoslavia, Malta and Egypt, and others went to the Pacific, Australia and India.

Cotton Valley (1943) was one of the T1-M-A-type tankers transferred to the Ministry of War Transport in 1943 for service in the Mediterranean. She was managed by F T Everard & Sons. In October 1944 she hit a mine off Port de Bouc and broke in two; the stern section was salvaged and a temporary new bow fitted. She was then used as a water carrier in Toulon. Her later commercial service in the Mediterranean region lasted until 2000, when she was finally broken up. (AUTHOR COLLECTION)

The C1-type *Flying Enterprise* saga, Christmas 1951

The following is from an Associated Press notice issued at Falmouth on 11 January 1952:

Safe ashore, Capt. Kurt Carlsen told the story today of his monumental fight with the raging Atlantic – a two weeks battle against the wind, waves and cold. He told a cheering crowd of thousands 'I deeply regret that I was not in a position to bring the '*Enterprise* back with me'. From the deck of the rescue tug *Turmoil* he watched the death throes of the 6,711 ton *Flying Enterprise* yesterday, minutes after he leaped into the water from the dying freighter. She went down in 40 fathoms of water, 37 miles off this fishing port…

'I commanded that ship for three years and made 44 crossings of the Atlantic. She was a very well built ship, she was an extremely solid ship.' Carlsen seemed calm as he described his ordeal, a solitary battle for a week after he ordered his crew of 40 and ten passengers to abandon ship on December 29, four days after the Christmas hurricane hit him … Things brightened up for him after a week of lonely battle, when the rescue tug *Turmoil*, coming close by, put aboard first mate Kenneth Dancy …

When he and Dancy finally got a towline, the freighter was 320 miles west of the tip of England, and the safety of Falmouth harbour on the rocky coastline of Cornwall lay four days away at snail's pace towing speed of 3½ knots. Even when the towline snapped 57 miles from Falmouth, hope was not abandoned. But gale force winds and high seas blocked all efforts to again hitch the *Flying Enterprise* to the tug. All day Wednesday and until noon yesterday they waited for a break in the weather, while Carlsen and Dancy balanced perilously on the slanting, bucking deck. As late as Wednesday night Carlsen radioed his belief 'the ship would come through all right' if the weather would ease a little. But it didn't. The *Flying Enterprise* dipped lower and lower into the water until waves splashed into her levelled funnel. Only then did Carlsen reluctantly admit defeat …

With a last fond look at his ship, Carlsen followed him [Dancy] into the water. The *Turmoil* came beside them and the deck crew helped them aboard …

The American C1-B-type cargo ship *Cape Kumukaki* (1944) was sold to Isbrandtsen Lines of New York in 1947 and renamed *Flying Enterprise*. She became the focus of the media when at the end of December 1952, on a voyage from Hamburg to New York with pig iron and coffee and also ten passengers, she hove-to in severe weather 100 miles off Land's End; a crack developed on the weather deck and the cargo shifted. Passengers and crew, save for Captain Henrik Carlsen, were taken off on 29 December; a tow was secured on 5 January, the ship now with a list of 60°; the ship finally sank on 8 January. (AUTHOR COLLECTION)

8 THE EMPIRE SHIPS BUILT IN BRITAIN

The prefix *Empire* was adopted for the names of all merchant ships built in Britain for the British government in the Second World War. This was a recognition that it was not just Great Britain that was fighting the Allies, but every nation within the empire. It was also a useful means of distinguishing between the British government standard shipping of the Great War, which had the prefix *War*, and the newer ships. The Empire ships included those acquired second-hand from America and elsewhere (see Chapter 6), as well as confiscated German tonnage. In all, about 1,300 ships carried the *Empire* name.

The Ministry of War Transport was established on 1 May 1941 by merging the Ministry of Transport and Ministry of Shipping, which it was hoped would better co-ordinate transport activities. The Ministry of Shipping, it should be remembered, was created in October 1939 out of what had previously been a department of the Board of Trade. The Ministry of War Transport had many and disparate roles, which included allocation of tonnage, ship management, management of ships owned, requisitioned or seized, and requisitioning, chartering and allocation of British merchant shipping. The responsibility for shipbuilding and ship repair had been removed from the Ministry of Shipping in February 1940 and vested with the Controller of Merchant Shipbuilding and Repairs, who sat on the Admiralty Board. Thus, although the Ministry of War Transport effectively owned the Empire ships, the responsibility for orders, designs and numbers of new ships was an Admiralty responsibility.

In reality, the Controller's office did little by way of design. Nevertheless, the Controller, Sir James Lithgow, of shipbuilding fame, did have a number of top-flight naval architects in his office at St Enoch station in Glasgow. Their key job was to scrutinise work submitted by invited shipyards and determine which ship types offered best practice in terms of speed, efficiency, deadweight capacity, and ease of operation and maintenance. Until then, approval for new ship orders was granted only if it was considered that the intended vessel fitted the overall plan of the Ministry of Shipping; the ordinary peacetime building programme was also still running its course, with ships being completed from orders placed before the war started.

The scrutiny and approval process that the Controller of Merchant Shipping and Repairs adopted was based firmly on lessons learnt from the Great War. Although it was accepted that standardisation had tremendous benefits in a shipbuilding environment, it was also recognised that the element of individuality in many British specialist yards would help to optimise output

Empire Southey (1942) was typical of the many tramp-type steamers that were built in the Second World War, all characterised by split superstructure. This one is of the PF(C) type with one 50-ton and one 30-ton derrick, along with ten 5- or 10-ton derricks. Post-war, she became Hollybank in the Bank Line Fleet, until she was sold in 1953 for further service under the Dutch flag, and later the Monrovian flag, before being broken up in 1967. (AUTHOR COLLECTION)

and quality of production. Michael Lindberg and David Todd described the process in their book *Anglo-American shipbuilding in World War II*:

The example of the general cargo ship, the indispensable tramp steamer, will suffice to show how the approach came to bear on merchant shipbuilding. At the Admiralty's behest, shipbuilders that had focussed on tramp steamers formulated several partly prefabricated designs that were further refined into standard cargo ships of the B, C, D and Y types. These ranged in size from 7,050–7,370grt (10,000–10,500dwt) with length of 446–449ft, the dispersion around the mean reflecting local yard conditions. Firms granted discretionary powers to build these extensions of their own prototypes included Barclay Curle and Charles Connell at Glasgow, Harland & Wolff at Belfast, Redhead on the Tyne, the Sunderland yards of Bartram, Doxford, Laing and Short, the neighbouring Hartlepool establishment of William Gray and that ardent supporter of standard ships since 1918, Burntisland on the Forth.

Thus the Great War approach of imposing standard designs on shipbuilders was deliberately spurned; instead each yard was given its head in the conviction that it would raise productivity by concentrating at what it did best. As a rule a British shipbuilder in World War Two only constructed ships of a type with which it was accustomed in the manner in which it felt most comfortable. On occasion this rule was broken – exigencies sometimes called for drastic measures – but the belief then current was that yards would give a good account of themselves by affirming their specialisation. The message that specialisation was a worthy end of rationalisation … had taken root.

The United States was shortly to undertake the world's biggest programme of constructing emergency standard ships. Lindberg and Todd, almost by way of an apology to the Americans for this British attitude to standardisation, continued:

This is not to say that standardisation was disparaged in any way; on the contrary, it came into its own with respect to the power, navigation, crewing, and lifting subsystems essential to the functioning of any ship. Practically this entailed the mass production of standard components built into the ship. Items such as winches, pumps, fans, electrical motors, controllers, switchboards, valves, heat exchange units, boilers and hatch covers all became interchangeable parts, 'commodities' rather than bespoke components built to fit the requirements of specific ships. Prominent among the subsystems subjected to standardisation of parts were marine engines. Just a few designs selected for volume production and components common to these designs were manufactured to standard blueprints, permitting their installation in any engine type.

This all seemed sensible and the best way forward. However, there were issues to be addressed, and a major one was that of engine-building capacity. At the start of the Great War, Britain had the annual capacity to produce 1.4 million horsepower, by 1920 it peaked at 1.8 million horsepower and thereafter declined through the years of the recession to just 0.6 million horsepower by the start of the Second World War. A considerable increase in engine-building capacity was required, as it also was in the shipyards themselves.

So what were the B-, C-, D- and Y-type standard ships, and what had happened to the A-type standard ship? Plans were, in fact, drawn up for the A-type standard cargo ship during the early part of 1941, following a survey of selected 'best practice' prototype ships, and based around a length of 425ft and a breadth of 56ft. The ships were to be constructed in large prefabricated units which would be brought together on the slipway, although only a few shipyards would be capable of handling the largest of these units. It was soon realised that this practical impediment greatly inhibited the prospects of mass production and, instead, the original plans were dropped in favour of a modified design, which incorporated a greater number of smaller-sized units in the construction phase. This was the Type B standard cargo ship, with a length between perpendiculars (bp) of 425ft (that is, from the centre of the rudder stock to the intersection of the stem with the load waterline), although this length between perpendiculars varied between shipyards. They had a split superstructure with a hatch between the bridge and the funnel, and were typically of 7,050grt. Their triple-expansion steam engine was intended to provide a service speed of 11.5 knots. The Y type was sim-

ilar, save that the funnel and the kingposts serving No. 3 hold in the split superstructure were closer together than in the B type.

The actual construction and degree of prefabrication was defined by each yard's facilities and experience. The extent of the use of welding was also discretionary, so that each type of ship became a variation on the critical design constraints provided by the shipbuilding controllerate, and on which each builder could apply his own variations. As more shipbuilders became involved in the programme, so the original design became more varied. But common to all were the engines, their component parts, the many and varied fittings, the cargo-handling gear and every other item that went to make a ship. All were mass-produced to specification, and delivered complete to the shipyards in the order required for their assembly into the ever-growing body of the ship. Clearly, this required careful planning and production control, especially after ships were launched and at the fitting-out stage.

In due course, there appeared a need for larger hatchways and better cargo-handling gear. In 1942 plans for the C type emerged to satisfy this need, not only with hatches giving better hold accessibility, but with an array of heavier derricks: a 50-ton derrick and a 30-ton derrick plus five 10-ton and five 5-ton derricks. The B type had one 30-ton derrick, two 10-ton and eight 5-ton derricks. The C and D types differed only in that the former had a topgallant poop of bulwark height, whereas the D type had a full-height poop erection. The average gross tonnage of the C type was 7,370 and the D type 7,370. A few ships were partly refrigerated with up to 250,000cu ft of space available, and for speed of construction many of the ships had square triangular-shaped sterns.

A total of forty-one B types, seventeen C types and ten D types were built between 1941 and 1946. The Y type and the variant X type continued to be constructed until 1945 by yards such as Harland & Wolff at both Belfast and Glasgow, Lithgows and William Hamilton at Port Glasgow, and Vickers Armstrong at Barrow. Redhead & Sons at South Shields also built to their own design a series of ships, with two being 432ft long and six at 406ft long. J L Thompson at Sunderland were sanctioned to build ships that broadly fitted the design criteria and one of these, *Empire Liberty*, was used as the prototype for the American- and Canadian-built Ocean-type ships (see Chapters 9 and 10). Of the other 11–12-knot, general-purpose, dry-cargo ships that could not be strictly classified as recognised types, 277 were built in British shipyards, with a further three built and delivered in Hong Kong; a further four were lost to the Japanese when Hong Kong was invaded and finally surrendered on Christmas Day 1941. All the ships conformed to the shipbuilding controllerate's requirements. It would seem that the freedom applied by the controllerate with regard to specific shipyard preferences had paid off handsomely with the production of such a large number of ships competing against the demands for other merchant ship types and, of course, the Admiralty's own military shipbuilding agenda.

By 1942 it was recognised that some of the fast cargo liners requisitioned by the Admiralty for military use required to be replaced for cargo carrying. To this end a fast cargo liner design was prepared by Furness Shipbuilding Company at Haverton Hill, to be fitted with steam turbine machinery for a projected sea speed of 15 knots. The prototype was *Empire Chieftain* launched on 20 May 1943, followed by *Empire Regent* two months later; both from the Furness yard. A total

Built as the Y7-type freighter *Empire Balfour* (1944) by Lithgows at Port Glasgow, and bought by Houlder Brothers and renamed *Barton Grange* in 1949. Unlike the B-type tramp ships, the Y types did not have a hold between the bridge and funnel. Houlder Brothers sold *Barton Grange* to the Western Steamship Company of Hong Kong in 1958, and she was eventually broken up in 1967. (AUTHOR COLLECTION)

Empire Might (1942) was one of nine refrigerated ships that were built and was of a class of three 13-knot ships with 300,000cu ft of refrigerated space, completed by the Greenock Dockyard Company early in the war. (AUTHOR COLLECTION)

of twelve ships, two with oil engines, were built under the controllerate's authorisation and others were built privately under licence. None were lost due to enemy action.

There was also a series of nine fast refrigerated ships built to a pre-war Shaw Savill Line design. The first, *Empire Song*, was laid down for Shaw Savill and completed for the Ministry of Shipping in October 1940. She was sunk by mine off Malta just seven months later. Her sister, *Empire Hope*, was also lost in a Malta convoy just over a year later, but the remaining seven ships in the class survived to take up civilian duties after the war.

Heavy-lifts were always a problem in wartime, as few ships were capable of handling such loads without assistance from dockside cranes or heavy-lift floating cranes. Ten ships were built to satisfy this demand and were known as the Bel-type heavy-lift ships, as their design was based on the Norwegian-owned heavy-lift ships whose names were prefixed by *Bel-*. The first pair, *Empire Charmian* and *Empire Elaine*, were motor ships of 10,000dwt, with a sea speed of 12 knots. They were followed by four, faster, 15-knot ships, equipped with steam

Empire Grace (1942) was one of four refrigerated motor ships built by Harland & Wolff at Belfast. She became the Shaw, Savill & Albion Line's *Wairangi* after the war and was scrapped in 1963 after a grounding incident. (AMBROSE GREENWAY COLLECTION)

turbine machinery, and four more 15-knot ships with turbo-electric drive. These all had a deadweight capacity of 9,750 tons. In all cases, the engines were aft and the bridge abaft the No. 1 hatch. Each ship was fitted with three 120-ton heavy-lift derricks, and they had an extra-long No. 3 hatchway that allowed access for large, heavy and bulky goods.

The Scandinavian-type, engines-amidships, small, general cargo ships had a deadweight capacity of just 4,700 tons. Some of these vessels were also equipped with heavy-lift gear (one 80-ton and one 50-ton derrick) for deployment overseas, particularly in Russian ports, where they acted as 'tenders' to other ships which otherwise would have to wait for an available heavy-lift crane berth. A total of thirty-eight of these handy little ships were completed, most built by William Gray & Company at West Hartlepool. They were a straightforward three-island-type ship, with a well deck forward and aft, and were equipped with a single triple-expansion engine to maintain a sea speed of 10 knots. The ships were particularly valuable in supplying the Allied troops with stores after the invasion of France in 1944. A further forty-two vessels were built in Canada to the same design, given *Park* names and registered in Canada (see Chapter 10).

William Gray also built a series of ten 4,310dwt, engines-aft, bridge forward of amidships, general-purpose ships known after the prototype as the *Empire Malta* class. The triple-expansion steam engine provided a sea speed of 10 knots. They were designed by the controller-ate specifically to carry dangerous goods such as cased petrol, but they could also be used for bulk cargoes and, as they had an 80-ton derrick, were useful for heavy-lifts as well.

All these ships were owned by the Ministry of War Transport. Each was, in turn, put out to a British merchant shipowner whose existing trade suited the type of ship, as did their expertise for managing and crewing the vessel. The faster cargo liners were managed by Blue Funnel, Clan Line, Union-Castle Line, British India and others, while the fast refrigerated ships went to Shaw Savill Line and Houlder Brothers. Some of the numerous tramp ship designs also went to liner companies, but most were managed by the traditional tramp ship operators who were mainly based in the northeast of England. The West Hartlepool Steam Navigation Company, for example, managed the B-type steamers *Empire Raleigh* and *Empire Spray*, taking delivery of them from William Doxford & Sons yard at Sunderland in 1941, and then passing them on to the Royal Netherlands government in 1942 and 1943, respectively.

The larger tramp ship operators had a correspondingly greater involvement. The Ropner Steamship Company of Hartlepool, or Ropner's Navy as it was affectionately called, initially managed seven former United States Shipping Board ships dating from the Great War: *Empire Bison* built as *West Cawthorn*; *Empire Cheetah*

Clan Line Steamers *Clan Macrae* (1942), formerly *Empire Might*, shows how the refrigerated ships were modified for commercial use postwar and how attractive they could appear in civilian livery. She was transferred to Bullard King in 1959 as *Umgeni*, and to Springbok Shipping Company (later Safmarine) in 1960 as *Gemsbok* and later *South African Financier*. She was finally broken up in 1962. (AUTHOR COLLECTION)

One of the Scandinavian-type, 4,700-ton deadweight capacity ships built by Wm Gray & Company was *Empire Harmony* (1943). In 1947 she was bought by The Aviation & Shipping Company of West Hartlepool in 1947 and renamed *Avisbrook*, and sold on in 1950 to Thomas Stone (Shipping), who renamed her *Menastone*, as seen here. She spent her twilight years under the Panamanian flag and was broken up in 1969. (AUTHOR COLLECTION)

built as *West Lianga*; *Empire Kittiwake* built as *Western Ally*; *Empire Merlin* built as *West Isleta*; *Empire Mouflon* built as *Memnon*; *Empire Ptarmigan* built as *Abercos*; and *Empire Woodcock* built as *West Cape*. Two of them were sunk by torpedo in 1940, with five passing to the Norwegian, Greek or Royal Netherlands governments in 1942, while *Empire Mouflon* was managed by Ropner throughout the war and bought by them in 1946, when she was given the name *Preston*.

The first new ship to come under Ropner's management was the X-type steamer *Empire Rainbow*, which came from the Greenock Dockyard Company in May 1941. The next three deliveries required them to send crews to Hong Kong to accept *Empire Moonbeam*, *Empire Starlight* and *Empire Moonrise* from the Hong Kong & Whampoa Shipyard; these were the only ships completed in Hong Kong out of an order of ten before the Japanese invasion. Ropner also took delivery of *Empire Grenfell* and *Empire Kingsley* from British yards in 1941, and *Empire Johnson* and *Empire Dryden* in 1942. Also in 1942 the company took over the management of *Empire Cabot* and *Empire Sunbeam*, both being bought by Ropner post-war and renamed *Clearpool* and *Swainby*, respectively. The Ropner management list goes on, and includes a variety of other British-built tramp ships of the B, C and X classes and ten Canadian-built Fort-type ships, as well as two Liberty ships.

It was realised from the outset that not only would a deficit of dry-cargo ships arise from the U-boat campaign, but so too would a shortage of bulk liquid tankers for the transport of oil and other products such as molasses and water. The

first tanker class was the Ocean type, which was based on a pre-war design adopted by the Shell group of companies. This was the Three-Twelves type: 12,000-ton cargo deadweight capacity, 12 knots speed and a fuel oil consumption of 12 tons per day for the oil engine ships. A total of thirty-five Three-Twelves ships were built between 1941 and 1946, the majority from the yard of Swan, Hunter & Wigham Richardson at Wallsend on Tyne. Some were disguised with uptakes aft for the engine exhausts, but with a dummy funnel placed just abaft the amidships superstructure. Seven of them were lost to enemy action, the rest remaining commercially competitive throughout the 1950s.

The slightly larger 14,500-ton cargo deadweight capacity, Norwegian-type tanker followed from 1942 onwards. These were based on a prototype built by Sir John Laing & Sons at Sunderland in 1938 for Norwegian owners. They were equipped with a triple-expansion steam engine, apart from five ships built by Laing that had oil engines. The steamers were fit for a service speed of little over 10 knots, but the motor ships could manage 11 knots. All but two of the twenty-one ships of this type, *Empire Lytton* and *Empire Norseman*, survived the war. Many of the survivors had a slightly longer post-war career than the Ocean-type tankers.

In 1944 a third type of tanker, the standard fast tanker, was introduced. Although they had a cargo deadweight capacity of only 12,000 tons, they were much faster and could maintain a loaded sea speed of 14½ knots. The idea was they would be able to sail independently, rather than in a slow 10-knot convoy where they would be prime targets for the U-boats; however, most were delivered too late to test this theory. Only thirteen of this type of ship was built, seven by the Furness Shipbuilding Company at Haverton Hill, five by Laing at Sunderland, and one by Harland & Wolff at Glasgow. Each was equipped with a single-screw steam turbine installation. All were transferred to the Royal Fleet Auxiliary after the war and adopted *Wave* names: for example, *Empire Evesham* became *Wave Ruler*; *Empire Mars*, *Wave Duke*, etc.

Fourteen small tankers were built between 1943 and 1946 specifically to support the Allied forces on the continent, although some did see service in other arenas. They comprised ten 5,000-ton cargo deadweight capacity motor tankers, known as the intermediate type, and four smaller steamships of the *Empire Pym* type.

As with the dry-cargo ships, the tankers were all owned by the government, but managed by commercial operators. The majority went to the oil company-owned fleets, with the Eagle Oil Company of London managed by Royal Dutch Shell, for example, managing the Ocean types *Empire Norseman* and *Empire Traveller*; the Norwegian types *Empire Airman*, *Empire Cobbett*, *Empire Coral* and *Empire Grenadier*; and the standard fast type *Empire Salisbury*, which eventually became *Wave Master*. Others went to the various companies involved in the tanker charter market, Ropner, for example, accepting the Ocean type *Empire Chapman* in June 1942 on completion by Harland & Wolff. She passed to the management of the British Tanker Company in 1944, who bought and renamed her *British Commando* in 1946.

A variety of coastal ships, 170 dry-cargo ships and coastal tankers in all, were built for the Ministry of War Transport. The largest was the *Tudor Queen* type, named after a prototype built

by Burntisland Shipbuilding Company in Fife for the Queenship Navigation Company. The ships had a deadweight capacity of 1,360 tons with engines aft and bridge forward of amidships, while some were equipped with triple-expansion steam engines; others had oil engines. Their sea speed ranged from a little over 7 knots to 9 knots. Some thirty-four ships of this class were built between 1941 and 1946. The ships were managed and crewed by companies experienced in the coasting trades, including James Fisher of Barrow, Queenship Navigation, Tyne-Tees Steam Navigation Company, etc.

A series of six 1,150dwt, engines-aft motor ships were built in 1941. These were overtaken by the *Tudor Queen* type, despite the former having a higher sea speed of 10 knots. Two of them, *Empire Gat* and *Empire Spinney*, both built by A & J Inglis on the Clyde, were managed for the Ministry of War Transport by the General Steam Navigation Company of London.

There was also a prefabricated coaster with a distinctive hard chine hull and transom stern known as the Empire F type, as all the ships' names began with *Empire F-*. They were much smaller ships than the *Tudor Queen* class, being of just 400dwt, but were useful units for coastal duties and near-continental work later on in the war. H Scarr at Hessle, on the Humber, built twelve of the ships from units both fabricated on site and in local steel fabrication works. The remaining thirteen ships were completed by the Goole Shipbuilding & Repairing Company. They were all equipped with oil engines situated aft along with the bridge and accommodation. They had two hatches served by derricks mounted on the foremast and mainmast. As built, there was a gun platform between the hatches and one on the poop, where defensive

Empire Cape (1941) was one of six 1,150-ton deadweight capacity, dry-cargo coasters built on the Clyde and at Belfast. She was managed for the Ministry of War Transport, initially by William Robertson of Glasgow, from 1943 by the Tyne-Tees Steam Shipping Company of Newcastle, and from July 1944 by the Dundee, Perth & London Shipping Company of Dundee. The Dundee company bought her at the end of the war and renamed her *Gowrie* and later *Lochee*, as seen here. (AUTHOR COLLECTION)

anti-aircraft guns could be mounted. These ships were variously managed by coastal and near-continental operators: for example, four by the General Steam Navigation Company: *Empire Fable*, *Empire Fang*, *Empire Facility* and *Empire Farringay*.

Scarr and Goole also built a prefabricated shelter-deck version of the F class specifically for service in the Far East, with all but one being completed in 1945. Scarr delivered twelve, and Goole another eleven. These ships all had names beginning *Empire S-*, such as *Empire Seabright*. There was also the B-type coaster of 1,200dwt capacity with names beginning with *Empire P*, such as *Empire Pattern*. These were modelled on the Coast Lines engines-aft, bridge-amidships motor ships of the 1930s pioneered by *Fife Coast*, although due to the shortage of diesel en-

gines they were equipped with triple-expansion steam engines. Finally, there was the smaller C type of just 300dwt capacity, with two hatches forward of the bridge served by a derrick on each of the two masts. They had names beginning with *Empire M-* and had the accommodation and bridge right aft, along with their steam propulsion machinery. Seven B-type

Empire Seabright (1945) was one of only twenty-three shelter-deck-type, dry-cargo coasters built especially for use in the Far East and was of slightly different profile to the Empire F class (see picture of *Empire Fairplay*). Like *Empire Fairplay*, *Empire Seabright* also went to Overseas Fish Import Company of Great Yarmouth as *Helen Seabright*, and then became *Ortolan* under the owner-ship of the General Steam Navigation Company, London, between 1951 and 1958. (AUTHOR COLLECTION)

LEFT: Empire Fairplay (1945) was one of twenty-five Empire F-type, dry-cargo coasters. She was launched as *Chant 40*, but given an *Empire* name when she was completed as a dry-cargo coaster. After the war she was bought by the Overseas Fish Import Company of Great Yarmouth, who renamed her *Helen Fairplay*, before she was sold to the Great Yarmouth Shipping Company to become their *Lynn Trader*, as seen here. They sold her to Egyptian owners in 1960. (AUTHOR COLLECTION)

and eleven C-type ships were built in British yards and a further fifteen B-type and twenty C-type ships were ordered from Canadian shipyards (see Chapter 10). The Canadian ships all had names beginning with *Ottawa*. The fall of Japan in August 1945 made a large part of the fleet redundant and few of them actually saw service in the Far East, all the Canadian-built ships being sold in 1946. Interestingly, *Empire Maysong* later became David MacBrayne's *Lochbroom*, but with a Polar diesel engine, and *Ottawa Maycliff* became their *Loch Frisa*, still with her steam engine, both supporting the Scottish West Highland cargo services.

The tanker version of the Empire F-type prefabricated ship was the Chant class (Chant – CHANnel Tanker). Scarr of Hessle built the prototypes in 1944 named sequentially *Chant 1* to *Chant 12*. The Goole company was responsible for *Chant 22* to *Chant 28*, and *Chant 50* and *Chant 51*. A total of forty-three Chant tankers were built, but clearly more were planned, as the Burtsland company delivered the four ships *Chant 66* to *Chant 69*, also in 1944. The ships did have a stability problem and four of them capsized, three at sea, *Chant 7*, *Chant 61* and *Chant 63*, while *Chant 66* capsized alongside at

Grangemouth whilst undergoing repairs. However, with additional ballast and a restriction on the deadweight at just below 400 tons, the surviving ships became useful commercial units, some lasting in service until the early 1960s.

The other important group of coastal tankers was the *Empire Cadet* type based on the design of Bulk Oil Steamship Company's *Pass of Balhama*, which was completed in 1933. Some twenty-three of this class were built, most by the Grangemouth Dockyard Company and A & J Inglis. They were distinguished-looking ships with a counter stern, a short poop and raised accommodation superstructure over the machinery space (triple-expansion steam engines and boilers). The cargo deadweight capacity was a handy 850 tons. They were variously managed in the war years by F T Everard, Esso and others.

The Goole Shipbuilding & Repairing Company also built a group of three larger 890dwt tankers: *Empire Boy*, *Empire Harp* and *Empire Faun*. The design evolved, so that the last ship *Empire Faun*, completed in 1943, was adopted as the prototype for the TED- and TES-type tankers (Tankers Eastern Diesel and Tankers Eastern Steam) for use specifically in the Far East. Twenty of these ships were built in 1945 and 1946, but none were available in time to assist with the war with Japan. They had a cargo deadweight capacity of 900 tons, with a distinctive rounded cruiser stern, machinery aft and a high bridge slightly forward of amidships. The TED motor ships all had names beginning *Empire Ted-*, and the TES steamers, *Empire Tes-*. The ships had a distinctive rounded cruiser stern.

Coastal colliers were also in demand. A key role was coal shipments from northeast England to the Thames, in the notorious North Sea con-

Empire Pattern (1945) was a 1,200-ton deadweight capacity, B-type, shelter-deck vessel built for service in the Far East by Smith's Dock Company, South Bank, Middlesbrough. In 1948 she was acquired by Elder Dempster Line and given the name *Forcados*, as seen here. She was resold in 1963 to Greek owners. In December 1966 she foundered off the coast of Cyprus. (AUTHOR COLLECTION)

William Watson's *Rumania* (1944) was completed as *Empire Susan*, one of fourteen deep-sea tugs. Powerful though she may well have been, she was wrecked on the North Long Sand in the Thames Estuary on 11 February 1956 while assisting the Brazilian vessel *Loide Honduras* which had run aground. (A DUNCAN)

voys to maintain the capital's supplies of electricity and coal gas. There were two main types of emergency standard collier. The first were the seventeen ships modelled on *Icemaid*, built by S P Austin & Sons for the Gas, Light & Coke Company in 1936, which had a deadweight capacity of 2,900 tons. The second was a class of nine ships with a larger deadweight of 4,100 tons which were all built by William Gray & Company at West Hartlepool. In addition, six small 350dwt motor ships with engines aft, the so-called Severn Collier type, were built to run from South Wales up to Gloucester power station and elsewhere in the Bristol Channel.

A number of miscellaneous small craft were also built for the Ministry of War Transport, of which the more interesting were the various types of tugs. The largest type of tug was the deep-sea type. Four were built at Goole between 1941 and 1943, and four at Willington by Clellands (Successors) at Willington in 1943 and 1944. They were all 135ft long with a beam of 30ft. Clellands built a further six of the class between 1944 and 1946 with a larger beam of 33ft, designed to accommodate the increasing amount of equipment the tugs needed to carry for rescue work. A number of large rescue tugs of the *Bustler* class, which were not distinguished with *Empire* names, were also built for the Ad-

miralty. They were over 1,000grt and comprised a fleet of eight ships with two more built in the early 1950s. Some were steam tugs, others motor tugs.

In addition, some 113 coastwise tugs were commissioned between 1941 and 1947. These were designed for estuarial and coastal duties, but were mainly used as harbour tugs. The smaller estuary tugs were built between 1941 and 1944. A total of fourteen of this type were commissioned. The small, prefabricated TID tugs were named sequentially *TID 1*, *TID 2*, etc. A number of these ended up in the Admiralty tug fleet based at Chatham, Portsmouth, Portland, Devonport, Rosyth and Harwich (see Chapter 16), and many were also sold for commercial service at the end of the war.

Delivering the coastal tugs to their intended area of use was no easy task. In 1942 Townsend Brothers Ferries were awarded a contract to deliver six of them from Hall, Russell & Company's yard at Aberdeen to the Middle East. In the event, none actually got that far, although one actually made it to Malta, as David Enticknap reported in *Sea Breezes*, March 1986:

The first two were the *Empire Gnome* and *Empire Minotaur* and I was second mate of the latter. We sailed on July 14 and took her through the Caledonian Canal to the Clyde. After a breather there we left for Milford Haven but, despite the time of year, the weather was so bad that we had to seek refuge in Douglas, Isle of Man. 'Minnie' was coal fired and when we ventured out of Milford on August 5 for the next part of the trip we had filled her up with coal in every available space and even had reserves in bags on the deck. These nearly proved our undoing for four days later we ran into more bad weather and they shifted and threatened to jam the steering rods. We heaved them over the side and then turned and ran back to Cork Harbour for shelter and to tidy up the ship. Because of Irish neutrality we were allowed to stay for only 24 hours and then, as the reserves of fuel had gone we went back to Milford with a short stop at Waterford on the way.

The two tugs tried twice more to head south, but both times had to abort the voyage and come back. *Empire Ned* and *Empire Fred* followed next, '*Ned* needing leak repairs at Glasgow and on arrival at Milford in December. Before they could sail, the pair were requisitioned by the Admiralty. The last pair was *Empire Ann* and *Empire Spitfire*. They were detailed to escort

a convoy of assorted landing craft destined for Gibraltar. A few hours out from Falmouth, one of the landing craft broke down and *Empire Spitfire* was ordered to tow her home. On return, she too was requisitioned, becoming the Admiralty tug *Prompt*. *Empire Ann* alone plodded on with her flock of little ships, occasionally fetching and carrying stores from the stores ship, and occasionally taking one of the landing craft in tow so that repairs to its machinery could be carried out. The convoy arrived in Gibraltar on 8 May, and on 23 May *Empire Ann* sailed alone for Malta, arriving safely on 30 May. Six days later, the delivery crew handed her over to the navy.

At Gibraltar, the crew of *Empire Ann* had a vision of considerable riches and salvage rights when they were ordered to assist a disabled Liberty ship, *Pat Harrison*. The dream was shattered when they offered up their heaving line as the master leaned over the rail and shouted, 'That's no use. They've blown the bottom out of her and she is sitting on the mud.' The stranded ship was still there several years later.

The tremendous effort in designing, building, managing and controlling the Empire fleet went a long way to frustrating the work of the U-boats. But Britain would not have won the war with just the ships it built in its own shipyards.

Of the many coastwise tugs, *Empire Palm* (1942) was typical of those built on the Clyde. She is seen flanked by Steel & Bennie's *Campaigner* (1911) on the left and *Chieftain* (1930) on the right. The similarity of *Empire Palm* to *Chieftain* reflects her pedigree. HMS *Howe* is lying alongside, about to leave the Fairfield shipyard on trials. (AUTHOR COLLECTION)

9 THE LIBERTY SHIPBUILDING PROGRAMME: 'BUILT BY THE MILE AND CUT OFF BY THE YARD'

I would be a stupid ass to come up here and tell you that we are running this with any degree of perfection. We are not. We are just doing the very best we can with the tools we have.

From Admiral Land's report to the United States Congress in
1944 on the Liberty ship programme.

The American merchant shipbuilding activity during the Second World War was extraordinary. In the peak year of construction, shipyards in the United States delivered 19.3 million tons deadweight capacity of merchant shipping, a rate of growth in capacity that is aptly illustrated by the tonnage for 1941, which was just 1.1 million tons.

Britain's initial involvement with the United States Shipping Commission was to negotiate for the construction of two new shipyards and place an order for sixty new ships. The design of the ship was to be based on Hull No. 611, then only a set of plans at J L Thompson's drawing office, later launched as *Empire Liberty* (see Chapter 2). Although the Thompson ship was to be all riveted, the sixty American vessels were to have an all-welded shell, or hull, riveted to the ship's frames or ribs. The cost to Britain was agreed at 'an initial payment of $2.8 million, and further payments of the same amount each month for the first three months, thereafter increasing to a maximum of $5.2 million between the tenth and fifteenth months of the contract, and thereafter falling'. This meant that each ship would cost around $1.6 million, a considerably higher price than that charged by British yards. However, it did include the costs of two new shipbuilding facilities, one at Portland, Maine, and one in Richmond, California. The contract was signed with the Kaiser-Todd-Bath consortium on 20 December 1940. The construction of another twenty-six ships of the same design was later contracted with three existing Canadian shipyards (see Chapter 10).

The Todd-Bath Iron Shipbuilding Corporation yard at Maine comprised three shallow basins cut into hard rock behind a long cofferdam. The ships were to be assembled in the basins, two in each of No. 1 and No. 2 basins, and three in the larger No. 3 basin. The first keel was laid on 21 May 1941. The Todd-California Shipbuilding Corporation shipyard was built on thousands of concrete piles over low-lying land and mud flats at Richmond. It had seven conventional slipways. The first keel was laid here on 14 April 1941. Alongside the basins at Maine and the slipways at Richmond were larger areas where prefabricated units could be assembled. Before the keels were laid, it was necessary to redraw many of the blueprints that came from the Thompson drawing office. Detail that was assumed in the United Kingdom could not be left out in the United States, where experience at the new yards was limited. To this end, the New York-based naval architects, Gibbs & Cox, were brought in to help with this work, and verify pipe and cable runs and other details, as Peter Elphick described:

It was Gibbs practice to make scale models of every part of the ship, models that were complete down to the smallest detail. So detailed was the engine room model, for example, that it showed the best lead for each one of the myriad number of pipes and electric cables involved. This information was then incorporated in the drawings. In other words, reported Cyril Thomson, 'nothing whatever was left to be arranged on the ship. This practice saved endless time and argument in the shipyards where local surveyors were responsible only for seeing that all plans were exactly followed'.

Detailed also were the stores management plans for the two shipyards, where every part and prefabricated unit arrived to a strict planning and production schedule. Elphick again:

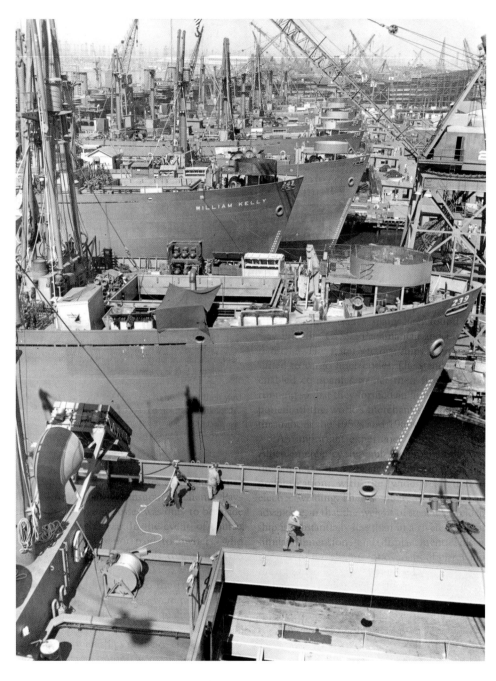

September 1944: un-precedented line-up of Liberty ships at the California Ship-building Corporation, Los Angeles, which set a wartime record by launching ten ships in eleven days; normally the yard launched a vessel every thirty-six hours. From nearest to more distant are *Thomas G Masaryk*, *William Kelly*, the first Liberty tanker *John Goode*, *Gutzon Bor-glum*, the second Lib-erty tanker *Henry C Wallace*, *David R Fran-cis* and *Joseph Reynolds*. (ACME NEWSPICTURES)

A necessary adjunct to prefabrication was that, on top of the necessity for materials and parts to arrive at the yard at the right time, all work processes and materials handling within the yards had to be co-ordinated and controlled to an extent never before achieved in the industry. And it was Kaiser who showed the way. Everything was planned ahead, nothing was left to chance. The storage, handling and movement of heavy materials within the yards, the order of precedence for lifting pre-assembled parts into position, welding sequences, and just about everything else, was planned down to the smallest detail.

The success of the yards was marked by the launch of the first ship at Richmond on 16 August 1941, just four months after its keel was laid. The ship's sponsor was Admiral Emery

Land's wife, but before she could break the champagne on the bow of the ship it had started to slide away from her! The ship was christened *Ocean Vanguard* after some deliberation about American sensitivities regarding the normal prefix *Empire*. The prefix *Atlantic* had been considered, but this raised sensitivities for Pacific-coast shipyards, and eventually the prefix *Ocean* was agreed for the sixty ships. All the Richmond-built ships had second names beginning with 'V' for victory. A week after *Ocean Vanguard* was launched, Thompson launched the prototype *Empire Liberty* back at home in Sunderland. Two more ships were launched at Richmond before the first pair, *Ocean Liberty* and *Ocean Freedom*, was floated out from their construction basin at Maine. *Ocean Vanguard* was taken over by her British crew in October 1941 and *Ocean Liberty* in March 1942.

The ships were 441ft long overall, had a breadth of 57ft, and their deadweight capacity was 10,500 tons. They had a sea speed of 11 knots and were powered by a triple-expansion steam engine supplied by coal-fired Scotch boilers. The engines were designed by the North Eastern Marine Engineering Company in Britain and the contract for their construction was awarded to the General Machinery Corporation of Hamilton, Ontario. Fourteen of the sets were diverted to other ships building for the United States Maritime Commission and consequently the last fourteen ships built at Maine had engines constructed by a variety of Canadian marine engineering companies built to a similar specification. The ships had five holds, Nos 1 and 2 forward, No. 3 being between the bridge and funnel in a split superstructure with

Nos 4 and 5 aft. Each hold was served by two derricks of varying capacity.

The agreed contract end date was December 1942. The Richmond yard delivered its last ship five months before this date and the Maine yard came home with one month to spare. Sixteen of the ships were lost in the war, and the others were all converted for peacetime duties with little difficulty.

During the early part of 1941 there was much deliberation whether to continue to build the sophisticated C2 dry-cargo ships and T2 tankers, or whether to switch to standardised volume emergency ship production. Admiral Land, as head of the United States Maritime Commission, veered from one side of the argument to the other as he came under severe criticism over the slow production of the C2 and T2 ships. The problem was a shortage of turbine machinery as American production of the units could not keep pace with demand. Eventually, Land had the commission prepare preliminary drawings of an emergency ship of its own, square and angular; the hull was simplified by removing all rolled and shaped plating at bow and stern to simplify construction. The response came from Gibbs & Cox, when William Gibbs outlined the delays likely to be experienced in starting an emergency shipbuilding programme with a completely new and untested design. In the end, Admiral Land agreed, and in January 1941 proposed to a congressional committee that an emergency standardised vessel be adopted and based on the British Ocean-type hull (from the prototype ship *Empire Liberty*). The committee agreed to the proposal and released funds for the commission to work on the

Precursor to the Liberty ships were the Ocean-type ships, *Ocean Glory* (1942) being the last to be completed by the Todd-Bath Iron Shipbuilding Corporation at Portland, Maine. She was bought by Clan Line Steamers in 1949 and given the name *Clan Macbeth*, and sold again in 1959 for further service before going for scrap in 1964. (AUTHOR COLLECTION)

details of design. The plans of the Ocean-type all-welded hull were given to the commission on 24 January by Britain.

The key differences between the proposed standard emergency 'five-year ship' and the Ocean type was that the new design would incorporate oil-fired water-tube boilers rather than coal-fired Scotch boilers. However, the same engine was proposed. The other difference was that No. 3 hold would be moved forward of the central superstructure and that all the accommodation would be in the superstructure above the engine and boiler spaces. The superstructure was box-shaped for ease of construction. The Maritime Commission gave the ship the classification EC2-S-C1, E for emergency, C2 indicating a length as in the existing C1, C2 and C3 classes, S for steam and C1 indicating the original unmodified design. In due course, tankers, troop transports and ships modified to carry crated aircraft were variants on the original design.

In February 1941 President Roosevelt broadcast the plans to build 200 of the five-year ships, announcing that orders had already been placed. In fact, orders had by then only been placed to build two new shipyards. The contracts had been issued to the Oregon Shipbuilding Corporation at Portland, an affiliate company of Henry Kaiser, and the Bethlehem Steel Company at Baltimore, under the name Bethlehem-Fairfield. Eight slipways were initially built at Portland and thirteen at Baltimore. In mid-March both companies signed contracts to build the first batch of 200 ships. The first keel was laid at Baltimore on 30 April 1941, and two were laid at Portland on 19 May. On 27 September the first, *Patrick Henry*, whose namesake said, 'Give me liberty or give me death,' was launched at Baltimore by Mrs Henry Wallace, the wife of the vice president of the United States. By the end of December 1941 each yard had delivered its first ship.

The title 'Liberty ship' overtook 'five-year ship' during the year. This came about because the term 'the Liberty Fleet' had become common parlance. It was not, as so often erroneously reported, a reference to the prototype *Empire Liberty*, which had been named after the *Empire* nomenclature had been initiated.

Admiral Land, at about this time and presumably when none of the British representatives were in earshot, is reported to have said:

In my judgement we are not interested in the type of ships proposed by the British, which type is for emergency use only. If it is decided to augment our own program, we shall build ships for 29 years life and have an eye on the future … we shall sell the ships to the British and be entirely clear of this design of vessel, which were suitable for their purpose, but would not be suitable for ours. Furthermore, if our emergency becomes equal to or greater than that of the British, we can always commandeer the vessels.

Although the names of the Liberty ships were all of famous people now dead, any group which raised $2 million in war bonds could name a ship. One, for example, was named for the founder of the 4-H movement in Kansas, others for the first Ukrainian immigrant to America, an organiser for the International Ladies Garment Union, and the woman who suggested the poppy as a symbol of American soldiers who died in the First World War. *Francis J O'Gara* was named after a seaman who was presumed dead, but who was unbeknown a prisoner of war. Francis O'Gara was the only person to visit his namesake Liberty ship!

During the course of 1941 a further seven new shipyards were constructed and contracts issued for the Liberty ship construction. Two more new shipyards were approved, subsequently providing a total of sixty-five slipways. Five of these new yards were controlled and managed by the Todd-Bath-Kaiser group. This was the start of a class of 2,710 ships, the Liberty ships: the greatest mass production of a standardised-type, prefabricated merchant vessel that the world will ever see. Eighteen shipyards would ultimately be involved in delivering the Liberty Fleet. The importance of the Liberty ship cannot be overstated and its role in defeating the Axis nations is indisputable; 215 of them were war losses, several on maiden voyages, particularly in the Russian convoys.

The first ship, *Patrick Henry*, was 150 days on the slipway and a further ninety-five days fitting out. Kaiser's first Liberty ship, *Star of Oregon*, was delivered the day after *Patrick Henry*, reducing the overall build time by thirteen days. Records were created and broken time and again. For example, the *Pittsburgh Post Gazette* announced on 31 August 1942:

Henry J Kaiser handed to his Government a 10,000 ton Liberty ship, the *John Fitch*, built in the breath-taking time of only 24 days. This shattered existing records for ship-

The first of the Liberty ships, *Patrick Henry* (1941), seen on trials on 26 December 1941. The caption to this press photo is 'By the end of 1943 the United States Wartime Commission will have hundreds of such ships in wartime service'. The newspaper that ran this particular photograph has partly scored out the name of the ship on the bows, presumably for security purposes, and responded to the prescribed caption by adding the price tag for each ship to the foremast – $1,660,000! (ACME NEWSPICTURES)

building and yet another record was broken when it was announced during the ceremonies that the engine that went into the *John Fitch* was completely assembled in just 30 hours.

By 1945, when the last ships were being built, overall construction times were just forty days. The all-time record was *Robert E Peary* which was launched just four days and fifteen hours after the first hull unit had been laid on the slipway on 8 November 1942, and was fitted out and delivered in a further three days. This record achievement was made at one of Kaiser's Rich-

mond yards as a propaganda exercise, with workers and machinery taken off other ships to speed the construction. Nonetheless, it was an

The Kaiser Permanente Yard No. 1 at Richmond in California seen from the air. The No. 1 yard was the original yard of Todd-California Shipbuilding Corporation, with seven slipways dedicated to building the Ocean-type cargo ship, before it was taken over by Kaiser for its Liberty shipbuilding programme. The two large buildings top right are the fabricating shop placed midway between No. 1 and No. 2 yards. The fabricated sections were transported to the slipways for installation. (THE PERMANENTE METALS CORPORATION)

incredible achievement, the more so as this ship did not suffer any structural problems from its all-welded construction which affected so many other Liberty ships (see Chapter 15). Admiral Dönitz, the man in charge of Germany's U-boats, had pronounced as early as May 1942 that 'the Americans are the largest enemy ship-builder', and added, 'I do not believe that the race between the U-boats and the enemy new ship constructions is hopeless.' The building of a ship within a week must surely have added to his concerns.

And the volume of ships that were turned out was phenomenal, Peter Elphick again:

From December 1941 when the first Liberty ship of all, the *Patrick Henry*, was launched, the flow of new ships grew and grew as construction times fell. By the end of 1942 no less than 511 Liberties had come off the stocks, 319 of them from yards controlled by Henry Kaiser. So great was the output of ships that by February 1943 newly constructed tonnage exceeded that sunk by submarines for the first time …

By the end of 1942 Liberty ships, together with their half-sisters the Oceans and the Forts, were already on their way to becoming ubiquitous. By D-Day in 1944 they

were exactly that, despite the structural cracking problems and intervening losses due to enemy operations …

About 250,000 parts were used to make one ship. The required material was largely marshalled in the pre-assembly areas, prior to being fabricated into sub-assemblies, and finally into about 120 units, some weighing over 100 tons. A conventional mould loft provided wooden templates for plates and rolled sections to be made and supplied to the pre-assembly area. In addition, large units such as engines and boilers were taken to the shipyard by road or rail in units limited in size and weight by their means of transportation. After the ship was launched, it moved to a fitting-out basin where a further two hundred or so pre-assembled items were installed, and the accommodation area completed and furnished. One of the key issues to be overcome was sagging of the hull at mid-length caused by the cooling and contraction of welded metal, mainly in the upper deck. Peter Elphick again:

[It was] recorded that at one of the yards engaged in naval shipbuilding, the bow of a cruiser under construction was raised over a foot above the level of the slipway after

The caption to this contemporary press photo reads 'The entire forepeak of a liberty ship is swung into place to speed ship production by revolutionary new prefabrication method'. The date and location are not given.
(PRESS ASSOCIATION)

completion of the welds on the top deck and after the cooling – and consequent contraction – of those welds. This raising of the extreme ends of a vessel, and the concomitant drop in the centre, is called sagging, and in Liberty ships was of the order of one or two inches. It was counteracted by raising the centre blocks on the slipway by a similar amount and it was of extreme importance to get the adjustment just right, otherwise the stern tube running from the engine to amidships to the propeller right aft, could be out of alignment with the most serious results on engine performance even amounting to engine failure.

Not surprising, then, that there were inherent structural issues with about 30 per cent of the ships. This was due, in part, to poor quality metal and the locked-in stresses in the hull that initiated failure. However, failure was initiated largely by poor-quality metal. For the most part, the stresses were eased by the flexibility of the structure, but in severe cold conditions, the low quality of the steel plating tended to lose tensile strength; it was a long time before this was recognised as the cause of the problem. The areas at most risk of fracture were right-angled hatchway corners, and at the deck edge where the top of the sheerstrake (vertical hull plating)

formed a right angle with the horizontal upper deck plating. These fractures occurred when the ship was most stressed by the sea and were accompanied by a loud cracking noise. Also contributing to failures was heavy over-, and incorrect, loading of the ships, which increased the stress on the hull. It was also found that the frames could have been spaced slightly further apart to give greater hull flexibility. This outcome was put into practice in the design of the Victory-type ships which would follow later (see Chapter 11). Nevertheless, only five Liberty ships were known to be lost due to hull fracture.

One of the first brittle fracture incidents concerned *Ocean Justice*, nearing completion at Portland to British account. One night in February 1942 the temperature had dropped to about -10°C by 6.30 in the morning, when a welder started to complete the welding of a heavy ash-chute insert plate, bearing in mind these ships were coal-burners, a very necessary piece of equipment. Immediately he did so, there was a loud cracking noise and fractures appeared in his vicinity on the main deck, 'tween deck, machinery casing and outer shell plating. This was the first of nine incidents affecting the sixty Ocean ships built in America; all the incidents occurred on ships built at Portland in Maine; none of the Ocean ships built at Richmond suffered any fracture defects, probably due to higher ambient temperatures. Thereafter, fracture failures occurred in quick succession, a few causing the loss of the ship. It was not only the Liberty ships that were at risk; the brand new T2 tanker *Schenectady* broke its back alongside the wharf following her sea trials, probably due to incorrect ballasting. The fractures passed through plates, rather than along welds, although they were initiated at welds (see Chapter 15). Two Liberty ships, *John P Gaines* and, later, *J L M Curry*, were both lost at sea due to explosive cracking, again through the plates and not along the welds. All of these cracking incidents occurred after the ships had been in sub-zero air temperatures for prolonged periods.

While the evidence for brittle fracture stacked up, one incident pointed directly at the weld. This was the T2 tanker *Esso Manhattan* on her approach to New York in low, but not sub-zero, temperatures. In this case, the initial fractures started on the main deck, where a dirty welded joint containing slag and porous metal was later identified.

It was not until after the war that scientific understanding of the processes involved in cold brittle fractures in otherwise ductile mild steel was fully achieved. As a consequence of wartime fractures, several 'belt and braces' measures had to be adopted, as this issue continued to bedevil not only the welded Liberty ships, but also other welded vessels. The measure adopted for the Liberty ship was the crack 'arrester', which is easy to build into a new ship, but is not easy to fit to an existing ship. In the former case, the purpose of the arrester was to connect the sheerstrake shell plate to the upper deck plating by means of a riveted steel angle section extending for nearly 300ft along the length of the ship about amidships. In the event of a crack propagating on a deck or shell plate, it would be relieved when it met up with a rivet hole drilled in the parent plate to take the rivets for the connecting angle, and would not continue on to an adjacent connected plate.

On existing ships, one method was to flame-cut a longitudinal slot in the deck plating extending for nearly 300ft of the length of the ship about amidships. A one-inch-thick steel flat bar was then riveted over the cut with two rows of rivets on each side of it. A similar arrangement was fitted to the sheerstrake where, over the same distance, a partial cut was made in the sheerstrake below the junction of the deck and sheerstrake plating, and a similar one-inch-thick steel flat bar was riveted over the

partial cut, again with two rows of rivets in the plate on each side of the partial flame cut. By this method, an effective crack arrester could be fitted to an existing ship. This arrangement was fitted for about 300ft on both sides of the ship, with each pair of arresters having some 3,500 rivets. The arrangement is clearly visible on the photographs of some ships, and it was found that this innovative 'belt and braces' type of arrester did work, and casualties were few thereafter – even when bomb damage had initiated the fracturing.

Owing to the relatively heavy weight of their machinery with its low centre of gravity, the Liberty ships were stiff, and in a heavy sea when lightly loaded, or in ballast, they rolled heavily. Because of their full-length bulwarks and bluff bows, they could become almost unmanageable in certain wind and sea conditions when in ballast. To correct this, and to ensure better propeller immersion, prescriptive guidance on ballasting was provided by the United States Maritime Commission in 1943, which advised carrying 1,050 tons of sand ballast, in addition to flooding the deep, peak and double bottom tanks. Some 600 tons of sand was to be distributed on the tank top, or bottom, of Nos 2, 3 and 4 holds, with the remaining 450 tons to be carried in the 'tween decks in order to raise the centre of gravity and reduce the period of the rolling. The British authorities issued a further memorandum in 1944, increasing this recommended solid ballast to 1,650 tons.

But despite these setbacks, the Liberty ships were a huge success, and a major factor in turning the battle of the Atlantic in favour of the Allies. But what of the ships themselves? Bernard Leek wrote in *Sea Breezes*, October 1990:

The product, knocked down in price and conceived as being short-term in service life, was conventional from stem to stern … transverse framing was used throughout. Two decks were worked into the hull structure, the second being continuous, and subdivision was effected by seven watertight transverse bulkheads carried up to the upper deck. In the basic design two deep tanks were included in the lower hold in the way of No. 1 hatch and a further deep tank was located abaft the engine room bulkhead, the tanks being available for either liquid cargoes or ballast. The hull was given a raked stem, a cruiser stern and an easy sheer. The

Launched by a bottle of champagne released by Crown Princess Martha of Norway, the Liberty ship *St Olaf* slides down the ways on 9 April 1942 on the second anniversary of the German invasion of Norway. It was the first time an American ship had been launched by a foreigner. *St Olaf* was later converted into a hospital ship. (ACME NEWSPICTURES)

upper deck was flat between the hatches and cambered with a slope at the sides, none of the deck area being provided with wooden sheathing ... the ship was provided with five hatchways, an inventory of derricks with SWLs ranging from 5 tons, a 50 ton heavy lift derrick being fitted to serve No. 2 hatch and a 30 ton derrick at No 4. Three masts were fitted and the derricks were mounted and pivoted on the masthouses. Ten simple steam winches completed the inventory of cargo gear.

The direct-acting, triple-expansion steam engines running at 76 revolutions per minute (rpm) drove a four-bladed propeller with a diameter of 18½ft. This maintained a service speed of 11 knots from a daily consumption of 30 tons of fuel oil. The water-tube boilers produced steam at 220 psi at a temperature of 230°C from a total furnace heating surface area of over 10,000sq ft.

Accommodation was amidships in a square-shaped block over the machinery spaces and in a deck house right aft. The after deck house contained the sick bay and was home to the DEMS gunners. Ship's stores were all amidships, except the munitions store, which was situated beneath the poop.

Many of the Liberty ships were retained by the United States during the war. A limiting factor was the availability of American crews to man the ships, but abridged wartime training courses and lower standards in certification allowed more ships to find crews than would otherwise have been the case. The shortage of trained seamen, however, was an incentive to outsource ships within the Lend-Lease scheme as the recipient government needed to find the crews for them, not the United States. Indeed, that Britain was able to find crews for all the ships it received from the United States during the war is a remarkable achievement in itself, with trained men being killed in considerable numbers, and others leaving the merchant service in favour of the Royal Navy. It is little wonder that crewing was difficult when set against the 29,000

The Liberty ship *Colin P Kelly Jr* (1943) was launched sideways into the water from the Alabama Dry-dock & Shipbuilding Company's emergency shipyard at Mobile on 8 January 1943. She was damaged by a mine at Tilbury in June 1945 and declared a constructive total loss. The Alabama yard suffered serious racial problems, leading to a new management team overseeing work from August 1943 onwards. (ALABAMA BUREAU ATL)

British merchant seamen who lost their lives during the Second World War.

A total of 177 Liberty ships were put under the auspices of the British Ministry of War Transport and managed by private British shipowners on its behalf. These were the Sam

Looking smart after refit, the Glen Line's *Glenshiel* (1943) was launched as the *Simon B Elliot* from the Bethlehem-Fairfield Shipyard in Baltimore, renamed *Samnesse* and sold to the Ocean Steamship Group in 1946 to become the Blue Funnel lines *Eumaeus*, before passing into the Glen Line fleet in 1952. She returned to Blue Funnel as *Euryrades* in 1957, before going to owners in Hong Kong for the final stage of her career. (JOHN CLARKSON)

ships, all but one being named with the prefix *Sam-*. The exception was the *Adolph S Ochs*, named after a former editor of the *New York Times*, which retained its name on transfer to the UK following lobbying. As before, the ships were managed by shipowners in the tramp and liner trades, with one or two exceptions: for example, the short sea trader General Steam Navigation Company managed *Sammex* until 1947, when she was sold to W A Souter & Company of Newcastle to become their *Sheaf Mead*.

The first variant to the original cargo-ship design was the Liberty tanker. This was classed as Z-ET1-S-C1 type, ET standing for emer-

Scholar (1945) was completed as *Samidway*. She came into Harrison Line ownership as *Scholar* in 1947. She is seen here at the end of her career with Harrison, laid up at Birkenhead in May 1964 awaiting a buyer. Shortly after the photograph was taken, she raised the Greek flag and was renamed *Konstantis Yemelos* – she was resold for demolition in 1969. (NICK ROBINS)

gency tanker, and was proposed in late 1942 because of the large losses of tankers, which had become prime targets for the U-boats. The tankers were built to the same standard design and dimensions as the cargo ships; they were delivered in 1943 and a few in 1944. The Liberty tanker retained dummy cargo-handling gear to confuse the enemy, and all pipework and manifolds were concealed in the 'tween deck spaces. They even carried deck cargo, typically vehicles and crated goods. The hatches were plated over save for paired 4ft diameter oil-tank hatches set into the dummy hatch covers; the tank hatches were not visible from the sea.

There were two pump rooms, one forward and one aft of the machinery space. The two deep tanks under No. 1 hold were removed, and part of the No. 3 deep tank was used for the forward pump room. Additional subdivision was provided along the centre line through the five hold compartments. Transverse bulkheads were built across the four larger hold spaces, but not No. 3 hold forward of the machinery compartment. Thus there were eighteen tanks, ten forward of the machinery compartment and eight aft. Vertical oil-tight bulkheads led down from the hatches through the 'tween deck to the lower tank spaces, and this trunking formed the expansion tanks. Either refined petroleum or heavy oil could be carried in the forward tanks, but only heavy oil was allowed in the aft tanks. The vents for the tanks were on the masts, and the forward petroleum product tanks were also provided with pressure relief valves and fire arresters. There was a steam smothering system, steam heating coils and a tank-cleaning system, just as there were in a conventional tanker. The

design work was carried out by the Delta Shipbuilding Company at New Orleans, who were contracted to build thirty-two ships, while the California Shipbuilding Corporation built a further thirty tank ships. The ships proved valuable units during the war, even though they were not quite as efficient as the normal engines-aft tanker. Almost all the survivors were converted to dry-cargo ships for peacetime duties, although a few were retained as built in the United States Reserve Fleet.

The Liberty collier (EC2-S-AW1 type) represented a major redesign to meet anticipated civilian requirements. The existing eastern seaboard collier fleet was old, and new emergency and, more particularly, peacetime tonnage was required. One of the principal changes was the relocation of all machinery aft in what had been No. 5 hold. This was a much more efficient arrangement that eliminated the need for a shaft tunnel and ensured that the bulk of the cargo was stowed in the fullest section of the ship. Standard Liberty ship components were used where they could be, and although the ships were very slightly longer than the standard vessel, they had the same breadth and depth. They were redesigned as single-deck ships with wing water ballast tanks in each hold. The Liberty collier had five holds, with No. 1 hold retaining the two deep tanks at its base. The wing ballast tanks were triangular in shape and had a maximum depth equal to the standard Liberty ship 'tween deck height and were located beneath the upper deck at the ship's side. The steel structure of these tanks added considerably to the longitudinal strength of the ship and, when full of ballast water, allowed the height of the centre of gravity of the loaded ship to be raised to reduce extreme rolling in a seaway.

A third deep tank was provided aft of No. 2 hold, and the double bottom ballast tanks under Nos 2, 3, 4 and 5 holds were retained. The forward accommodation was located on top of No. 5 hold and was occupied by the deck officers, with the engineer officers and the remainder of the crew being housed aft. All accommodation could be sealed during loading and discharge to prevent the percolation of coal dust. A total of twenty colliers were built during 1945, each with the geological suffix *Seam* to their name.

Other specialist units were the modified boxed aircraft transports (Z-E2-S-C5 type) which had four large holds instead of the customary five, and four sets of kingposts rather than three tubular masts. A total of thirty-six of this type were delivered from January 1945, but they were too late to help the war effort. Most were retained by the military after the war. The other special ships were the army tank transports (Z-EC2-S-C2 type), which were similar to the boxed aircraft transports. They differed slightly in hatch sizes and cargo-handling arrangement. The other key difference was that the tank transports not only had a 'tween deck, but also had a third mezzanine deck for cargo. Only eight ships were constructed in this way, all delivered between November 1943 and February 1944. They served a valuable wartime role, but all of them joined the Reserve Fleet after the war, until they were withdrawn and scrapped.

As the Allies finally got the upper hand, attention turned to the construction of Victory ships, and then returned to a focus on the C2 freighter and T2 tanker. Shipyards used to mass production of Liberty ships found that they were diverted to other tasks, including building landing craft for likely assaults in the Pacific. *Time* Magazine, 10 July 1944, reported the launch of *Benjamin Warner*, the last conventional dry-cargo Liberty ship to be built on the west coast:

The West Coast came to the melancholy end of a shipbuilding era last week. In Henry J. Kaiser's record-holding Richmond Shipbuilding Corporation Yard No. 2 in California, the S.S. *Benjamin Warner* (named after the father of Hollywood's Warner brothers) slid into San Francisco Bay. It was the 1,147th Liberty ship launched on the West Coast – and the last.

A few Liberties are still being finished at East Coast yards. But no more keels will be laid, East or West. Already Richmond No. 2, and most of the other yards, are building the faster Victory ship (15 knots) and a shoal of Navy craft, C4 troop transports, LSTs, frigates. But the feverish shipbuilding in which Richmond No. 2 built a Liberty in seven days is ended.

Benjamin Warner (1944) was built in Yard No. 2 at the Kaiser yards at Richmond, California. The keel was laid on 13 June 1944 and the ship was launched on 1 July 1944. *Benjamin Warner* was the 519th Liberty ship built at the Kaiser Richmond shipyards and the last Liberty ship launched on the west coast. She was laid up on the Hudson River after the war and was scrapped at Bilbao in 1971. (THE PERMANENTE METALS CORPORATION)

In waving good-bye to the Liberty ship program, Rear Admiral Howard L Vickery, vice-chairman of the U.S. Maritime Commission, said: 'Mass production of ships will have to end with the war. The yards will compete for a maximum number of ships we can hope to build, about one hundred a year. What will happen to the other yards? We don't know the answer.' But the tin-hatted workers in Richmond No. 2 could make a sound guess. The payroll at Kaiser's four Richmond yards has dropped from 93,000 to 73,000. It is still going down.

Benjamin Warner was the 519th Liberty ship built at the Kaiser Richmond shipyards and was to spend her entire life laid up in the Hudson River until scrapped in 1971. The shipyards had done their job and helped to win the war. The crews of the wartime Liberty ships had also done their job, but under the most uncomfortable, hazardous and sometimes appalling conditions. As it turned out, the careers of the surviving Liberty ships, the 'five-year ship', were just beginning (see Chapter 14).

Henry J Kaiser (1882-1967)

Kaiser was born 9 May 1882, in Sprout Brook, New York. He left school at the age of thirteen and was soon employed as a salesman. By 1903 he owned a group of photography shops in Florida, each based on the burgeoning photographic industry. He met his first wife Bess as a photographer. His future father-in-law insisted that he move to a more secure job with an income of at least $125 per month. He sold his business and moved to Washington to become a very successful salesman, earning a lot more than the salary he had been charged to earn to win his wife. His first construction company focused on road paving and was formed in Oakland, California, in 1913. By 1931, he was chairman of the executive committee overseeing the construction of the Hoover Dam. He was also involved with the Grand Coulee, Bonneville, and Shasta dams. He supervised the construction of the Bay Bridge between San Francisco and Oakland.

In the late 1930s Kaiser established the first organised healthcare programme for his employees. His legacy, the Kaiser Permanente Medical Care Program, rose from the humble beginnings of a twelve-bed desert field hospital to reach more than eight million subscribers as America's largest not-for-profit healthcare organisation.

His work in shipbuilding and the steel industry during the war made a great contribution to the war effort. Kaiser was a larger than life character and a self-publicist, but above all a wonderful leader and inspirer. That led to achieving what many said could not be done: 'When your work speaks for itself, don't interrupt.'

In 1945 he established Kaiser Industries, and was chairman until his death in 1967. That umbrella company held majority interests in numerous industries, including Kaiser Aluminum and Chemical Corporation, Kaiser-Fleetwings, which produced dishwashers and other items, as well as in magnesium, real estate, and tourism.

10 CANADIAN SHIPBUILDING AND SHIPOWNING, AND AUSTRALIA'S RIVERS

Another large-volume contribution of wartime tonnage to the Allies was that from Canada. By no means on the scale that was achieved by the United States it was, nevertheless, important. It started with the visit by Cyril Thompson of the British Shipbuilding Mission to the United States, which also visited Canada, as Peter Elphick recounts:

During their time in Canada Cyril and his companions met with C D Howe, the Canadian Minister of Munitions and Supply, and the Director of Shipbuilding, D B Carswell. The possibility of building ships, over and above those already being built in that country, were explored, for there was some spare capacity in Canadian yards though far from enough to satisfy the present British needs. The Dominion laboured under some special difficulties; there was concern over the country's ability to manufacture ship engines and there was a general shortage of materials. The main problem, however, was a geographical one; the shipyards were so far north that those in Eastern Canada had to contend with severe ice conditions in winter.

But Canada most certainly rose to the challenge, Elphick again:

Within a month of signing the Kaiser-Todd-Bath contract [in the United States] and as a direct consequence of the Thompson Mission's visit to Canada, British representatives in that country signed deals with three existing Canadian shipyards for the building of another twenty-six ships. The ships were called the 'North Sands' type after the name of the Thompson yard at Sunderland, and were to be even closer to the *Empire Liberty* design than the ships about to be constructed in the States for they were to be mostly riveted throughout. At about the same time the Canadian Government itself placed orders for ships to the same design and specifications.

The contract for the first twenty ships was signed in January 1941. Eight ships were to be built by the Burrard Dry Dock Company in North Vancouver, five by Canadian Vickers at Montreal and seven at the Davie Shipbuilding & Repairing Company at Lauzon, just upriver from Quebec City. The ships were coal-fired,

The North Sands-type ship *Fort Babine* (1942) on sea trials in Burrard Sound off Vancouver in June 1942. In September 1943 she was attacked by aircraft and bombed off Cape Finisterre. She later sank while under tow. She was one of the ninety Fort ships transferred to Britain under the American Lend-Lease terms. (NORTH VAN SHIP REPAIRS)

with the same arrangement as the American Ocean type, with a heavy triple-expansion steam engine designed to sustain a service speed of 11 knots. The first of the North Sands type was laid down by Burrard on 23 April 1941, launched 176 days later with the name *Fort St James*, and fitted out and delivered in a further 105 days. This could not be paralleled on the St Lawrence River, which froze over for much of the winter. Here ships were launched before the ice formed, so that they could be fitted out over the cold winter months, ready to leave when the river thawed the following spring. Springtime launches had to be fitted out before autumn, to clear the river before it froze over.

Canadian Vickers' first ship was *Fort Ville Marie*. She was launched on 9 October 1941, six days before *Fort St James* entered the water, and the race was on to clear her from the river before she got trapped for the winter. A British crew was sent to the yard, and the partly completed ship steamed the 150 miles downriver to Quebec, complete with an army of shipyard workers. At Quebec, the holds and 'tween decks were completed, but the accommodation and some of the cargo-handling gear remained unfinished, despite contracting in other local companies to help. Two weeks after she arrived at Quebec, she loaded a general cargo and sailed for Halifax. Here, essential work was finished to allow her to sail for Britain, where the finishing touches were undertaken. The first ship delivered by Davie was *Fort Tadoussac*, launched into an icy river on 6 November 1941 and delivered the following spring on 18 April.

The ships had a deadweight capacity of 9,300 tons, but were given a 700-ton wartime extension to include deck cargo, bringing the total to 10,000 tons. They had three masts, the mizzen being a simple pole communications mast. The foremast supported derricks to serve Nos 1 and 2 hatches and a heavy 30-ton derrick. The arrangement aft at Nos 4 and 5 hatches was similar, while the central hold, No. 3, situated between the bridge and the engine and boiler rooms, was served by a single derrick and Samson post.

All but one of the ships from the original order of twenty was commissioned by British crews during 1942, with the last commissioned in spring 1943. In the meantime, additional orders had been placed with a variety of new and existing shipyards by the Canadian government, and a steady stream of North Sands-type ships were completing from mid-1942 onwards. Many

of these came under the Lend-Lease agreement, whereby the United States paid Canada to build the ships, which were then bareboat-chartered to Britain. This resulted from a meeting between the stakeholders in London on 21 April 1942, known as the Hyde Park Agreement. Granatstein & Cuff described the Agreement as:

'Done by Mackenzie and FDR at Hyde Park on a grand Sunday April 20 1941.' So Franklin Roosevelt inscribed the original typed copy of one of the most significant economic agreements between Canada and the United States during World War II. The simple six paragraph statement expressed the desire of President Roosevelt and Prime Minister Mackenzie King that in 'mobilizing the resources of this country each country should provide the other with the defense articles which it is best able to produce ...'

President F D Roosevelt saw the agreement as securing his northern border, while still being neutral. He also saw it as a valuable means of supplying Great Britain with the equipment it so desperately needed. Under the agreement, ninety vessels of the North Sands type were delivered to Britain between February 1942 and March 1943. A further fifty-six North Sands-type ships were built to British order. All these ships had the characteristic *Fort* prefix to their name.

There was considerable rivalry between yards on the west coast and those on the east coast, and both were rivals of anything American, as reported in Montreal by the *Globe and Mail* on 20 August 1943:

Workmen in the United Shipyards aimed their sights tonight at the shipbuilding records of Henry Kaiser, United States shipbuilder, after breaking all Canadian marks by sending three 10,000 ton steel freighters down the ways within four hours, placing one of them in the water in the record time of 39 days. The previous 47 day keel-to-launching record was held by a Vancouver shipyard ...

Mrs G C Clarke, wife of a shipyard official, sent the *Fort Moose*, the first of the ships, on the way. An hour later the *Fort Covington*, with Mrs F P Shearwood breaking the traditional bottle over the massive prow, dipped into the water. Who sponsored the *Fort Romaine* remains a bit of a mystery, but officially Mrs John Rennie, wife of the shipyard manager did the honours ... When spectators returned for the final launching they were amazed to find a complete keel – all 465 feet of it – firmly in place on the slipway that held the *Fort Moose* less than two hours before.

Canada, unlike her situation in the Great War, was now an independent state and a Dominion within the empire. As such, she could not necessarily look to Great Britain for her own security, both in terms of military defence and food security. Once the Pacific arena opened up in December 1941, Canada's position became even more precarious, and she was almost solely reliant on the United States for providing cargo space for her international trade needs. By the end of 1942 over half the Canadian sea-going merchant fleet had been lost, leaving just twenty-five ships. Oil imported from the Caribbean was at a premium, and petrol rationing was introduced at the start of April 1942. In consequence, Canada started a shipbuilding programme to its own account, both merchant and military. Canada created a Crown Corporation, the Park Steamships Company Limited, in order to manage the merchant ships it built in its own yards. Michael Hennessy explained in his chapter within the book *The Merchant Marine in international affairs*:

Formed by Order-in-Council on 8 April 1942, Park Steamships Company Ltd became responsible for taking over Canada's new merchant ships. The company operated by assigning these new vessels to private operating firms. All Park Steamships remained subject to assignment by the Canadian Shipping Priorities Board. Though subject to

oversight by higher Allied shipping control bodies, the vessels served as credit with the Allied shipping pool. They also greatly relieved the shortage of space available to Canadian priority cargoes. These ships served as a lever when dealing with the Allied shipping boards; the Allies could either ensure carriage of the Canadian goods through assignment of vessels or watch the Canadians employ ships inefficiently. Realizing the many advantages of this kind of operation, Park Steamships eventually controlled over 115 merchant vessels, manned by some 12,000 Canadian merchant mariners. Moreover Canada retained ownership of many vessels loaned to Britain. Through these steps, Canada's merchant fleet rose from virtual extinction to become the third largest in the world by 1945.

Between June 1942 and July 1944 the Park Steamships Company commissioned forty-four North Sands-type 10,000dwt cargo ships. These included eight ships launched with a *Fort* name and destined for British registry that were renamed with the Park Steamships' own nomenclature of *Park* names. Thus, for example, *Fort Norway* built in 1943 by Burrard should have come to Britain, but was completed for Park Steamships as *Mohawk Park*. In 1944 she was finally released to Britain and given the name *Fort Spokane*, along with two other ships originally destined for the United Kingdom.

The North Sands type did not altogether suit Canada's needs, being coal-fired, steam reciprocating-engined ships. Oil fuel was a cheaper option than coal for the Canadian fleet, and a new type of ship was developed that had oil-fired

Cedar Hill (1944) was built as the North Sands-type ship *Dentonia Park* for the Park Steamships Company, and was sold by the Canadian government to the British government in 1946, joining Halifax Overseas Freighters in 1950 and Counties Ship Management in 1964. Counties Ship Management had the largest fleet of Canadian-built standard-type ships on the British register in the 1950s and early 1960s. (NICK ROBINS)

water-tube boilers instead of coal-fired Scotch boilers. This required some internal rearrangement to replace coal bunkers with oil tanks, and the removal of redundant ash chutes and bunker hatches. The new class was named the Victory type, and for clarity is referred to here as the Canadian Victory type. The basic design of the ships was otherwise essentially the same as the North Sands type, except that the butts of the hull plates were now welded, although the seams were still riveted, so that a distinct linear overlap occurred along the seams of shell plating on both the later North Sands and the Canadian Victory types. The easiest way of distinguishing the two classes was that the North Sands type had a lifeboat port and starboard on the bridge island and one on the engine island boat deck aft of No. 3 hatch, while the Canadian Victory type had two lifeboats port and starboard on the boat deck and none on the bridge island. This was made possible because the bunker hatches prevented two lifeboats being mounted on the boat deck of the North Sands type, so the second boat had to go on the bridge island.

One North Sands type, *Point Pelee Park*, and twelve Canadian Victory-type ships were completed as 'tankers' between August 1942 and March 1944. Outwardly, they looked little different from their dry-cargo counterparts, although raised trunking was laid over the central part of the main deck along the entire length of the three cargo spaces. This contained the expansion tanks for the main cargo tanks, which were built into the holds. All but two were converted to dry-cargo ships after the war.

A total of forty-nine standard Canadian Victory-type cargo ships were built for Park Steamships between August 1943 and November 1944. Some twenty-one of these were launched with *Fort* names, with the intention that they should go to Britain with British crews. Agreement was made that they should be retained by Canada when assurance was given that Canada could find a sufficient number of trained merchant seamen to crew the vessels. This arrangement suited Britain, which was finding it hard to maintain specified crew levels on some ships. Canada built an additional thirty-two Canadian Victory-type ships for Britain, all with *Fort* names; the last to be delivered was *Fort Island*, built by Burrard, which was accepted on 15 March 1944. Some of the Canadian Victory-type ships had twenty-five refrigerated compartments built into the 'tween decks for the carriage of perishable goods. The prototype Canadian Victory-type ship was *Fort Columbia*, launched from Burrard South Yard at Vancouver and accepted by a British crew in July 1943.

Britain ordered twelve more Canadian Victory-type ships in 1943. These were specifically for use as stores-issuing ships to supply the naval presence then required in the Pacific. One of them, *Fort Langley*, was equipped as an aircraft stores-issuing ship, while the other eight ships were equipped with refrigerated chambers in the 'tween decks with a total capacity of 111,500cu ft. The lower holds were used for other goods, such as non-perishable and dry foods, general stores, equipment and spare parts. The ships had one or two mezzanine or plat-

Aspen Park (1944) was a product of the Burrard Dry Dock Company, Vancouver. The seams of the plates are riveted and the butts welded, leaving a visible horizontal bulge line along the overlap of the seams. She was a Canadian Victory-type ship. In 1946 she was one of a group of ten Canadian Victory-type ships purchased at the same time by Western Canada Steamships. She was renamed *Lake Athabasca*, as seen here. In 1949 she was sold to Panamanian-registered owners and ten years later went to the Greek Registry, and was eventually broken up in 1969. (AUTHOR COLLECTION)

Atwater Park (1944) was one of the forty-nine Canadian Victory-type ships built in 1943 and 1944. She remained under the Canadian flag during the war, was renamed *Lake Atlin* in 1946, and became the Monrovian-registered *Halcyon* in 1953. She was broken up following collision damage in 1969. (AMBROSE GREENWAY COLLECTION)

form decks for stowage of lightweight goods (*Fort Dunvegan*, for example, was described as a four-deck ship by Lloyd's). Three more refrigerated Canadian Victory-type ships were transferred from Park Steamships Company to Britain in 1945: *Buffalo Park*, *Cornish Park* and *Queensborough Park*, which, respectively, were renamed *Fort Charlotte*, *Fort Beauharnois* and *Fort Duquesne*. These three were later transferred from the Ministry of War Transport to the Admiralty along with *Fort Dunvegan*, *Fort Constantine* and the specialist stores ship *Fort Langley*. All these ships were managed for the Ministry of War Transport by larger liner companies operating to and from Pacific and Far Eastern ports. Lloyd's Register shows that the ownership of the latter three vessels was retained by the 'Dominion of Canada', and that the ships stayed on bareboat charter to the United Kingdom until they were purchased outright in the 1950s.

A third iteration of the North Sands type was the Canadian type. Basically very similar to the North Sands and Canadian Victory types, the Canadian type was fitted with Scotch boilers that were suitable for coal-firing or oil-firing. Back came the bunker hatches on the boat deck, so the distribution of lifeboats reverted to the configuration in the North Sands type – one boat forward and one aft of No. 3 hatch. The fuel option followed a suggestion by Britain that this would allow the ships to use fuel chosen for its favourable cost. In the event, little use was made of the coal-burning option, as all the ships were retained by Park Steamships, during the war none coming to Britain, where coal remained the preferred fuel. One Canadian type was launched with a *Fort* name, *Fort Simcoe*, but she was commissioned as the Canadian *Elgin Park* in February 1945. The first Canadian type of the twenty-eight ships completed for Park Steamships was *Sunalta Park*, delivered by United Shipyards in September 1944, and the last was *Seven Oaks Park*, delivered by the Victoria Machinery Depot Company in July 1945.

Three more Canadian-type ships were completed by United Shipyards for the British Ministry of Transport, just after Germany surrendered in May 1945. These were *Fort*

Fairmount Park (1945) was launched at the end of January 1945 from the South Yard of the Vancouver Dry Dock Company, but completed by parent Burrard Dry Dock Company in North Vancouver. She was of the 'Canadian' type. *Fairmount Park* was sold in 1946 to the Bristol City Line of Steamers, later rebranded Charles Hill of Bristol and renamed *Montreal City*; she is seen here leaving Swansea. She served on the liner duties between the Bristol Channel and east-coast American and Canadian ports, until she was sold in 1959 for further duty under the Polish flag as *Huta Baildon*. (JOHN CLARKSON)

Rosalie, *Fort Sandusky* and *Fort Wayne*, and they were each equipped as heavy stores and ammunition carriers, with a suitable array of cargo-handling gear to suit this role. The first two of the trio were transferred to the Admiralty in 1947 and 1949, respectively, while the third, *Fort Wayne*, was returned to Canada in 1950 and sold for commercial use.

The remarkable aspect of this shipbuilding frenzy was that the first North Sands-type ship, *Fort St James*, was the first large ocean-going ship built on the west coast of Canada for twenty years. Precious few had been delivered from the yards on the St Lawrence River and elsewhere in the east in that same time. Canada had come from nowhere to become one of the world's biggest shipbuilding nations, with output reaching a peak in 1943.

James Pritchard commented on the success of the west-coast yards in *A Bridge of Ships*:

Two thirds of all the cargo ships constructed in Canada was built on the west coast, together with 78,849 displacement tons of steel-hulled warships, which account for about 18 per cent of all naval tonnage in the country. Burrard Dry Dock Company produced more than one quarter of all the merchant tonnage built in Canada. Although half of the company's cargo hulls were built by Burrard South Yard at Vancouver, all engines were installed by Burrard North Yard at Vancouver. During 26 months between April 1941 and June 1943, Burrard completed 50 North Sands ships, or 500,000 tons of shipping. During the war, Burrard constructed 109 large cargo ships, North Van Ship Repairs and West Coast Shipbuilders each constructed 54, Victoria Machinery Depot and Prince Rupert Dry Dock built 19 and 13 respectively, and Yarrows built 2 before being transferred to naval construction.

Canada did not just build 10,000dwt cargo ships, but had a prodigious output of smaller vessels from its yards situated in the Maritime Provinces. These yards were responsible for building fifty-eight cargo ships, mostly single-deckers, of the British Scandinavian type with a deadweight capacity of 4,700 tons (see Chapter 8). Plans were obtained from William Gray & Company of Hartlepool, which had been responsible for building most of this type of vessel in the United Kingdom. The ships were delivered in 1943 and 1945. Ten of the ships delivered between 1944 and 1945 had 'revised' cargo-handling gear and altered accommodation layout, and were known as the Revised type, and six of them completed in 1945 had two decks and were known as the Dominion type. Of these, five were given *Canadian* names after the war: *Canadian Observer*, *Canadian Highlander*, etc. They were then laid up at Halifax, only to be scrapped in 1965. The others did see commercial service after the war, at least one, *Liverpool Packet*, coming under British ownership between 1960 and 1963 for the Bowater Steamship Company.

Two types of dry-cargo coastal ships were built for the Park Steamships Company specifically for use in the Far East. The first batch were ordered by the Ministry of War Transport in London in January 1945, and they were intended to serve as feeder ships to support troops around the smaller ports in the Pacific arena. These were the same as the British-built B-type coaster modelled on the 1930s Coast Lines motor ships, although equipped with steam engines, and the smaller coasters of the British C type with engines, accommodation and bridge right aft (see Chapter 8). The C type was built by yards in the Great Lakes and in the Maritime Provinces. The B type had a deadweight capacity of 1,200 tons and the C type of 300 tons. The fifteen B-type ships were always referred to in Canada as the China type and were all built on the west coast. The ships all had names beginning *Ottawa* rather than *Park*, and like their British counterparts, the second name of the B type all began with the letter 'P' and of the C types with the letter 'M': for example, *Ottawa Pangis* was a B type, whereas *Ottawa Mayhill* was a smaller C type. None of the ships were delivered before the fall of Japan in August 1945, with only one, *Ottawa Maycove*, being delivered in 1945, the remainder being completed the following year. As a consequence, the remainder were redundant; all the ships were sold part-completed, the B type or China type almost entirely going to owners in the Far East, and the C type sold locally in Canada.

Six 3,600-ton cargo deadweight capacity, motor tank ships were built by Collingwood Shipyards, Ontario and Marine Industries at Quebec during 1943 and 1944. They were twin-screw ships with machinery aft and a bridge forward of midships, and were propelled by twin Sulzer diesel engines, which with twin rudders made them highly manoeuvrable. Their role was specifically to provide tanker access with refined oil products to the Great Lakes ports; they were 259ft long, giving just one-foot clearance between the lock gates in the Lachine Canal, and had an optimum loaded draught of 14ft. They were unique in the Canadian wartime building programme, as they were all-welded. A special capital assistance grant of $148,000 had been given to Collingwood in order to acquire the equipment for welding, which included machine tools, welding equipment and electrical transformers. The design prototype was *Lakeshell*, built by Marine Industries for Shell and launched on 1 June 1940. James Pritchard reported:

> Two tankers, the *Nipiwan Park* and *Norwood Park*, were completed at Collingwood in November 1943 and hastened to the sea before the navigation season closed. Marine Industries completed the *Otterburn Park*, *Eglington Park* and *Millican Park* at Sorel in May, June and August 1944, respectively. The final Great Lakes tanker, the *Springbank Park*, was completed at Collingwood in September. All were delivered to Park Steamships Company, who nominated the Imperial Oil Company of Toronto to manage them. These tankers went on to transport high-octane aviation gasoline, particularly to Newfoundland, to meet the needs of streams of bombers being ferried to the United Kingdom.

Four of the tankers went to Sorel-based Branch Lines after the war.

Eighteen large steam tugs of the modified *Warrior* type, of 233grt, were ordered by Britain and were built in Ontario by the Midland Shipyard and the Canadian Shipbuilding & Engineering Company. They were powered by steam engines, with an indicated horsepower in the region of 1,000. These tugs were mostly delivered in 1945 with a couple in 1946 and had names beginning *Rock-*, as in *Rockforest*, *Rockswift*, etc. Only two came to Britain, *Rockland* joined the Admiralty fleet as *Flare*, along with *Rockpigeon*, which retained its original name, both transferred in 1947 from the Ministry of Transport.

Canada also built wartime classes of harbour tug, referred to as the Glen type and the Ville type, mainly for use by the Royal Canadian Navy. They were of about 100grt and provided useful towage capacity. Many of them were released for civilian duties in Canadian ports after the war.

Some 265 small tugs of the TANAC type were built by Canadian shipyards during the Second World War, and the majority transferred to the British Ministry of War Transport. Early in the war, the British Ministry of War Transport recognised the need for a considerable number of small tugs that would be suitable for harbour service around the world. Designs and specifications were accordingly prepared so that construction could be undertaken by workers with little experience in shipbuilding. The tugs were largely built in prefabricated sections in various locations and were brought to and assembled at several different shipyards. The powering of these tugs was revised during the building of the series, being increased from 200–375bhp.

Particular attention was paid to the accommodation for the six-man crew. Living quarters were all insulated, with mechanical ventilation being arranged in the engine room and accommodation. In order to increase the utility of the vessels, fire pumps with a monitor and deck hose connections were fitted. The vessels served across the world, and were even involved in the invasion of Europe.

They mostly had sequential names TANAC 1, TANAC 2, and so on, but were universally known as TANACs, a name that is believed to have been intended to be the Canadian equivalent of the TUSA tugs that were built for Britain in American yards (see Chapter 7). TANAC is T for tug and the first four letters of Canada spelled backwards. Names with a letter 'V' before the number signify that they were equipped with a Vivian engine built in Vancouver, rather than the Cummins engine installed in all the other tugs. The motor tugs were 65ft long and 55grt. All but thirty-five of the 265 tugs that were built were steel-hulled, the remainder had wooden hulls. The first TANAC was delivered in late 1942 and the last in 1946; those that crossed the Atlantic did so as deck cargo. Some were returned to Canada after the war and the last fifty were sold as surplus, fifteen of them going to China, the remainder staying in Canadian waters. During the war, thirty-eight of them served in the Royal Navy and a further nine served in the Royal Canadian Navy with names ending -*wood*.

Concern over the war in the Pacific prompted a British order for twenty-one maintenance and repair ships, the *Beachy Head* class. In the event, only sixteen were commissioned, all using Canadian Victory-type hulls and named after British promontories, such as *Girdle Ness*, *Portland Bill*, *Hartland Point*, etc.

A typical TANAC tug equipped with a Vivian diesel engine was *TANAC-V-209* (1945), built by Russel Brothers at Owen Sound in Ontario and completed in 1945. She was equipped as a fire-fighting harbour tug. (AUTHOR COLLECTION)

The first in the Beachy Head class of maintenance Canadian Victory-type ships was HMS *Beachy Head* (1945), built by the Burrard Dry Dock Company at Vancouver. In 1947 she was loaned to the Royal Netherlands Navy and renamed *Vulkan*, reverting to the name *Beachy Head* in 1950. Two years later she was sold back to Canada, joining the Royal Canadian Navy with the new name *Cape Scott*, as seen here. She was scrapped in Texas in 1978. (AUTHOR COLLECTION)

Many outstanding orders were cancelled towards and after the end of the war. Once again, peacetime spelled the end for Canada's shipbuilding industry. James Pritchard wrote:

With shipbuilding contracts quickly running out, the Ministry of War Transport ordered eighteen 105 foot modified *Warrior* class tugboats. Thirteen were delivered before the end of 1945 and the remainder declared surplus. The ministry also ordered 35 China … [and] three diesel powered cargo ships, each 7,500 gross tons, completed after 1945. Five maintenance ship contracts were also cancelled. For the second time in the twentieth century, the Canadian shipbuilding industry proved that it was an emergency product of war. Despite its accomplishments, it had no reason to exist in peacetime. An examination of the prices, costs, and value of ships built shows why this was so.

The cost of building ships in Canada was

high … During the Second Word War, market forces were not in play, and although several factors reduced the cost, experience, volume, and efficiency gained by building numerous ships of the same type enabled Canadian shipyards to turn out 10,000 ton cargo ships at a relatively low cost …

By way of complete contrast with Canada, the Australian wartime emergency shipping programme was modest in the extreme. Its standard ships were few in number and all built to conform with Lloyd's 100 A1 classification. The Australian Shipping Board was created in March 1941 to control overseas ships chartered for the Australian coastal trade and all ships built by Australian shipyards. By 1942 it was apparent that new ships would need to be built to replace losses and the board adopted the pre-war-built *Scottish Monarch* as the prototype of its proposed A-class standard ship. *Scottish Monarch* was completed in 1938 by the Caledon Shipbuilding & Engineering Company at Dundee for the Glas-

gow tramp firm Raeburn & Verel. She had five holds, No. 3 hold placed in the split superstructure between bridge and engine compartment. The A class, or River class, was commissioned from mid-1943 onwards; eight of the thirteen ships in the class were completed by the end of the war. The ships all had names beginning with *River*: *River Derwent*, *River Fitzroy*, and so on. They had a deadweight capacity of 8,570 tons and were ideal for the Australian coastal trades. They were equipped with a single triple-expansion steam engine and were capable of maintaining a speed of 11 knots. Five of the ships were built by Evans Deakin & Company at Sydney, four by the Broken Hill Propriety (BHP) shipyard at Whyalla, South Australia, and two each at the Cockatoo Island Docks & Engineering Company at Sydney, and the Commonwealth Naval Dockyard at Williamstown, Victoria. The first pair, *River Burdekin* and *River Clarence*, were delivered in 1943, four more were delivered in each of the years 1944 and 1945, two more in 1946, and the last, *River Burnett*, in 1947.

River Loddon (1944) was one of the Australian River-class, dry-cargo steamers intended for the Australian coastal trades. Built at Williamstown in Victoria, the conventional all-riveted hull plate assembly of these ships is apparent from the photograph. Her ownership passed from 'Australian government' to the Australian Coastal Shipping Commission in 1957, and she was eventually sold for demolition at Osaka in Japan in 1963. (AUTHOR COLLECTION)

During 1945 ten B-class cargo ships were ordered, six coal-fired, two oil-fired and eventually three as motor ships, making a total of eleven. These were of a similar design to the A class, though slightly smaller in overall dimensions, with a deadweight capacity of 6,312 tons. They did have a vastly improved system of cargo-handling gear, and proved valuable units in the general international trades. This class of ship had names beginning with the letter 'B': *Barrigun*, *Balarr*, etc, and were delivered between 1947 and 1952.

There was no C class constructed, but of the D class, ten were ordered in 1945. These were either coal- or oil-fired, with the exception of the last, which was a motor ship. These ships had limited refrigerated cargo space and were smaller ships than the A- and B-class ships, with a deadweight capacity of 3,081 tons. The ship names all began with the letter 'D', and the ships were delivered between 1946 and 1950. Finally, five E-class ships were ordered in 1946. They were engines-aft motor coasters of 632dwt, of similar design to Coast Lines *Hibernian Coast* and *Caledonian Coast*. The last of the E-class ships, all with names beginning with 'E', was delivered in July 1950.

The coastal ships were transferred from the Australian Shipping Board to the newly formed Australian Coastal Shipping Commission in 1956, the ships coming under the ownership of the Australian National Line in January 1957.

Prototype for the Australian River class of cargo ship was the British tramp steamer *Scottish Monarch* (1938), which had been designed and built by the Caledon Shipbuilding & Engineering Company at Dundee for the Glasgow tramp ship operator Raeburn & Verel. *Scottish Monarch* was a war loss, torpedoed and sunk in the South Atlantic on 1 June 1941. (AUTHOR COLLECTION)

The Normandy Beaches, from an article by Thomas Wilson that first appeared in *Sea Breezes*, June 1994

Fort Gibraltar was one of many of her type, wartime Canadian-built 7,100 gross tons, 440 feet long. She looked vast as I viewed her for the first time from the dockside and when I joined she was being fitted with what seemed to be a huge armoury of gunnery …

On June 6 at breakfast time, when loading was almost complete, we heard an announcement from the BBC that the invasion of Europe had started with beach landings in Normandy. Next day we moved out into the Thames estuary and joined a large convoy of all types of ships, merchant ships of the Liberty and Fort variety like ourselves, naval landing ships and landing craft.

Everyone was tense on that trip, each one, I suppose, like me, concerned about his immediate future. However, although expecting something to happen at any minute, nothing did and the convoy had a completely quiet passage, arriving off the Normandy beaches the night of June 9/10. Approaching them we were spellbound by a brilliant violet light on the horizon. The knowledgeable ones said a tanker must have gone up but we heard later that she was an ammunition ship. This introduction didn't seem to augur too well but we came to anchor, I suppose about a mile off the beach, without further incident.

With daylight, as far as the eye could see, there were ships of all descriptions with landing craft coming and going between the anchored ships and the shore. Immediately offshore from us was a large cruiser which turned out to be HMS *Belfast*. At about 1 minute intervals she was firing her 6 inch guns over our heads, which made us feel slightly uncomfortable.

Our captain posted me on one wing of the bridge with an Aldis lamp and instructed me to call up any landing craft that passed within range: he was anxious to deliver our cargo as quickly as possible and get off home. I had no response whatever to my message, 'Am ready to discharge' until, eventually, from one landing craft came the laconic 'Everything comes to those that wait'.

Patience was eventually rewarded and a landing craft arrived followed by a peculiar large raft, which seemed to be controlled from a small structure like a garden shed at one end of it. This was a 'Rhino' with a crew of one naval petty officer and one seaman …

On June 24 … a sister ship of ours, the *Fort Norfolk*, set off a mine underneath her a few hundred yards from us and slowly broke her back at No. 3 hatch. Her crew poured over the side as naval craft rushed to the scene to pick them up. Her bow and stern came up, and down she went inside half an hour …

For the rest of July and half of August the *Fort Gibraltar* plied between London Docks and Gold, Juno or Sword beaches, making a total of seven round trips. We had another incident when an acoustic or magnetic mine had our name on it and as we left the beach there was a tremendous explosion below us and the ship rolled gunwale under. This seemed to be the end of her but up she came and steamed on.

And so the *Fort Gibraltar* survived the summer of 1944, and although mined, bombed, shelled and attacked by E-boats she came through unscathed, a tribute to her builders in North Vancouver and to her deck and engine-room officers and crew who kept her going through thick and thin without an unscheduled stop.

Normandy landings, Omaha Beach: a Liberty ship discharges army lorries onto a 'Rhino', ready for transit to the beach. This was an operation that was weather-dependent and could only be carried out in light seas and low winds. (AUTHOR COLLECTION)

11 LIBERTY'S SUCCESSOR, THE VICTORY SHIPS

In time, there was an idea that the Liberty shipbuilding programme should be scaled down in favour of building a more robust and better-equipped type of vessel. Such a vessel would contribute to the Allied war effort, and would also serve a useful role in getting international trade and commerce back onto its feet post-war. However, this was also an idea that was anathema in some quarters of the United States administration. Some saw the concept of equipping the merchant fleets of Britain and her Allies with such ships as likely potential competition to America's own merchant marine, while others saw it as an essential precursor to the post-war resumption of international trade. There was always an underlying feeling in the United States that the Liberty ships were good enough for Britain and the Allies, even though America had got the C-class cargo ships to promote trade once hostilities ended. Besides, it was well known in the United States that Britain had already embarked on building its own fast cargo and fast refrigerated ships (see Chapter 8).

In autumn 1942 the preliminary design for a 15-knot, fully welded and prefabricated cargo vessel of 11,000dwt began. It was decreed that the design 'should be generally such as to utilize to the greatest possible extent the principles found effective in the production of the present Liberty ship', in terms of its simplicity and standardisation. The Liberty ship, it was said, was too slow, while the C2 cargo ship took too long to build.

There was considerable debate over the need for the new type of fast ship and the United States Maritime Commission found itself at loggerheads with the War Production Board. Intervention from the military chiefs eventually found in favour of the Maritime Commission, and work was able to continue on the design of the new type which was now designated as EC2-S-AP1, and later termed the Victory ship. Two factors were in the commission's favour. The first was that Liberty ship production now exceeded U-boat destruction and the second was that steel production was finding it difficult to keep up with the increasing pace of the Liberty shipbuilders. The *Victoria Advocate* reported on a speech by the chairman of the commission on 10 March 1943:

'There is no limit to the need for ships in a total, global war' says Rear Admiral Emery S Land, Chairman of the Maritime Commission, and that explains why plans have been made to continue the huge American shipbuilding program well into 1944 and 1945, with some interesting changes in the original schedule.

Prize project of the new program will be the new, bigger, faster, better Liberty ship, which it is proposed to call the Victory ship. This Victory ship is still in the design stage and no keels have been laid. A number of experimental hulls are being run through the Navy's model testing basin here in Washington to determine the perfect shape, and the first full size model of a Lentz-type engine is undergoing tests. This Lentz engine is really something. It operates on the poppet-valve principle, like your automobile, instead of on the sleeve-valve or turbine principle used in most steam engines.

The design specifications for the new type of ship were a length of 445ft and a beam of 63ft, later reduced to 62ft, as many slipways could not accommodate the larger width. The deadweight capacity was to be about 11,000 tons, similar to that of the Liberty ship, and a projected speed of 15 knots. The Liberty ship hull was not suitable for the faster operational speed and the C-type construction methods were too slow for an emergency shipbuilding project. A completely new hull design was developed, again eliminating the need for bent frames as much as was possible. The hull was designed with a long forecastle and a parallel middle-body with no sheer other than at the bow and stern, and a 'V'-shaped bow and cruiser stern. The design was for a full scantling ship with machinery and accommodation amidships with five holds, two decks and the forward three holds also with a mezzanine deck.

In the event, the Lentz engine, a double compound steam engine developed in Germany before the war, was not adopted for the new class of ships, although it was being used in the German Hansa A-class emergency standard ships (see Chapter 12). The Lentz engine had two complete compound engines connected to a common crankshaft and was, in effect, a four-cylinder engine. Tried and tested in Europe, and highly regarded for its efficiency, it was little known in the United States. The American Shipbuilding Company at Cleveland had some experience of the engine, but otherwise it was recognised in the United States by reputation only.

In 1941 a number of steam turbine manufacturers had been set up by the United States Maritime Commission to construct machinery for its C-class ships. By 1943 they were on top of the task and claimed to have the capacity to furnish the proposed Victory class of ship as well. Designs were drawn up to use the standard

C2 turbine and the higher capacity C3 turbine, the class designation being EC2-S-AP2 and EC2-S-AP3 respectively. The connection to the single propeller shaft was via double reduction gearing. Once the name Victory had been ratified in April 1943, the ships were reclassed as VC2-S-AP2 and VC2-S-AP3 types.

The attraction of turbine machinery was that it was already in production. Design of the machinery varied slightly from manufacturer to manufacturer, so the shipbuilder was given some leeway in how to arrange the seating for the turbines and gearing, and its connection to the single shaft. Two oil-fired water-tube boilers generated steam at a pressure of 465 pounds per square inch (psi) at 750°F and at a rate of 27,500 pounds per hour for both the C2-type turbines and the C3-type turbines. However, the bigger C3 machinery was expected to provide one knot over the required 15 knots.

The original contracts were issued, as they had been for the Liberty ships, on a cost plus bonus fee rate, the shorter time it took to build the ship, the higher the bonus. From late 1944 the contracts were awarded at a fixed price to ensure that yards actually delivered in a reasonable time. The concern was that yards would be tempted to waive the bonus in order to keep staff employed on a ship on which rates of construction had been slowed down.

Orders were placed with only a few yards. The V2S-AP2 type was constructed at the Bethlehem-Fairfield Shipyard at Baltimore, California Shipbuilding Corporation at Los Angeles and yards Nos 1 and 2 at Permanente Metals Corporation at Richmond. The VC2-S-AP3 was built by the California Shipbuilding Corporation, the Oregon Shipbuilding Corporation at Portland and Permanente Metals Corporation Yard No. 1.

A press release from the Kaiser shipyard in Richmond on 22 November 1943 announced progress at the yard:

> The Henry J Kaiser shipyards laid the keel of their first Victory ship Tuesday and started production of new 'pint size' cargo vessels in an industrial changeover heralded as a major step to speed the offensive against Japan. The new Victory ships, larger and faster than the Liberty ships which have been produced at unparalleled speed, gradually will supplant the 10,500 ton vessels, company officials announced. 'Liberty ships slowed down the convoys and were too big to enter small

VC2-S-AP3-type Victory ships lined up during completion at the California Shipbuilding Corporation yard at Los Angeles during June 1944. The nearest six ships from right to left more distant are: *Lincoln Victory*, *Panama Victory*, *Joplin Victory*, *Colombia Victory*, *Bluefield Victory* and *Sapulpa Victory*. (LIBRARY OF CONGRESS)

Cooper Union Victory (1945) was a product of the California Shipbuilding Corporation. She was sold by the United States government in 1951 to become *Green Harbour* for the Central Gulf Steamship Corporation of Wilmington. She was lengthened by 90ft in 1960, and was eventually sold for demolition in 1970. (AUTHOR COLLECTION)

harbors of the South Seas' a spokesman said. 'Therefore we have started production of two new types: the Victory ship with three decks instead of two, more powerful engines for greater speed, and the "pint sized" cargo vessel, about half the size of the Liberty ship and designed to go almost anywhere in the South Pacific.'

The 'pint-sized' ship was the C1-M motor ship designed specifically for use in small shallow harbours in the Pacific (see Chapter 7). The Maritime Commission had agreed to stop production of the steam-engined C1 types in favour of the Victory type, and to start to scale down its Liberty ship programme.

A plan of the general layout of the four yards at the Kaiser shipyards at Richmond, California. (THE PERMANENTE METALS CORPORATION)

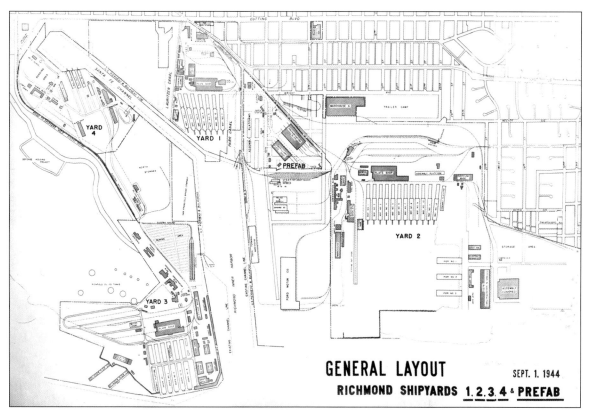

GENERAL LAYOUT
SEPT. 1. 1944
RICHMOND SHIPYARDS 1. 2. 3. 4 & PREFAB

Slipway No. 5 in Yard No. 1 at the Kaiser shipyards in Richmond. *Nicaragua Victory* (1944) was a Type VC2-S-AP3. The keel was laid on 16 May 1944, she was launched on 10 August and delivered on 23 September 1944. *Nicaraguan Victory* was managed by the Isthmian Steamship Company in 1944 and 1945 for the United States War Shipping Administration in San Francisco. She was sold to Argentinian owners in 1946, and eventually broken up after a long service career in 1979.
(The Permanente Metals Corporation)

Delays in getting the War Production Board to sanction the plans of the Maritime Commission meant that the first ship, *United Victory*, was only launched at the end of February 1944. *United Victory* and her sisters had a deadweight capacity of 10,750 tons and were subdivided by seven watertight bulkheads to create the five hold spaces, the machinery compartment, and the fore and aft peak tanks. There were three deep tanks on either side of the propeller shaft tunnel.

Altogether, the Victory ships were better equipped than the Liberty ships, and greater care was taken over detail. For example, in the Liberty ships, the master's cabin was on the bridge deck with a steel deckhead that made it unbearably hot in the tropics; in the Victory ships, the master's suite, comprising cabin bathroom and office, was situated beneath the bridge and, in addition, was comfortably insulated.

The Victory ship hatches were just over 22ft wide and Nos 3 and 4 hatches were 34ft long. The smaller hatches, Nos 2 and 5, were each 24ft long, with No. 1 hatch, which was built into the 73ft-long forecastle, being one foot longer. Cargo handling gear comprised 5-ton derricks in pairs, supported on either side of the three masts, and pairs of derricks supported by king-

posts forward and aft of the superstructure. There was also a 50-ton jumbo derrick serving No. 3 hatch mounted on the mainmast, and a 30-ton derrick plumbing No. 4 hold mounted on the mainmast. The topmasts were telescopic to provide reduced air-draught for passing under bridges. Although the main deck was without parabolic camber, the central part of the deck in the way of the hatches was flat, but the outer 21ft of the deck to port and starboard sloped down towards the sheerstrake at 1.5° in order to shed any water on deck.

The ships had electrically driven cargo winches. These were positioned in two groups of four around the foremast and mainmast, with a further two located forward, and two more aft of the superstructure. Ten single-drum, single-speed winches served the 5-ton derricks, and four single-drum, two-speed winches the 30-ton and 50-ton derricks. Each winch was driven by a 50hp, watertight, enclosed motor, and the control equipment, resistors and brake were arranged on a common bedplate under waterproof enclosures. The electric, horizontal shaft-type anchor windlass on the forecastle deck was capable of raising two anchors simultaneously from a 30-fathom depth of water at a chain speed of 30ft per minute.

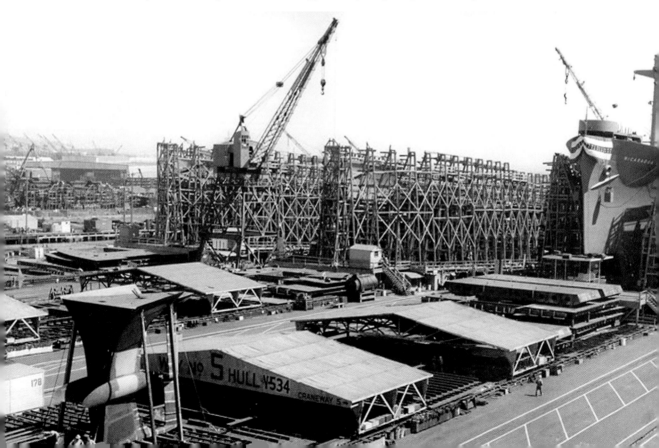

Yale Victory (1945) was laid down on 13 December 1944 and was launched on 1 January 1945. She was delivered to the US Maritime Commission's War Shipping Administration on 24 February 1945 and managed by the Olympic Steamship Company for the United States Maritime Commission War Shipping Administration. She was transferred to the United States Army in 1946 and was renamed *Sgt Archer T Gammon* in 1947. In 1950 she was transferred to the navy for use in the Military Sea Transportation Service. In early 1973 *Sgt Archer T Gammon* was transferred to the United States Maritime Administration for disposal and was scrapped at Kaohsiung, Taiwan. (THE PERMANENTE METALS CORPORATION)

Natural ventilation was supplied below decks through four 36in cowls, two 24in cowls and two 18in cowls. Each kingpost served as an exhaust trunk from the holds with 30in diameter Breidert exhaust heads installed at the top of each. Two 20,000 axial flow supply fans with ducts led to several terminals in the machinery spaces, with a single 12,000 axial flow fan with ducts leading from the boiler room.

The wheelhouse was recessed by 3ft from the front of the superstructure, allowing access across the front of the bridge. The bridge was equipped with a magnetic compass in a compensating binnacle, engine-room telegraphs, bells, foghorn, rudder angle indicator, echo depth sounder and inclinometer. Telephones for shipboard communication were available. The accommodation deck house on the cabin deck and boat deck below were recessed in the same manner as the wheelhouse. An article in *Marine Engineering and Shipping Review*, April 1944, described the accommodation aboard the new Victory ships:

The captain's stateroom and office are on the cabin deck, starboard side. The quarters for deck officers, engineers and radio operators are on the cabin and boat decks. The quarters for the crew are on the main deck. The officers' mess and pantry are located at the after end of the deckhouse on the starboard side of the boat deck. The crew's mess and pantry are located on the deck below the officers' mess. The galley is located at the after end of the deckhouse on the main deck. The hospital is on the portside on the main deck. The quarters for both the officers and crew are comfortably and conveniently arranged. Built-in berths are provided for the officers' staterooms and pipe berths for the hospital and crew's quarters.

Following *United Victory*, the next thirty-three ships were named after member countries of the United Nations. *Brazil Victory* and *USSR Victory*, for example, were built by California Shipbuilding Corporation, Los Angeles, and *Haiti Victory* by Permanente Metals Corporation, Yard 1, Richmond. The ships that followed were named after cities and towns in the United States and included *Ames Victory* built by Oregon Shipbuilding, *Las Vegas Victory* built by Permanente Metals Corporation, Yard 1, and *Zanesville Victory*, built by Bethlehem-Fairfield Shipyards, Baltimore. Finally, American colleges and universities were adopted, such as *Adelphi Victory* and *Yale Victory*, both built by Permanente Metals Corporation, Yard 2. The 117 Victory attack transports (VC2-S-AP5) were named after state counties and did not include the suffix *Victory* in their names. One was given the name *Marvin H McIntyre*, after the secretary to President Roosevelt. Despite some commentators erroneously stating otherwise, all the Victory ships were built in American yards, and none were sublet to Canadian yards. It is presumed that this confusion has arisen over the Kaiser yard at Vancouver that built thirty-one Victory attack transports for the United States Maritime Commission. This

Ethiopia Victory (1944) was laid down on 20 January 1944 and launched on 20 April 1944. She was delivered to the US Maritime Commission's War Shipping Administration on 17 July 1944 and managed by Agwilines (Atlantic, Gulf & West Indies Steamship Lines), which took delivery of the ship on 17 July 1944. *Ethiopia Victory* was laid up in reserve after the war. In 1964 she was renamed *Victoria* and modified to carry missiles, refrigerated provisions, submarine torpedoes, spare parts and fuel. She provided support services for the bases at Holy Loch and Rota. She was eventually scrapped in 1987. (THE PERMANENTE METALS CORPORATION)

Kaiser Vancouver yard, however, was located at Vancouver in Washington in the United States, and not at its Canadian namesake.

The occurrence of plating fractures, which had dogged the Liberty ship, was almost absent in the Victory ship. The Victory had a less rigid structure, with the frame spacing being 6in further apart than in the Liberty. In addition, the sheerstrake had a double-riveted angle connecting it to the deck plating, to prevent fractures from spreading from the deck plating to the hull, or vice versa. Finally, the bulwark plating was not welded to the sheerstrake, but left free above it, so that any corrosion in the bulwark plate could not spread into the body of the ship. The gap between bulwark and sheerstrake provided a continuous water freeing area.

Two features of the design, neither of a major nature, were found to be susceptible to failure on the Victory ships. One was the bulwark plating cap rail, where fractures in the butts of the plating manifested themselves, and the other was fractures in way of the bulwark stays and their connection to deck and bulwark plating. The significant area for cracking of the bulwark plating was where the plating was butt-welded to the adjacent superstructure on the upper deck. The forecastle bulwark stays were also liable to failure, where it was believed the weight of water washing over the deck in head seas was the cause.

Some 414 Victory cargo ships and 117 Victory attack transports were built. The majority of them, 272 vessels, were VC2-S-AP2 type with 6,000hp C2-type machinery, followed by 141 VC2-S-AP3, 8,500hp C3-type engines, and there was one experimental diesel-powered ship, *Emory Victory*, of the VC2-M-AP4 type. Contracts for an additional 132 vessels were cancelled in 1945. Three further Victory ships, two AP3-type and one AP5, were completed in 1946 as VC2-S1-AP7 ships, modified as post-war passenger and cargo carriers by the Alcoa Steamship Company of New York. The total number of Victory hulls built in the United States was 534.

Ninety-seven of the Victories were converted to troop carriers. Conversions allowed for berthing up to 1,600 troops in the 'tween decks. Galleys and messes also needed to be built and fitted out, along with showers, toilets, equipment and store facilities, plus recreational space for the troops. The accommodation spaces were well ventilated and electrically heated. In addition to the four standard boats stowed on gravity davits, lifesaving equipment included extra lifeboats that were stowed in cradles, life rafts and floats, and a personal lifejacket for all personnel on board.

The attack transports (VC2-S-AP5), known as the *Haskell* class, were designed to take troops and their equipment to battle. They were basically troop ships, save that they had a greatly enlarged crew complement of 535, and different cargo-handling equipment. Up to 3,000 tons of heavy stores, including vehicles, could be stowed in the lower holds, and up to 1,600 troops were carried in the 'tween decks. The foremast was replaced by the two kingposts that would normally have been at the front of the superstructure, and the boat deck was extended over No. 3 hatch forward and No. 4 hatch aft. The extended boat deck was used to stow up to twenty small landing craft on special davits. More landing craft could be accommodated over Nos 2 and 5 hatches. The topmasts of the mainmast and mizzen were extended, and a radio aerial attached to the funnel.

A number of yards contracted to deliver Victory ships were instructed during the construction phase to change the completion of the ships to attack transports. The lead ship, *Haskell*, was laid down at the California Shipbuilding yard in March 1944 and launched on 13 June. Three of the ships, *Logan Victory*, *Hobbs Victory* and *Canada Victory* were lost to kamikaze attack at Keram Retto and Okinawa in April 1945. The loss of these three ships, with cargoes that included 24,000 tons of munitions and nearly all the United States supply of 81mm mortar ammunition, was a setback to the Okinawa invasions.

Towards the end of the war, production of the Victory-type ships was slowed down, and during August 1945 numerous contracts were cancelled. The cancellations included nine AP2-type ships at the California Shipbuilding Corporation in Los Angeles, and twenty-one at Bethlehem-Fairfield Shipyard at Baltimore, as well as seventeen AP3 types at the Oregon Shipbuilding Corporation at Portland. All orders placed with Permanente Metals Corporation, Richmond, had been fulfilled, or nearly so, at the time of the cancellations.

The Victory ships provided an important service, helping to draw the war to a satisfactory and early conclusion. They maintained the all-important Atlantic ferry, sustaining the American troops stationed in Europe, and were able to support the numerous outstations and posts dotted around the Pacific. The adaptability of the basic design was a key feature so that the normally configured cargo ship could easily be converted into troop ship or attack transport for military use.

With the war over, the life of the Victory ships was just beginning. Many of the military conversions were decommissioned and reverted to cargo-ship configuration, while some of the troop ships were converted for passenger and cargo liner use. Three of the hulls that were cancelled at the Oregon Shipyard in August 1945 were intended to become two AP3-type cargo ships and one AP5 attack transport. The keels had been laid during the week preceding the cancellation, and much of the preparatory assembly and prefabrication of units was already at an advanced stage. The shipyard advertised the hulls for sale, and the offer was quickly accepted by the Alcoa Steamship Company of New York, a company that served the Caribbean region. The ships were launched as passenger and cargo liners between March and September 1946 as *Alcoa Cavalier*, *Alcoa Clipper* and *Alcoa Corsair*, each with accommodation for ninety-eight passengers.

The Alcoa brand was that of the Aluminium Company of America and each ship loaded bauxite (aluminium ore) at Trinidad for unloading at Mobile, and there loaded general cargo for return to Los Angeles. Aluminium also featured in the redesign of the three ships, where for the first time on a merchant vessel, each vessel had an aluminium superstructure, while the funnel, lifeboats, davits and handrails and 'tween deck hatches were also made of aluminium. An

De Pauw Victory (1945) was one of the many American Victory ships that served briefly during the latter months of the war and was then placed in the Reserve Fleet, in this case at Suisun Bay in California. She was eventually sold for demolition in 1989. (AUTHOR COLLECTION)

additional deck, the promenade deck, infilled the well between the bridge front and the forecastle, and there was a similar structure aft of the superstructure to the forward end of No. 5 hatch, with Nos 2 to 4 hatches being trunked to the promenade deck. The after part of the upper deck was used for a variety of two-, three- and four-berth staterooms. Other staterooms were distributed around the main superstructure, and the officers and crew domiciled within the lower deck area, now designated as 'B' deck. The dining saloon, which could accommodate sixty-five passengers at one sitting, was forward on the upper deck. There was a swimming pool over No. 4 hatch, a cinema and all the trimmings expected by a holidaymaker destined for the Caribbean. The three ships proved extremely popular with travellers and shippers alike on the three-week round voyage. Typical passenger loadings were around a comfortable 66 per cent capacity.

The three Alcoa sisters caused quite a stir in shipping circles when they were commissioned. Not only did they demonstrate the role that the Victory-type ship could adopt as peacetime passenger and cargo liners, but they also demonstrated the value of lightweight aluminium construction in merchant shipbuilding. Aluminium was a means of both reducing the weight of a ship, whilst helping to reduce the height of the ship's centre of gravity, measured above the keel. As it turns out, the three ships were to be the first of many such conversions.

The most radical post-war conversions were three troop ships, *Cranston Victory*, *Costa Rica Victory* and *La Grande Victory*. *Cranston Victory* was managed by the South Atlantic Steamship Company, *Costa Rica Victory* by the American Hawaiian Steamship Company and *La Grande Victory* by Shepard Steamship Company, on be-

half of the United States War Shipping Administration. Their role as American troop transports was short-lived, as they were soon laid up and in 1946 were on the Maritime Commission's sale list. All three ships were purchased in 1947 by the Dutch government as troopers to the Dutch East Indies (Indonesia), and later to Dutch New Guinea. They were renamed respectively *Zuiderkruis* and *Groote Beer*, both under the management of Stoomvaart Maats 'Nederland', and *Waterman*, managed by NV Rotterdamsche Lloyd. On her return voyage to the Netherlands, *Zuiderkruis* transported those who wished to leave the former Dutch East Indies as repatriates.

In 1951 they were sent in turn to the Netherlands Dock Company in Amsterdam to be rebuilt as immigrant ships. An extra deck was added and the bridge relocated forward. Their original accommodation was gutted, and cabins were fitted to accommodate up to 830 passengers in the lower deck and the upper deck, while two entirely new passenger decks were built almost the length of the ship.

Zuiderkruis started in her new role in June 1951, sailing from Rotterdam to New York, with her next voyage being to Canada. Then in August she departed with around eight hundred migrants for New Zealand. In November 1951 *Waterman* left the shipyard for trials after conversion, and then began her first voyage to Australia. *Groote Beer* made three voyages to Australia before her reconstruction, which was started late in 1951, and she commenced in her new role in May 1952. Thereafter, the schedules of the three ships varied between transatlantic voyages and sailings to Australia and New Zealand. Management of the ships on behalf of the Dutch government remained the same, save that *Groote Beer* soon came under the manage-

ment of the Nederlandsch-Amerikaansche Stoomvaart Maarts NV (Holland-America). Holland-America also acted as agents for the ships in America and Canada.

Slightly less ambitious was the conversion of six ships owned by Flota Argentina de Navegacion de Ultramar of Buenos Aires. These were reconfigured in the late 1950s to carry about eight hundred passengers in cabin class. This was achieved by building over the upper deck aft and converting the entire lower deck into passenger accommodation.

One British liner company also rebuilt Victory ships into passenger and cargo liners. Don-

aldson Brothers & Black, the Donaldson Line, of Glasgow, managed the troop transport *Medina Victory* for the Ministry of War Transport when she was transferred to Britain in June 1946. In September the following year, she was bought by Donaldson and the troop accommodation stripped out to become a cargo ship, with the original passenger accommodation refitted with just twelve berths. She was renamed *Laurentia*. With help from the Scottish Tourist Board, Donaldson were persuaded to reconstruct the ship to accommodate fifty-five first-class passengers, to serve between Glasgow and Canadian ports, west coast in summer and east coast in winter.

A consort was purchased, the identical troop transport *Taos Victory*, which had been under the management of Furness Withy. She was renamed *Lismoria*. She too was converted by extending the superstructure aft to the edge of No. 4 hatch and extending the boat deck to accommodate an extra pair of lifeboats port and starboard. No. 4 hatch was built over and extended

Waterman (1945), built as *La Grande Victory*, seen in the Suez Canal with her decks lined with troops, as she was before conversion to an immigrant ship in 1951. (AMBROSE GREENWAY COLLECTION)

Ambitious conversions of three VC2-S-AP3-type (8,500hp engines) Victory ships, *Cranston Victory*, *La Grande Victory* and *Costa Rica Victory* into the Dutch emigrant ships *Zuiderkruis*, *Waterman* and *Groote Beer* were undertaken in 1951. *Zuiderkruis* (1945), seen here at Cape Town, had accommodation for 900 emigrants and voyaged to Australia, New Zealand and America. (AMBROSE GREENWAY COLLECTION)

Impressive post-war conversions of standard Victory ship types were the Donaldson Line's passenger cargo steamers *Laurentia* (1945), seen here, and *Lismoria*. They were built respectively as *Medina Victory* and *Taos Victory* (1944), and were taken in hand in 1948 to be reconfigured with fifty-five first-class passenger berths and public rooms for the passengers. (AUTHOR COLLECTION)

upwards by trunking as far aft as the mainmast. By all accounts, the accommodation was comfortable, and described in advertising literature as being 'airy and spacious', although it is hard to believe that such a conversion could really fit this description.

There were many other conversions as time went on; some Victory ships were even converted into container ships. But their greatest role was as the basic twelve-passenger cargo liner that was bought by many of the world's liner companies, although not in significant numbers by UK shipowners, as at that time Britain was almost out of dollars. Captain Michael Jones speculated on the reason why only fourteen Victory ships came to British owners in a letter published in *Marine News*, June 1969:

> Looking at the fourteen Victory ships which were purchased for service under the Red Ensign or by British shipowners, there is a rather curious pattern in that the majority would operate on dollar earning trades and, therefore, I speculate that the UK Treasury would only release their precious Dollars to purchase these relatively expensive ships when the ships would bring back more Dollars to the UK in return.

Of the fourteen Victory ships purchased by Great Britain, the four Blue Funnel ships (together with two Dutch ships owned by NSMC) operated on a full round-the-world service based in the United States, as did the *Silvermaple* of Silver Line and the *British Prince*. I remember seeing the second Furness Victory, the *Pacific Stronghold*, in Aden in 1948 so I suspect she was also operating at that time with Prince Line round-the-world. I suppose Donaldson Line could be said to be earning Dollars with their two Victory ships trading to North America, but I would not wish to speculate how the tramp ship owner Billmeir managed to convince the Treasury that he should buy his two vessels which he sold to P&O in less than a year.

Treasury insistence on potential dollar earning is reflected in an unsuccessful request from Union-Castle Line to buy two Victory ships. The Union-Castle Line traded to southern and eastern Africa and did not earn dollars; the request was rejected by the Treasury. The Treasury restrictions were not as strict regarding purchase of the cheaper Liberty ships, and many of these ships were to fly the Red Ensign post-war (see Chapter 14).

12 GERMAN STANDARD SHIPS BUILT IN THE SECOND WORLD WAR

A wide range of German standard ships were built in the Second World War. They ranged from the fragile F-lighter and KT ships operating in the Mediterranean and Black Sea, to the robust and sophisticated Hansa A-class cargo ships designed for work in the Baltic and Atlantic. The Hansa A class added greatly to the logistical capacity of the Axis nations, but the even more sophisticated and larger Hansa B- and Hansa C-type ships arrived too late to help their cause. A key issue in the construction of these latter ship types was the availability of the Bauer Wach exhaust turbine systems, which significantly delayed completion of all but the lead ship in both classes. A dozen tugs were also completed under *das Hansa Bauprogramm*.

The German naval supply capacity in the Mediterranean was severely depleted in 1941. Many of the vessels available in February at the start of operations in North Africa had been lost by the end of the year, amounting to about 70,000 tons out of 124,000 tons. Given the ongoing need to supply German forces in North Africa, and the lack of ships available elsewhere that could be transferred into the Mediterranean, an emergency construction programme was envisaged.

A small type of prefabricated steamship of easy construction called the Kriegstransporter

was planned. Deutsche Werft in Hamburg was given responsibility for drawing up the detailed plans for the ship and constructing the prototype. This was *KT 3*, launched on 1 August 1942 and completed six weeks later on 16 September. It was planned that the remainder of the ships would be built in Italy. Prefabricated parts were to be made in Germany for the first batch of twenty ships and sent south by train, to be assembled initially in Genoa by Ansaldo Sestri. The first two Italian-built ships were *KT 1* launched on 5 September 1942 and completed on 14 November, and *KT 2* launched on 12 September and completed on 9 December. No other vessels were completed that year. The principal dimensions as reported by Wilhelm Donko in his book *Die Kriegstransporter KT 1 – KT 62 der Deutschen Kriegsmarine* were:

Length: 62 metres
Width: 11 metres
Height to main deck: 4.2 metres
Draught: 2.9 metres
Displacement loaded: 1,200 tons
Stowage space: 980 cubic metres
Hatch 1: 6.75 by 5.4 metres
Hatch 2: 9.8 by 7.4 metres.

The outline of the Kriegstransporter-type ship used in the Mediterranean and Baltic Sea from 1941 onwards clearly shows her flat-plated bow shape, transom stern and unbalanced deck profile.
(AUTHOR COLLECTION)

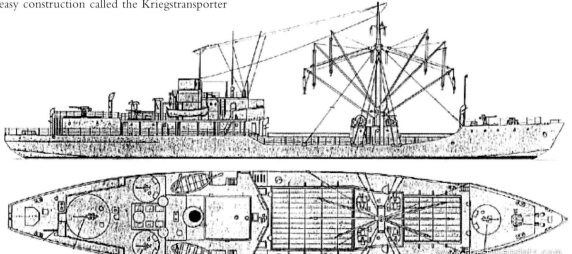

The Kriegstransporter was additional to the numerous small flat-bottomed Marinefährprähme (literally, 'navy ferry barge', but known as 'F-lighters' by the British). These were small ships with bow doors and diesel engines aft, with a deadweight capacity of 105 tons and a speed of 10½ knots. They were designed to run across the Mediterranean in convoys supplying the smaller ports. A total of thirty Marinefährprähme were ordered in October 1941, of which twenty-two were to be built in Palermo, and eight in Varna, Bulgaria. In November the order was increased by another fifteen, and in December another twenty were planned to be built, with the ultimate target of about a hundred vessels. The first batch of ten Marinefährprähmee was commissioned in Palermo in November 1941: *F 146* to *F 154* and *F 160*. In the first half of December the remaining five of the first order, *F 155* to *F 159*, were completed.

The F-lighter crew consisted of fourteen men. The Marinefährprähme was, nevertheless, vulnerable both to the weather and the Allied patrols, and one of the first lighters to be built foundered on her maiden voyage.

The larger Kriegstransporter had a deadweight capacity of 400 tons and could carry six tanks in the single hold, two via the forward hatch and four via the after hatch. They had two coal-fired water-tube boilers, supplying steam to twin triple-expansion steam engines which provided a maximum speed of 14½ knots. The bunker capacity was 400 tons of coal, which gave them a range of up to 1,500 miles. The Kriegstransporter could unload tanks and other heavy equipment using its own 30-ton derrick mounted on the mainmast situated between the two hatches. The KT ships also had four 5-ton or three 5-ton and one 10-ton derrick, similarly mounted. They had a crew complement of fifty-three.

The ships had a blunt raked bow to halfway down to the waterline with the forefoot cut away below this at a steeper rake. This was a simple design feature that avoided the use of shaped frames and plates. The ships had a short, triangular-shaped forecastle and the machinery spaces were aft, over which was the accommodation for officers and crew. The transom stern was slightly raked.

The building programme was presented to the commander of German naval transport in Italy at Genoa on 24 January 1942. An officer from the German naval high command supported by the director of Deutsche Werft made the presentation, when it was hoped that the first keel could be laid in March. At a meeting three days later with representatives from the four shipyards designated to carry out the building programme, along with the Italian naval ministry, it was concluded that twelve ships should be built by the end of the year, with the remaining eight of the first batch to follow in 1943. This meeting was followed by another during the morning of 28 January in the naval ministry, at which the Germans learned that intervention by the Italian Minister for Transport required the programme to be halved. This reduction was necessary in order not to jeopardise the existing Italian shipbuilding programme. The new German programme now foresaw five completions only in 1942, with the remainder coming in the fourth quarter of 1942. In the event, only two were completed in 1942: *KT 1* and *KT 2*.

By the end of the war, forty KT ships had been completed in Italian yards (at Genoa, Ancona, Iva, Trigoso and Livorno), thirty of them by Ansaldo at Genoa. Two were built at Toulon and others were built in Austria (Linz, Korneuburg), Hungary (Obuda) and Russia (Nikolajev). Although sixty-two were planned, contracts for the last two ships were never issued.

Only one of the KT ships ever flew the Red Ensign post-war. This was *Empire Stevedore*, which was the original prototype Kriegstransporter *KT 3*. She was captured towards the end of the war and was taken over at Hamburg in October 1949 by the Royal Engineers, who moved her to Marchwood, minus her engine, for use as a military stevedore training ship, replacing *Empire Flamian*. *Empire Stevedore*, it seems, was haunted. Her last German captain shot himself when the ship was captured and his ghost, looking through binoculars towards the bow of the ship, regularly appeared in the wheelhouse shortly after midnight. Those aboard ship after midnight often reported hearing the captain's footfalls as he climbed the ladder to the bridge.

By 1942 the German merchant navy, *die deutsche Handelsflotte*, was under as much pressure in the Atlantic and Baltic as it had previously been in the Mediterranean. Germany had suffered considerable losses while ships tried to reach home at the outbreak of war, while others in Allied ports were confiscated. The occupation of Denmark and Norway increased the stress, as ships were needed to supply the occupying forces. Some vessels had also been requisitioned for alteration and training preparatory to *das Unternehmen Seelöwe*, Operation Sea Lion, the planned invasion of England. In addition, many ships, such as fast cargo liners, had been requisitioned by the navy. On the plus side were the few vessels captured during the war, but these were not enough to make up for the losses. The consequence was that the Deutsche Handelsflotte could no longer cope with the demands placed on it, and it was recognised that an urgent shipbuilding programme was needed. The ships were to be built to simple, no-frills designs and were to be largely prefabricated to speed construction, even though German shipyards then had little experience of such techniques. However, the ships would be well equipped and built to classification standards.

It was proposed that the shipbuilding programme would involve both government and shipowners. The Shipping Trust, Der Schiffahrt Treuhand GmbH, was established in Hamburg and registered in August 1942 to facilitate German shipping companies acquiring the new tonnage. Hans Jürgen Witthöft in his book *Das Hansa-Bauprogramm* wrote:

Gesellschafter der Schiffahrt Treuhand GmbH … Shareholders appointed in the new company were those shipowners that had suffered the greatest losses:

Bock, Godeffroy & Co., Hamburg
Deutsche Dampfschifffahrts-Gesellschaft 'Hansa', Bremen
John T Essberger & Co., Afrika Linien, Hamburg
Hamburg-Amerika-Linie, Hamburg
Hamburg Südamerika-Dampfschifffahrts Gesellschaft, Hamburg
Norddeutscher Lloyd, Bremen
Schulte & Bruns, Emden
Rob M Sloman, Hamburg

The Company Board comprised four and at most eight people (later nine). Its members were elected for a term of three years … The development of the three basic types of ship to be built in the Hansa shipbuilding programme took six months to complete and comprised cargo ships of 3,000, 5,000 and 9,000 tons deadweight, also a 1000 horsepower and a 600 horsepower tug.

Some 420,000 tons of steel had to be made available for the programme, and slipways needed to be freed so that construction of the ships could begin. Competition with the navy was always going to be a problem. The shipbuilding committee, *das Hauptausschuss Schiffbau*, co-ordinated the allocation of shipbuilding capacity, established priorities between military and civilian needs, and encouraged efficient building methods for the proposed standard ships. In June 1942 Hauptausschuss Schiffbau planned 120 Type A 3,000dwt, sixty Type B 5,000dwt and twenty Type C 9,000dwt cargo ships. Ship types were designed by renowned naval architects and engineers with input from the Shipping Trust shareholders. The ships were to be a compromise between the needs of the liner and tramp trades. Materials shortage, and supply of equipment of lower, but acceptable, quality, characterised the designs.

For each type of ship, a separate shipyard was made responsible for the final design details. Close liaison was maintained between the appointed shipyard and the Shipping Trust as well as with the German classification society, Germanischer Lloyd. Dialogue was also maintained with the military regarding the demand for new ships. Some allowance was also given for individual shipyard preferences in interpreting the design drawings, but both shortage of materials

The profile of the Hansa A-type steamers is well illustrated in this picture of *Sheldrake* (1944), owned by General Steam Navigation Company of London. She was built by Stettina Vulcan at Stettin as *Njong*, confiscated by the Allies in 1945 and renamed *Empire Garland*, before becoming *Sheldrake* in 1947. She was sold in 1958 to Monrovian owners, and served three further Greek owners before being scrapped in 1972. (J K BYASS)

and damage due to air strikes could also affect the design of individual ships. The ships were to be built as plainly as possible, but were to be sea-going ships in every respect and classified accordingly as 100A/4.

The smaller Hansa A type was based on *Casablanca* and *Oldenburg*, built by Deutsche Werft in 1936 for Oldenburg-Portugiesische Dampfschifffahrts Rhederei AG of Oldenburg. (*Oldenburg* had already been sunk by torpedo in April 1940.) They were cargo ships of 3,230dwt capacity, having engines and officers' accommodation amidships with Lentz double compound steam engines. The two water-tube boilers were coal-fired and generated steam at 310°C. They had a service speed of 12 knots (the Lentz engine had also been a serious contender for the Victory ship, see Chapter 11). The crew were accommodated in the poop.

Deutsche Werft was entrusted with the final design drawings for the Hansa A type, which had a slightly smaller hull than its prototypes, but with a slightly higher deadweight capacity; the Lentz engines were less powerful and the design speed was 10 knots. The Hansa A type comprised shelter-deck ships with three holds, two forward and one aft of the engine compartment. Each hold was plumbed by two 5-ton derricks mounted on the foremast situated between Nos 1 and 2 holds and the mainmast serving No. 3 hold. Some ships also had a 30-ton derrick forward and a 10-ton derrick aft.

The first ship was laid down at the Finkenwerder yard of Deutsche Werft on 15 December 1942 and launched as *Hansa I* on 30 April 1943. Fitting out took a further seven weeks. On completion she was handed over to a crew from Hamburg Südamerika-Dampfschifffahrts-Gesellschaft as shareholder in the Shipping Trust, Der Schiffahrt Treuhand GmbH. Each 3,000-ton ship had a crew complement of thirty. *Wesergau*, to be owned by Norddeutscher Lloyd, Bremen, was the next launch in May and the first ship built at the Reiherstieg yard of Deutsche Werft. She was followed by *Cuxhaven*, which was launched in July and was owned by the Hamburg-Amerika-Linie in Hamburg.

During 1943 construction of the Hansa A was also undertaken at Lübecker Machinenbau Gesellschaft and Lübecker Flenderwerke AG, both at Lübeck. Their first ships were *Wesermarsch* for Norddeutscher Lloyd, launched in November, and *Heiligenhafen*, launched in September for Hamburg-Amerika-Linie. At Rostock, Neptun Werft completed *Eckenheim* in December 1943.

Experience with the ships showed that they cost about one-third more than a similar ship would have cost in 1939. The wartime cost was around DM1.7 million. The difference was resolved by setting the commercial value of the ships at DM1 million, and this was the price the German shipowners paid for the basic Hansa A-type ship. The other issue for the shipowner was that the ships were allocated quite late on during their construction, and the subsequent owner had little control over the precise fitting out of each vessel.

Construction of the Hansa A-type ship was extended during 1943 and 1944 to selected shipyards in the German-occupied countries in northern Europe. The shipyards employed their own workers, and construction was undertaken under strict military supervision in order to prevent sabotage.

Dutch yards delivered a total of seventeen basic A-type ships, and one modified and enlarged 3,550dwt vessel to German owners during the war. Four more were under construction at the end of the war, which were completed privately between 1948 and 1952, the last, greatly modified and updated as *Stahleck* for Deutsche Dampfschifffahrts-Gesellschaft 'Hansa'. The ships were built in twelve separate Dutch yards. Building times were extensive compared with those of the German yards, reflecting both difficulties in accessing supplies and the indifference of the labour force. For example, De Merwede at Hardinxfeld laid down yard number 502 in the summer of 1943 and delivered her as *Elmenhorst* in April 1945. The first ship completed in Holland was *Hendrik Fisser VI*, completed in April 1944, and *Brunhilde*, which was launched in October 1943 and delivered at the end of May 1944 by Van der Giessen at Krimpen for the Hamburg Südamerika-Dampfschifffahrts-Gesellschaft.

Two Belgian yards were employed on the Hansa A programme. John Cockerill at Antwerp built two, *Weserstrum*, which after the war became the General Steam Navigation Company's *Albatross*, and *Aeolius*. Both ships were completed in 1944. J Boel & Fils at Tamise constructed a further four ships, also delivered in 1944, and had another four under construction at the end of the war. They laid down two more after the war was over. These were all completed privately to various configurations at the preference of their new owners.

Four Hansa A-type ships were built in Danish yards between 1943 and 1944. These were

Irene Oldendorff for Egon Oldendorff, Lübeck; *Friedrichshafen* for Hamburg-Amerika-Linie; and *Asnaes* and *Rosnaes* for service with the Danish government under the Danish flag.

By 1944 plans were drawn up for a modified and enlarged version of the Hansa A with an increased deadweight capacity of 3,550 tons. Seven ships of this type were built by Deutsche Werft at Finkenwerder, including *Betzdorf*, which later became *Baltrader* in the United Baltic Corporation fleet, and one, *Hendrik Fisser VII*, which was subcontracted to J & K Smit's yard at Kinderdijk in the Netherlands. These ships were all completed in 1944 and 1945. They had four holds, two forward and two aft. The foremast was placed on the forecastle and the mainmast right aft on the poop, each supporting two 5-ton derricks to serve Nos 1 and 4 holds. There were two sets of kingposts, which also served as ventilators to the cargo spaces, one forward of the superstructure and one aft. These supported two more pairs of derricks to plumb Nos 2 and 3 holds.

At one time, 128 Hansa A-type ships were planned. However, the total production of Hansa A-type ships amounted to just seventy vessels, including seven ships of the 3,550-ton, four-hatch type. Eighteen of the ships were lost during the war. Some thirty-three Hansa A-type ships were built in German yards, one being completed as late as 1950, and included in this total were six 3,550dwt ships of the modified Hansa A type. Holland built twenty-three, including one of the modified version

and four 3,000-ton ships completed after the war; Belgium built four during the war and a further six after the war; and Norway built four ships, with two modified for Norwegian government use. Some fifty-two ships were completed before the German capitulation on 7 May 1944, but nineteen contracts were cancelled at the end of the war.

After the war, a number of the Hansa A types were brought into British waters awaiting allocation to the various Allied nations. The description of one of them in the *Glasgow Herald*, 31 January 1946, illustrates some of the peculiarities of the ships and the frugal nature of some of the ship's fittings:

The *Empire Eden* is a German standard ship, a 'Hansa' as they called them. Built for no longer passages than to the Norwegian coast, she is only 1,923 gross tons. With a soft raking stem and cruiser stern she is a trim little ship, but difficult to handle when light. She carries 3,900 tons of cargo, and has one derrick capable of lifting 30 tons. Her patent lifting gear has caused considerable interest. She also has new type gravity davits of good design. Inside her ordinary ship's wheel a small car wheel is fitted, which is easily handled.

When taken over, crew accommodation was a curious mixture of the very good and the pretty poor. Seamen were still accommodated in open fo'c'sles (three-berth cabins have now been installed), and there was

General Steam Navigation Company's *Albatross* (1943) seen from the quarter, was built by John Cockerill at Antwerp as the Hansa A-type steamer (3,000-ton deadweight capacity) *Weserstrom*. Taken by the Allies in 1945, she adopted the name *Empire Galena* until sold to GSN in 1947. (AUTHOR COLLECTION)

no running water in the cabins, where basins had to be emptied over the side. Yet the galley and officers' accommodation were very good for a ship of this size.

German shortage of material was evident in the lavish use of wood in this 1944-built ship. Cupboard doors had wooden hinges, while key holes were made of compressed wood, handles were of Bakelite. Altogether there was a great scarcity of brass and copper and an increased use of nickels, alloys, and wood.

A number of British owners bought the Hansa A-type ships and adapted them for their own trades. The Currie Line of Leith, General Steam Navigation Company and United Baltic Corporation, both of London, as well as the Indochina Steam Navigation Company of Hong Kong and the Straits Shipping Company of Singapore were the biggest investors.

The Hansa B 5,000dwt capacity programme amounted to thirty-one ships, twenty-six of which were still under construction at the end of the war. Bremer Vulkan at Bremen were the champions of this type of ship, and had the

drawings completed and preparatory prefabrication work done ready for the first keel to be laid at their yard on 10 March 1943 and launched 30 October. This was *Haussa*, which was handed over to Deutsche Afrika Linien GmbH (John T Essberger & Company), Hamburg, on 30 December 1943, having taken nine and a half months to build and fit out. A total of forty-nine ships were planned for this class, later increased to fifty-five ships.

The Hansa B had a raked bow and a cruiser stern, machinery and bridge amidships and was flush-decked apart from a raised forecastle. The officer's accommodation was amidships and the crew were accommodated in the poop. The crew complement was thirty-eight and they also had seventeen anti-aircraft gunners to accommodate. The ships had two hatches forward and

two aft serving the four holds. They were two-deck ships, although a few were completed as single-deck ships. The foremast was situated between Nos 1 and 2 hatches and supported a 65-ton derrick and three 5- or two 5- and one 10-ton derricks. The mainmast supported one 30-ton derrick and three 5-ton derricks serving Nos 3 and 4 hatches. The peacetime deadweight capacity of this class of ship lay between 5,100 and 5,965 tons.

As with the Hansa A type, the Hansa B ships were also equipped with Lentz double compound steam engines. In the Hansa B design, however, the exhaust steam was passed through a low-pressure Bauer Wach turbine, and this arrangement could maintain the design service speed of 12 knots. The steam was supplied at 325°C by three water-tube boilers. The ships were coal-fired and had a bunker capacity of 716 tons.

By the end of the war, only five Hansa B ships had been commissioned, as the delay in their completing was caused by the shortage of parts for the exhaust turbine system. The first Type B ship, *Haussa*, delivered by Bremer Vulkan was followed by *Wangerooge*, which was laid down on 4 November 1943 and launched on 25 March 1944. She was delivered to Norddeutscher Lloyd on 6 May 1944. The ship had a short life and was sunk by a mine off Stadtlandet, Norway, just four months after she was commissioned. Helsingör Werft built and fitted out *Kronenfels* in a few days under twenty-one months and delivered her to Deutsche Dampf-schifffahrts-Gesellschaft 'Hansa' in March 1945. Naksov completed *Millerntor* also in twenty-one months and delivered her to Hamburg-Amerika-Linie Lloyd in March 1945, and Odense Staalskibsvaaerf were about to hand *Dammtor* over to Hamburg-Amerika-Linie in

the same month, having taken eighteen months to complete the ship, when she was destroyed alongside the fitting-out quay in an Allied air strike. In each of the last three ships, the period from keel-laying to launching was between four and eleven months, and it was the fitting out and completion of the machinery that delayed the commissioning of the ships. As a consequence, only *Haussa* made any real contribution to the Axis war effort.

Work was suspended on the Hansa B-type ships that were still under construction on 7 May 1945. In due course they were completed, but usually to the specification of their new owners, so that a large variety of slightly different profiles and cargo-handling arrangements appeared. A total of twenty-nine recognisable Type B ships were completed between the second half of 1945 and 1948. *Marianne*, for example, built by Bergens MV, and the only Hansa B type to be built in Norway, was delivered in July 1947 to a local Norwegian owner as a motor ship; two ships built in Sweden were completed for the Norwegian registry with double compound Lentz steam engines.

If the Hansa B-type ships made little contribution to the Axis war effort, the larger Hansa C ships made even less. Although twenty ships of this 9,000dwt class were planned, only one, *Nikolaifleet*, was delivered before the war ended. She was laid down at the yard of F Schichau at Danzig on 15 March 1943, launched just before Christmas and delivered to Hamburg-Amerika-Linie on 15 June 1944. However, she was sunk by torpedoes fired by two motor torpedo boats of the Royal Norwegian Navy off the German coast less than seven months later. Carrying a full cargo of iron ore, the ship went down quickly with considerable loss of life. She carried a crew of forty-six and about twenty gunners.

The Hansa B-type ship (5,000-ton deadweight capacity) *Jorge Velho* (1946) was built as *Klostertor* by Odense Staalskibs in Denmark. She was sold on completion to D/S Jutlandia A/S and renamed *Jens Toft*; was resold to Cinaba Comercio Industria e Nav Bandeirante SA of Santos, Brazil, and renamed *Jorge Velho* as seen here, and eventually sold for demolition as *Sao Mateus*, although still registered in Santos, in 1973. (AUTHOR COLLECTION)

The Hansa C type had a peacetime dead-weight capacity of 9,270 tons (10,200 tons under wartime allowances). To all intents and purposes they were an enlarged version of the B type, with two holds forward and two aft of the machinery spaces and two decks. Apart from an increased length and wider beam, the main outward differences were additional cargo-handling gear and a more substantial superstructure, with open alleyways on either side on the upper deck. The cargo-handling equipment comprised three 5-ton, three 10-ton and one 65-ton derrick supported from the foremast, five 5-ton and one 30-ton derricks to the main-mast and two sets of kingposts, one aft of the forecastle and one each before and aft of the superstructure, each with two 5-ton derricks.

The propelling machinery was a Lentz double compound engine with a low-pressure turbine working on the Bauer Wach principle. As with the Hansa B-type ships, the turbine units were scarce. Steam was generated in three separate boilers, which were fired by coal; the bunkers could carry 1,070 tons of coal. The design service speed of the class was 12 knots.

Two Hansa C-class ships were completed after the war by Burmeister & Wain at Copenhagen as motor ships. These were *Colombia* and *Venezuela*, completed in 1947 and 1948, respectively, for Danish owners. *Colombia* was laid down in February 1944 and launched in December 1945, when work ceased, awaiting a buyer. The keel of *Venezuela* was laid down on 25 November 1944, the name *Katherinenfleet* (Hamburg-Amerika-Linie) was allocated to the ship, but she was launched in August 1946 for her new Danish owners. Wilton-Fyenoord at Schiedam was subcontracted to build three Hansa C-class ships by F Schichau, but these ships were never started due to commitments on other projects. Plans to build at Gothenburg, Malmö, Landskrona, Rotterdam and St-Nazaire also came to nothing, although a number of

ships based on the Hansa C design were built after the war, but were so modified as to be un-recognisable as Hansa C-type vessels.

The final tally for the number of Hansa standard type ships completed by 7 May 1945 was:

	A 3,000 tons	B 5,000 tons	C 9,000 tons
German yard	35	4	1
Belgian yard	4	0	0
Dutch yard	11	0	0
Danish yard	2	1	0
Total	52	5	1

There were also designs drawn up for three types of standard steam tug – of 1,000, 600 and 350hp. *Das Schlepperprogramm* was undertaken as part of *das Hansa Bauprogramm,* although planning was modest, with just six of the larger and six of the intermediate powered tugs envisaged, despite considerable losses due to air strikes by the RAF. The need for the larger tugs arose out of the initial training exercises for *das Unternehmen Seelöwe*, the invasion of England, in 1940. Tugs and barges were planned to play an important role in the invasion. Three 600hp tugs were built in Germany and three in Finland by Ruona at Raabe, and six 1,000hp tugs were built in Germany by Nordwerft Köser & Meyer in Hamburg. In addition, eight 350hp tugs were to be built in Italy by Cantieri Riuniti dell' Adriatico at Monfalcone; none were competed before the end of the war.

The 600hp tugs were all built by the Johann Oeklers shipyard in Hamburg and based on a 1938 design. They required a crew of twelve, as did the larger 1,000hp tugs. Two 350hp tugs were laid down at Elmshorner Werft in January 1945 and completed after the war. Another contract placed with D W Kremer & Son was cancelled in 1946.

The plans for the 9,000-ton deadweight capacity Hansa C ships illustrate a conventional-looking tramp steamer of 1930s vintage. Although twenty ships of this class were planned, only one, *Nikolaifleet* (1944), was delivered before the war ended. She was sunk by torpedoes fired by two motor torpedo boats of the Royal Norwegian Navy off the German coast, less than seven months after she was commissioned. (AUTHOR COLLECTION)

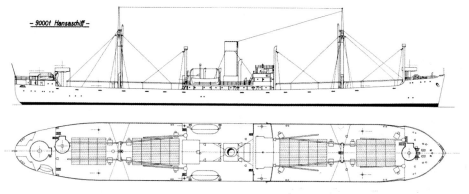

13 JAPANESE STANDARD SHIPS

In the Great War, Japan built ships for its own shipowners and for the Allies, including the British Ministry of Shipping. During the Second World War, Japan built ships to its own account for use against the Allies.

Until 1865 it was forbidden to build ships in Japan for international trade, in order to inhibit the spread of foreign beliefs in the islands. Consequently, Japan had only six yards capable of building ships greater than 1,000 tons at the start of the Great War. From this small beginning, Japan was able to produce standard design ships of 3,000, 7,500 and 9,000dwt by 1915. These were largely laid down on a speculative basis, but all of them soon found buyers. Japan's merchant fleet almost doubled in capacity to 2.5 million tons during the course of the Great War. At the end of the war, the six original major shipyards had blossomed into a staggering fifty-seven different major shipbuilding sites, at least one of which was designed and constructed with British assistance.

Japan built 236 ships to six different wartime standard designs during the Great War. The largest was the Type A, a two-deck, shelter-deck ship of 11,600dwt. They were propelled by two sets of triple-expansion steam engines driving twin screws, to give a sea speed of 12 knots. The Type A ship came in two sizes: a 475ft vessel and a single-screw shorter version. They had a long, low superstructure amidships, with a high bridge structure. The Type A design was similar to the class of ship built by Mitsubishi for NYK, such as *Toyama Maru* built in 1915, and *Durban Maru* completed after the war. There was also

the T type, based on a pre-war Clyde-built ship acquired second-hand by Japan, and these were essentially similar to, but smaller than, the A type. They were all well-equipped, top-of-the-range ships, and were built to a high-quality specification.

The United States bought forty-five new ships from Japan in 1917 and 1918. These ships comprised A-type and T-type steamers, but over half the order was for the United States standard Hog Island Type A freighters – the Emergency Fleet Corporation Design 1022. Britain also bought twenty standard ships from Japan in 1917 and 1918 through agents such as Furness Withy and Federal Steam Navigation Company. The largest was the Japanese A-type *War King*, built by the Kawasaki Dockyard at Kobe. Britain also acquired a series of eight of the smaller 9,500dwt single-screw ships. The smallest of the twenty ships was *War Amazon*, a 305ft-long vessel built by the Harima Dockyard at Kobe. Contracts to build a further four ships were placed through the Federal Steam Navigation Company. A problem with steel imports from the United States arose in April 1917, when America gave up her neutrality. Shipbuilding in Japan then slowly ground to a halt until steel imports were again resumed in the spring of 1918. However, by 1919 the keels of the four ships ordered through the Federal Steam Navigation Company had still not been laid, and the orders were cancelled.

In the Second World War Japan was no longer sympathetic to the Allied cause. Japan saw opportunities for expansion which it took in

Durban Maru (1919) was one of a class of sophisticated ships built largely by Mitsubishi at Nagasaki for Nippon Yusen Kaisha KK. Together with six A-type ships, NYK acquired nineteen standard cargo ships between 1916 and 1920, all built to a high standard, and equipped either with steam turbine or triple-expansion steam engines to provide service speeds of between 12 and 13 knots. These ships served between the wars and many were lost in the Pacific during the Second World War to American aerial and submarine attacks. (B & A FEILDEN)

War Soldier (1917) was one of twenty similar ships built for Britain in the Great War. She was a product of the Kawasaki Dockyard Company at Kobe and was a spar-deck ship with a deadweight of 10,400 tons. In 1921 she was bought by Union-Castle Line and renamed *Ripley Castle*, as seen here, and later sold for scrap in 1932. (AUTHOR COLLECTION)

conjunction with its notorious attack on Pearl Harbor in December 1941. As an island nation, it depended heavily on its own shipping to sustain its trade and to supply its occupied territories in the Pacific arena. At an early stage in its siding with the Axis powers, it embarked on an emergency standard shipbuilding programme, the basic design work having been initiated as far back as 1937. However, the emergency programme did not start during 1942 because of conflict between the Imperial Japanese Navy, which acted in the same capacity as the United States Maritime Commission, and the army. The argument was heavily in favour of military ship-

building until it was almost too late. Nevertheless, the implementation of the emergency shipbuilding programme in December 1942 was rapid, and the ships built were very much in response to the emergency Japan itself had created. Yoshiwa Miwa wrote of Japan's economic planning and mobilisation during the war:

Despite increased demand for more ships and faster production, the industry continuously missed deadlines, leading to a policy of planned shipbuilding between December 1942 and April 1944. This policy focused entirely on volume-oriented production.

War Pilot (1917) was one of the smaller ships built to the order of Furness Withy by the Kawasaki shipyard. She was sold by the British government to the British and African Steam Navigation Company in 1920, who renamed her *Jekri*, laid up in the River Fal in the Depression (as seen here), and scrapped in 1933. (AMBROSE GREENWAY COLLECTION)

Revising the Industrial Equipment Corporation Act, the government designated ships, aircraft and liquid fuel as top priority equipment. By inserting the phrase 'by building ships according to government standards and instructions' into the Act, the government instructed the corporation to order ships in bulk; it also arranged loans to enable ships to be ordered.

S C Heal wrote in his book *Ugly Ducklings*:

Intelligence reports from 1943 onwards referred to the mounting losses of the Japanese Merchant Marine and how it appeared to be causing severe shortages of all types of imported materials in Japan, as well as slow strangulation of the supply links to her many island garrisons. Parallel to these reports were suppositions as to what was being done by the Japanese war effort to cover the loss of merchant ships. Sources of much of this intelligence came from Allied submarine commanders who found that while targets of larger vessels were becoming more difficult to find there appeared to be no shortage of small freighters of the 1,000 ton range and smaller. These simply constructed vessels could be quickly built, but the strategy must have put a considerable strain on finding sufficient skilled personnel, particularly officers, to man the vessels. The idea was that by providing a large array of small potential targets, the losses when they did occur, would be less harmful to the war effort. This was true to some extent, even though it meant sacrificing the operating economics of larger vessels, there was to some degree safety in numbers.

These small ships were the so-called Types C, D and E small cargo ships. The Type 2E, of just 1,580dwt and all completed in 1944, was the largest group, comprising a total of 457 ships.

Heal had earlier written in *Sea Breezes*, May 1991:

The Japanese ships … most closely resembled the concept of a quickly built, floating expendable steel box designed to keep going for as long as they could hold together or avoid a torpedo. No attention was paid to the niceties of design and little to the economics of efficient ship operation; the increasing desperation of Japan's worsening plight left no room for such considerations.

Indeed, one senior government official, Ariyoshi Yoshyia, commented after the war that 'the wartime standard ships were really miserable tubs'. He added the observation that government officials in charge of the programme seemed to be mainly concerned about the number of ships built, not their quality, and that repairs were neglected.

There were six standard designs built by Japan, of which the 131 ships of the Type 2A, built in 1944, were the largest, with a deadweight capacity of 11,200 tons. Heal again:

As originally built the design called for machinery aft, navigation bridge forward of amidships and five hatches. The ships were flush decked without sheer and had two hatches forward and three aft of the bridge in a tanker-like configuration. Hull construction was straight framed throughout with angled bilges, a heavily raked stem and a squared cut-off stern. The midships house was a box-like structure relieved only by two simple bridge wings and the aft accommodation structure was equally simple.

Daiya Maru (1944) was typical of the Type 2A ships with engines aft, flush-decked, and noticeably without sheer. She was sold after the war to the Taiwan Navigation Company and renamed *Tai Peh* (as seen here), and was broken up in Taiwan in 1959 in her original configuration. (AMBROSE GREENWAY COLLECTION)

War Dream (1919) was a British N-type prefabricated ship built in the Great War, this one by Harland & Wolff at Belfast, who had done the design work for this class of ship. She became *Glenshane* in the Glen Line fleet in 1919 and after several other owners she was sold to Shoryu Kisen KK at Dairen, and renamed *Shoryu Maru*. She was one of two N-type Great War standard ships then owned in Japan, *War Melody* having become *Hakatatsu Maru* in 1924 and also registered at Dairen. These two ships provided the outline hull design of the Japanese A-type standard ship. (AUTHOR COLLECTION)

The Type 2A pedigree was the British N-type fabricated steamer dating from the Great War. In 1943 an earlier class of three Type 1A ships had been constructed, based directly on the design of two British N-class ships which had come into Japanese ownership between the wars. These were the former *War Melody* and *War Dream*, both built by Harland & Wolff at Belfast in 1918. *War Melody* was bought by the Dollar Line in 1919 and sold to Japan in 1924, being renamed *Hakatatsu Maru*, and in 1937 renamed *Ryuun Maru*. *War Dream* became *Glenshane* in the Glen Line fleet in 1919, and after several other owners was sold to Shoryu Kisen KK at Dairen in 1938, and renamed *Shoryu Maru*. Both ships were measured up in the late 1930s and used to create drawings for new ships to be built to the same, or at least similar, hull design. The squareness and absence of sheer or tumblehome showed the pedigree of the drawings, which also included the square cut-off stern, avoiding the need for shaped frames.

But there the likeness ended. They had three holds forward and three aft of the amidships superstructure, a deadweight capacity of 10,425 tons and were powered by a triple-expansion steam engine. Nine ships were ordered, but only three were completed to this design, the remaining six becoming machinery-aft Type 2A ships. The attraction of placing the machinery right aft was that it minimised the length of the shaft and the space occupied by the shaft tunnel, thus offering further shortcuts to the builders and a greater cargo space. The Type 2A hull was also modified, with a slightly more raked stem, and

the blunt stern was squared off to an even greater amount than before. This arrangement reduced the hatches and holds to four, each served by a motley collection of twelve 5-ton and one 30-ton derricks.

In 1945 a further modification was the Type 3A, where the bridge was brought aft, giving a clear run of four hatches before it. Only six of the machinery- and bridge-aft ships were completed before Japan capitulated, and many ships on the stocks, or fitting out, were abandoned or destroyed. In none of the A-type variants was there any attempt at having shaped plating at bow or stern; indeed, the forecastle deck was almost a perfect triangle in shape.

Much use was made of prefabrication. For example, the entire bridge structure for the Type 2A ships was assembled as one unit and lifted aboard, complete with fittings and outside companionways in place. One saving in the Type 2A was the absence of an outer funnel casing, there being just a hot stovepipe leading up from the fiddley. This was clearly liable to severe corrosion, as it could not be painted, and the deck was protected only by a circular flange to deflect water. This was changed in 1945, when the Type 3A ships came out with a proper outer funnel casing to protect the exhaust uptake.

The butts of the hull plating were welded and the seams were riveted. Australian prisoners of war were used in some shipyards, and a favourite act of sabotage was to use undersized rivets in oversized holes, thus weakening the integrity of the hull. In his book on Japan's wartime emergency shipbuilding programme,

published some years after his article in *Sea Breezes*, J C Heal wrote:

The deck had all straight crossbeams, thus eliminating camber. The bilges were constructed using standard formed quarter-round plate and were brought up to pinch out at the angular forefoot and stern … Every effort was made to economise on materials and methods to speed up the production process by using standardisation throughout. There was no classification society supervision, and a number of innovations would never have been approved by such organisations (which provide the design and construction standards that guide most world shipping). One such innovation and probably the most critical, was the elimination of tank tops and, therefore, a double bottom in the cargo holds. This would have left the ships vulnerable to bottom damage with far greater consequences, virtually guaranteeing a total loss when a partial loss might have occurred to a regularly constructed ship in the same circumstances.

Lack of classification meant that the ships could not be insured commercially, and a government compensation scheme was started with the proceeds of the sale of the ships to commercial shipowners (see Chapter 2).

Desperate for tonnage, the Japanese even salvaged vessels that would normally have been abandoned. One such was the Z-type standard tanker *War Sirdar* (1919), which was transferred to the Admiralty in 1920 and used as a fleet oiler between the wars. In the Second World War she was bombed and badly damaged by Japanese aircraft on 28 February 1942, and subsequently stranded in the Strait of Sunda. She was then raised and salvaged by the Japanese to become the Japanese naval oiler *Honan* in 1943. She was sunk by a torpedo fired from an American submarine in March 1945.

In January 1945 the United States Division of Naval intelligence issued a description of *Standard classes of Japanese merchant ships*. In it was a description of the Type 2A ship:

Large engines-aft cargo vessel with pronounced 'economy' hull. Note kingposts against bridge which is located almost amidships, small stack, and heavy stick masts centered in fore and after wells. One observed variation has wide cargo hatches extending three-fourths the beam of the ships. Ships of this class are under construction at Tokyo and have been observed being built near Nagasaki. No prefabrication of hull sections is apparent.

The description also stated that the ships were equipped with triple-expansion steam engines and the boilers, which could be fired either by coal or oil, provided a sea speed of 10 knots. The issue here was oil scarcity, and providing the coal-fired option allowed use of Japanese-mined coal as a substitute fuel.

The intelligence report summarised all the known standard class of ships and was essentially

The Z-type Great War standard tanker *War Sirdar* (1919) was transferred to the Admiralty in 1920 and used as a fleet oiler between the wars. In the Second World War she was bombed and badly damaged by Japanese aircraft on 28 February 1942, and subsequently stranded in the Strait of Sunda. Raised and salvaged by the Japanese, she became their naval oiler *Honan*, but was sunk by a torpedo fired from an American submarine in March 1945. (AUTHOR COLLECTION)

Outline of the Type 2A standard ship with engine aft, two holds forward of the bridge and two aft. This class had an acutely raked bow and the blunt stern was squared off. These were the ships that were rebuilt after the war with engines and accommodation amidships. (AUTHOR COLLECTION)

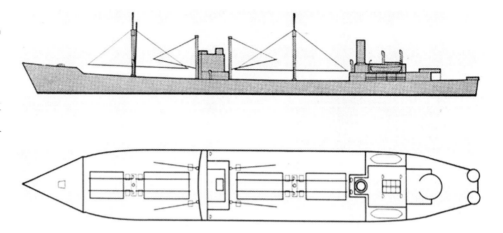

accurate, save for some detail. In February 1946 the United States Naval Mission to Japan estimated the total number of ships built in each class with the help of the Japanese. Post-war analysis by Heal, however, suggests that more ships were built than were recorded in the official report.

The most likely statistics are as follows, although actual numbers of ships are sometimes difficult to ascertain, with losses largely unrecorded. In the numbers built column, an asterisk denotes a possible over-estimate. The prefix 1 denotes the 1943 programme, 2 that for 1944, and 3, ships built in the 1945 programme.

Type	Gross tonnage	Deadweight tonnage	Numbers built
Type 1A (general cargo)	6,400grt	10,430dwt	3 built
Type 2A (general cargo)	6,600grt	11,200dwt	121 built
Type 3A (general cargo)	7,200grt	10,230dwt	6 built ★
Type 1B (general cargo)	4,670grt	7,340dwt	15 built
Type 3B (general cargo)	5,100grt	7,000dwt	3 built ★
Type 1C (general cargo)	2,700grt	4,480dwt	33 built
Type 1D (general cargo)	1,900grt	2,850dwt	22 built
Type 2D (general cargo)	2,300grt	4,000dwt	80 built
Type 3D (general cargo)	3,000grt	4,750dwt	14 built ★
Type 1E (general cargo)	830grt	1,320dwt	14 built
Type 2E (general cargo)	870grt	1,580dwt	386 built
Type 3E (general cargo)	880grt	1,565dwt	25 built
Type 1F (general cargo)	490grt	770dwt	21 built
Type 1K (ore carrier)	5,240grt	8,430dwt	21 built
Type 1TL (large tanker)	9,980grt	15,600dwt	18 built
Type 2TL (large tanker)	9,950grt	16,600dwt	27 built
Type 3TL (large tanker)	9,960grt	15,070dwt	1 built
Type 2AT (tanker, ex-cargo)	6,700grt	11,000dwt	34 built
Type 3AT (tanker, ex-cargo)	7,240grt	10,000dwt	2 built
Type 1TM (medium tanker)	6,400grt	10,430dwt	26 built
Type 2TM (medium tanker)	2,850grt	4,720dwt	34 built
Type 2ET (tanker, ex-cargo)	830grt	1,608grt	145 built
Type 3ET (tanker, ex-cargo)	833grt	1,608dwt	1 built
Type 1TS (small tanker)	1,020grt	1,480dwt	5 built
Type 2ET (tanker, ex-cargo)	6,400grt	10,425dwt	3 built

The ships constructed in the first programme in 1943 were all built in small numbers. The more successful types were then modified, as was the case of the Type A ships with the machinery being moved aft, and built in greater numbers. The volume-type ships of this programme were the small Type 2E cargo ships, although the larger Type 2D ships were also constructed in large numbers. Tankers were also built in this phase, although their numbers were small due to the relative complexity of the ship type; the predecessor of the Type 1TM medium tanker was the TM-class fleet oilers, such as *Palembang Maru* launched in 1942. The large and medium tankers were equipped with single-screw steam turbine machinery, as also was the 1945-built Type 3D general cargo ships. Some 175 Type 2A ships were reconfigured before completion as tankers, with tanks built into the original hold spaces so that they could easily be converted back to dry-cargo ships. A further 135 of the smaller Type 2E ships were also dealt with in the same way.

Prefabrication became important, and even the tankers were assembled in large welded units ready to be brought to the slipway to be integrated into the ship itself. There was no sophistication about any of the ships, which were all built to a minimum standard as quickly as time and resources would permit. The persistence in design of having the engines right aft did, indeed, save on building time and on materials. However, it generated interesting problems with trim when lightship. As a consequence, large ballast tanks were needed forward of amidships, to bring the vessel to a level trim, and the volume of these nullified any cargo deadweight benefit by not having a long shaft tunnel below the aft hold spaces.

The traditional Japanese craft of wooden shipbuilding was not overlooked, and five sizes of coastal cargo ship ranging from 70–250grt were built in large numbers. Some 2,278 wooden ships were built between 1942 and 1945, mainly as 100-, 150- and 250-ton versions, totalling a massive aggregate 327,000grt. The Japanese also sent shipyard officials to Syonan in occupied Singapore to supervise construction of 150-ton vessels described as 'half western in style'. A new company was formed to manage these little ships, Yusen Kinkai Kisen KK, overseen by Nippon Yusen Kaisha.

A great many Japanese ships were lost due to military engagement with the Allied forces, notably to American submarines. Many new ships were still incomplete after Japan's surrender, and work on them was halted. After VJ Day, Japan found that the majority of its merchant

The Type 2A post-war converted steamer *Kenkoko Maru* (1945), stranded in 7ft of water on 28 April 1951 at Black Point, seventy miles north of the Golden Gate, San Francisco. She was on passage for San Francisco when she went aground in a storm. Later re-floated and repaired, she was put back into service and eventually broken up eleven years later in 1962. (CLEVELAND PRESS – ACME TELEPHOTO)

fleet, greatly depleted as it was from the beginning of the war, comprised unclassified and uninsurable tonnage, most of which had already outlived its useful life. As an island state, Japan needed ships badly and consequently it took thirty of the forty surviving Type A ships in hand for major conversion under the supervision of the classification societies. This task was completed by 1950, and in subsequent editions of Lloyd's Register the thirty ships slowly appeared on the record for the first time. A number of the ships retained their original machinery-aft and bridge-amidships configuration, although they were largely rebuilt and fitted with steam turbine machinery. Two of these lasted into the 1960s, *Enchu Maru* surviving in service until 1967, latterly as the Hong Kong-owned *Eastern Trader*, and *Ehiko Maru*, latterly *Eastern Carrier*, which was only broken up in 1966. Heal reported in *Sea Breezes*:

> The standards were taken in hand and provided the first new units of Japan's post-war fleet. So far as can be determined they were gutted right down to the essential elements of their hulls, double reduction steam turbines replaced the three cylinder reciprocating engines originally installed and an entirely new engine room was built amidships over which the new single island superstructure was placed. The flush deck was replaced by a long bridge deck starting at the forward bulkhead of No. 2 hold and ending at the aft bulkhead of No. 4 hold. This was created by simply cutting in new well decks at Nos. 1 and 5 holds. No. 3 hold was sited in a conventional position

through the accommodation island and between the bridge and engine room. Probably most bulkheads remained substantially as built, except for the bulkhead aft of No. 5 hold as this was the location of the original engine room.

These rebuilds finally allowed the ships to be insured on the international market and gave them a new twenty-year lease of life. Nearly all of them remained in Japanese ownership until, one by one, they were slowly withdrawn from the mid-1950s onwards and scrapped. The last ships of the class to be completed were *Tonegawa Maru* in 1946 and *Etorofu Maru* in 1948; however, both were completed in the original reciprocating engines-aft configuration and later rebuilt. Other classes of ships were modified sufficiently for classification purposes and took up commercial post-war service. The coastal motor ships were the longest lived, some surviving in service through the 1950s. The large and medium tankers did not last long in service and were soon overtaken by the American standard T2 and T3 tankers. Nevertheless, some of these former naval auxiliaries served in the Pacific and Far Eastern waters until the end of the 1950s. The longest serving Type A was *Einin Maru*, which was converted to a fish-factory ship in 1969, having been used in the whaling industry since 1953. Although her original twenty-year classification expired in 1963, she continued in service until demolished in 1976, presumably reclassified as a static industrial vessel.

Some classes were built with a view to a longer life, notably some of the earlier built small vessels and the small, medium and large

Enshu Maru (1945) was a Type 2A ship that was initially owned by Nippon Yusen Kaisha. She retained her original profile post-war, although she was partly reconfigured to gain classification. In 1951 she was renamed *Kyoan Maru* when she was sold to Kyoritsu Kisen KK, and resold in 1957 to become *Shinei Maru*. In 1964 she left the Japanese registry to become *Eastern Trader* for E-Hsiang of Hong Kong, but was sold for demolition three years later. (D EDGE)

tankers; both types built in the 1943 Phase 1 programme. The large tankers had a design speed of 18 knots, the medium, 15 and the small units, 12 knots. However, the Phase 2 and 3 products were built to much lower standards. Many of the economy vessels built in the Phase 2 and Phase 3 periods of 1944 and 1945 were assembled at newly laid out yards, where prefabrication and mass production copied that of the United States. One big difference was the limitation in crane capacity, and units for assembly were generally less than 30 tons in weight, whereas 50 tons and over was the norm in the United States shipyards. In addition, as time went on, the distance between the transverses supporting the longitudinal frames was increased, an economy measure that also weak-ened the integrity of the hulls. Other issues involved the use of old-style hot-bulb oil engines in the smaller coastal vessels; the engines, of Great War vintage, were notoriously unreliable and difficult to reverse.

Ironically, in 1950 Japan found itself with a surplus of ships, as explained by Chida and Davies:

> In an effort to reduce the amount of redundant tonnage the Government undertook to purchase a number of vessels of inferior quality for scrapping – these were mainly Japanese wartime standard ships which had been constructed during the Second World War. It was planned to put these measures into practice in August 1950; however, there had been a fundamental change in the situation because of the outbreak of the Korean War. The world shipping market then reflected the changed circumstances, and by November 1950 a sharp rise in freight rates was underway. While these increases affected all routes, those involving Japan were particularly affected, owing to her geographic position near to the actual fighting. The consequent shortage of Japanese ocean-

Ehiko Maru (1945) was also a Type 2A ship that led a similar career to the *Enshu Maru*, ending her days as *Eastern Carrier*, owned by E-Hsiang Steamship Company of Hong Kong. As such, she was wrecked off the port of Shimotsu in Japan in March 1966. (AMBROSE GREENWAY COLLECTION)

138

Before: the Type 2A *Kocho Maru* (1945) as built by Mitsui at Tamano. (AMBROSE GREENWAY COLLECTION)

After: *Kocho Maru* (1945) as rebuilt after the war to satisfy classification rules. She was broken up at Osaka in 1963. (AMBROSE GREENWAY COLLECTION)

Tonegawa Maru (1946) was one of the few Type 3A ships that were converted into three-island-type ships for classification and commercial service post-war. She was built by Mitsubishi Zozen KK at Tokyo and was owned by Toyo Kaiun KK. She survived in commercial service under the Japanese flag until she was eventually sold for scrap in 1965. (AUTHOR COLLECTION)

going ships was then amplified by other factors that were unique to Japan, which included the wartime impetus given to her imports and exports and, it is believed, the American tonnage which had previously been carrying relief cargoes from the United States …

Thus it became necessary to reverse the policy which had been adopted earlier that year and the government withdrew a part of its plans for the purchase and scrapping of inferior ships. Those that had been released from purchase were therefore available to be re-registered. This enabled classification to take place, and once insurance cover had been arranged they were then available for

ocean-going service. The tonnage recommissioned in this way was estimated to have been about 57 ships totalling 217,000 tons deadweight, and although they would have been uneconomical in normal times they were operated on a fully profitable basis for the remainder of the boom period.

The boom period lasted until 1955, when once again the economic viability of many of the standard vessels was in doubt. This was when many of the ships were withdrawn. Besides, there were now many purpose-built ships currently available that had been designed and built after the war which were far better suited to the modern trades.

Descriptions of the Japanese standard ship types after United States Naval Technical Mission to Japan Report, February 1946, and Heal, *The Ugly Ducklings*

The cargo ships had light pole masts with 5-ton derricks mounted on them along with a 30-ton derrick forward. Note prefix 1 denotes 1942/43 programme, 2 that of 1944 and 3, the 1945 programme.

Type 1A 6,400 gross tons, six-hatch cargo ship, coal or oil-fired boilers, triple-expansion steam machinery amidships along with bridge and accommodation

Type 2A 6,600 gross tons, four-hatch cargo ship, coal or oil-fired boilers, triple-expansion steam machinery right aft, bridge forward of amidships.

Type 3A 7,200 gross tons, four-hatch, coal or oil-fired boilers, triple-expansion steam machinery right aft along with bridge and accommodation

Type 1B 4,670 gross tons, five-hatch cargo ship with turbine machinery and coal-fired boilers and accommodation separated from the bridge structure amidships. The split profile accommodates the coal bunker hatch and No. 3 hatch.

Type 1C 2,700 gross tons, four-hatch general cargo ship with coal-fired boilers and triple-expansion steam machinery but otherwise similar to the 1B type with accommodation and bridge in one island amidships. Well decks fore and aft. Double bottom throughout.

Type 1D 1,900 gross tons, two-hatch cargo ship with coal-fired boilers and triple-expansion steam machinery, bridge and accommodation amidships, No. 1 hatch was short forward of the bridge and the longer No. 2 hold was aft.

Type 2D 2,300 gross tons, cargo ship had the bridge accommodation boilers and machinery moved right aft and the deadweight capacity increased with a hull 10ft longer and 4ft wider than the Type 1D.

Type 3D 3,000 gross tons, cargo ship was equipped with coal-fired boilers and turbine machinery situated three-quarters aft along with the accommodation and bridge. There were four hatches, one aft of the engine and accommodation structure.

Type 1E 830 gross tons, small coastal cargo ship equipped with an oil engine (a Japanese design 700hp hot-bulb engine). Engine accommodation and bridge were amidships with well decks and No. 1 hold forward of the superstructure and No. 2 hold aft

Type 2E 873 gross tons, small coastal cargo ship equipped with an oil engine. Machinery, bridge and accommodation were right aft and one hold with two hatches, each served by a 5-ton derrick mounted on the foremast and mainmast at each end of the well deck. They were prefabricated with a square-shaped hull cut off triangular stern and a 'V'-shaped bow. Some 457 of these ships were built, the most populated type of all the Japanese standard types.

Type 1F 490 gross tons, small coastal cargo ship, a motor ship with a counter stern, otherwise essentially similar, although smaller, to the type 2E.

Type 3F 1,000 gross tons refrigerated fish carriers – four built.

Type 1K 5,244 gross tons, ore carrier equipped with coal-fired boilers and triple-expansion steam machinery amidships with accommodation and bridge. Long, low, well decks forward and aft had cargo-handling gear at the ends of the well decks.

Type 1TS 1,020 gross tons, coastal tanker with bridge amidships and oil-fired boiler and triple-expansion steam machinery aft.

Types 1TL, 2TL and 3TL 10,000 gross tons, large oil tanker with oil-fired boilers and turbine machinery aft, bridge and accommodation forward of amidships. The 1TL had either four or five tanks, the later ships had seven tanks. These ships were adopted as naval auxiliaries and three were converted into escort carriers.

Type 1TM 6,400 gross tons, medium tanker with oil-fired boilers and turbine machinery aft, bridge and accommodation forward of amidships. They had fourteen tanks and sub-tanks. Again, many of these served as naval auxiliaries.

Type 2TM 2,850 gross tons, medium tanker. A scaled-down version of the Type 1TM equipped with oil-fired boilers and turbine machinery aft along with bridge and accommodation. They had four main tanks.

Type 2ET 873 gross tons, coastal tanker equipped with an oil engine aft, with bridge and accommodation over the engine compartment. Some 135 of these ships were built.

14 THE BIG SELL-OFF AND POST-WAR COMMERCIAL SUCCESS OF THE STANDARD SHIPS

With the world at peace once more, the reigning maritime powers discovered that there was a massive surplus of merchant shipping available for the trade on offer. Although this would become a deficit in five years' time due to the Korean War, for the moment there was a glut of dry-cargo ships. Many of them were the slow and poorly equipped types, such as the Liberty ships and the British- and Canadian-built ships. Japan was worse off, as its wartime-built ships were nearly all built out of class and needed considerable rebuilding, even to get them insured.

Michael Hennessy observed from a Canadian perspective:

> Before October 1945, few Canadian ocean-going vessels experienced difficulty loading full cargoes for the United Kingdom, Australia, India, South Africa or the Baltic and Mediterranean regions. Canadian tonnage had been integrated into the international scheme of interim post-war shipping control reached by the Allies in late 1944 that created the United Maritime Authority. The UMA ensured that merchant shipping remained available to the Allies after the surrender of Germany and for resettlement and reconstruction work. As soon as the war with Japan ended, however, international shipping went from a condition of overall scarcity to overall surplus. This led to a series of negotiations, beginning in Washington in October 1945, to discuss the issue of over-capacity. There, the United States expressed concern that this overcapacity should not result in rabid competition. To maintain the harmony of the war effort, the United States Maritime Commission proposed rationalizing its war-built fleet by volunteering to lay up some 2,000 vessels, roughly 50 per cent of the American war-built Liberty fleet.
>
> Few Allies proved willing to reciprocate. A number of European nations, particularly Denmark and Norway, argued their problem was lack of tonnage, not surplus. The Europeans all expressed the opinion that any lay-up should come solely from Canada and the United States. Recognizing that international competition would be fierce and that many nations would seek to employ their ships for currency generation, the Canadian Cabinet was prepared to accept disposal of a large portion of the war-built merchant fleet of Canadian registry, but would take actions to encourage the maintenance of a substantial Canadian registered merchant marine.

In the post-war years, ships were decommissioned in large numbers and put in reserve while others were sold off. Both Canada and the United States were aware that their vast fleets of slow cargo ships would soon become uneconomic and redundant, as new, modern and more efficient ships were developed. As a result, their tenure as important international merchant navies was, at best, time-limited.

As for Britain, it was paying £500,000 a month to the United States for the continued use of 400 Liberty ships from autumn 1945 onwards. These ships were essential for Britain to redevelop its trade and its role as an international maritime shipowning and operating nation. In February 1947 the United States called the cards in and requested that Britain send the ships back, although some of them could be bought. The initial allocation for bidding for the Liberty-type ships was Italy, a former Axis country, 100; France, seventy-five, including twenty-five bought in one block by Compagnie Generale Transatlantique, the largest single purchase of all; Netherlands, twenty-nine; Norway, twenty-six; China, eighteen; but there was no mention of Britain. One of the favoured countries was Greece, which was allocated ninety-eight Liberty ships and two coasters: the 'Greek shipping miracle', from which Greece became one of the world's most prominent shipowning countries.

It was also the foundation for the fortunes amassed in due course by shipping magnates Niarchos, Onassis and Goulandris. The Greek seamen referred to the ships as *Vasilovapora*, or 'Queen vessels', as their accommodation far outstripped anything they had known before the war!

Peter Elphick summed up the distribution of the Liberty ships:

In all, including those chartered or sold to American companies, about 900 Liberties traded commercially after the war, most of them in their original condition except for the removal of wartime appurtenances such as guns, gun tubs and magazines. The remaining two thirds did not trade commercially. Some stayed in the service of the American Army and Navy, but most ended up moored and mothballed in harbours on both sides of the United States as part of the Reserve Fleet.

About 450 Liberties were allocated to American shipping companies and another odd beneficiary this time was Panama. American companies had flagged-out to Panama, with the glut of post-Great War ships and the emergence of stricter American maritime regulations. This time they flagged-out in droves and like Greece, Panama was on the way to becoming one of the major shipowning nations of the world, albeit as a flag of convenience.

There was considerable commercial sensitivity over which nations could bid for American wartime surplus shipping. Britain, it seems, was not to be one of those favoured nations, while American shipping companies fretted over the likely competitive outcome of bolstering the British mercantile marine. Stanley Bonnett wrote in *Sea Breezes*, December 1963:

After a great deal of haggling the then Labour Government of Mr Attlee agreed that British owners could bid for 100 Liberties at £135,000 a time. Mr Alfred Barnes, Minister of Transport, authorised a further bid for 40 Victories at about £250,000 each. A lot of Americans were determined that we should have none. A resolution was submitted to the US Congress Maritime Committee by Representative Fred Bradley of Michigan. He demanded their instant return on the grounds that the ships 'are coming to the United States and directly competing

against American ships on terms greatly unfavourable to American operators.' What was hurting the Americans was that it cost them in those days £2,000 a month in wages for a Liberty crew while our [British] crews cost just £800.

By March 1947 Britain retained some 229 Liberty ships on bareboat charter from the United States. Of these Britain was eventually allowed to bid for 106 of them, although precious few Victory ships ever came to the British registry. *The Times* newspaper commented:

The wartime agreement, under which the United States concentrated on the building of merchant ships and the United Kingdom that of warships, has inevitably hit British shipping hard. While the United States merchant fleet has grown since before the war from roughly 7.5 million tons to 38 million tons, including 12.5 million tons now held in reserve, the United Kingdom's fleet, which suffered war losses of 11 million tons, has fallen on balance from over 17 million to 13 million tons. At sea, perhaps more than on land, this country needs a respite in which to rebuild her resources.

Britain was able to buy its ships, albeit at a high price. But the cost of a Liberty ship rose and rose: by January 1949 they were changing owners for £180,000, and by 1952 that investment was worth £600,000, rising to £700,000 by the start of the Suez crisis. But there it peaked, and the value rapidly fell as new purpose-designed ships became preferable, even in the tramp trades. In the early 1960s the Russians were buying up redundant Liberty ships for just £60,000.

Various British Liner companies bought Liberties, including P&O, Ellerman and Cunard. Even Holt's Blue Funnel Line bought them, eight in total which it had managed and trialled during the war. The ninth Liberty ship under Holt's management was *Samcree*, but she was returned to America promptly when distorted tank top plating was discovered in No. 3 hold. Blue Funnel was also able to purchase six Victory ships at £227,000 each (two of them for its Dutch-flagged associate company). In all, British shipowners were only able to acquire fourteen Victory ships.

The transactions with the United States Maritime Commission were settled in dollars.

Blue Funnel Line's *Mentor* (1945) was a typical VC2-type Victory ship, completed as *Carthage Victory*. She is seen manoeuvring in Gladstone Dock, Liverpool, towards the end of her career with the Blue Funnel Line in March 1965. She was one of only a few Victory ships bought by the British liner companies after the war. *Mentor* was sold to Greek owners in 1968 and, after being registered in Panama by three subsequent owners, was scrapped in 1971, having given twenty-six years of reliable commercial service. (AUTHOR COLLECTION)

However, not all British shipowners had access to enough United Sates currency to pay their way. Elphick again:

The British Ministry of Transport bought some Liberties directly from the US Maritime Commission, afterwards selling them on to British shipping lines. Other British companies purchased their ships direct, but as dollar expenditure was involved and Britain had little in the way of dollar reserves, the approval of the Exchequer was required for every purchase. Some lines adopted novel ways to pay for their ships, ways that circumvented the restrictions on dollar expenditure. The *E H Sothern* became the *Sammont* after being launched at Los Angeles in September 1943. She was purchased by Ben Line in 1947 becoming the Line's *Salmonier* by an arrangement made with Saguenay Aluminium Company at Chicoutimi, Canada, a subsidiary of an American company. The ship was manned and run by Ben Line for four or five bauxite-carrying voyages between Georgetown, British Guiana and Chicoutimi, after which the ship became Ben Line property. (It is possible that the bauxite cargo itself, which could have been paid for with sterling cred-

its as it was mined in what was then a British colony, somehow entered into this transaction.) A similar but longer term arrangement and covering several vessels seems to have been made by Furness Withy Line, which used Liberties to convey pipes for an American oil company from the States to the Middle East. At the conclusion of the contract the ships belonged to Furness Withy.

But there was more on offer from the United States Maritime Commission. The Type T2 tanker was on the sale list at $2,026,500 and the T3 tanker at $1,903,125, while the little N3-type tanker was priced at $380,000. The C1 cargo ship came with a price tag of $640,000, the fast and well-equipped C2 cargo ship was valued at $1,650,000, and the faster C3 at $1,230,000. But there were allocations, the C-type ships were built to modernise the American Merchant Marine and this they did, with sales initially restricted to American (and therefore also Panamanian) companies, but resale soon found them flying the Australian flag.

During the sell-off in 1947, some fifty-two tankers were bought by British owners from the residue of the vast fleet of 525 tankers built in American shipyards to the order of the United States Maritime Commission. Of the large T2-

Standard T2 tanker *Esso Glasgow* (1944) was built as *Wauhatchie* for the United States Maritime Commission. She was one of nine T2 tankers sold to Anglo-American Oil Company in 1946, when *Wauhatchie* was renamed *Esso Glasgow*. She was lengthened in 1957 when the mid-section was completely replaced. She was the last of the T2s to remain in service with what by then had become Esso Petroleum Company. She was sold for demolition in 1971. (AUTHOR COLLECTION)

and T3-type tankers, 196 went to United States registry and seventy-one more to Panamanian registry. Britain was next best served, followed by Italy with twenty; France, eighteen; Norway, seventeen; and smaller numbers to Canada, Greece and Holland, and one or two ships to a number of other countries.

The British Board of Trade also found itself the proud owner of a great number of unwanted ships after the war. The first tranche of government sales to British shipowners was announced in January 1946. It included a large range of ship types, including the diverse array of standard ships built in Britain during the war, as well as those built in North America and bought by Britain, but only those ships acquired outwith the Lend-Lease scheme. An alternative to buying outright was a three- or five-year lease

arrangement with an option to purchase. Some of the Empire ships had been sold during the war to private companies who had lost equivalent types of ship to enemy action. As a consequence, some of the British-built standard ships were in private hands even as the war ended, although they were still working at the behest of the ministry. The standard fast cargo-liner type was one that was also ordered privately by shipowners, while other ships of this class were bought on the stocks in 1946 and completed to owners' own requirements. The colliers and coasters were also built to private order during the war.

Shipping companies were dealt with on a priority basis according to the tonnage each company had lost during the war. Many companies preferred to buy ships they had managed for the Ministry of War Transport, knowing their foibles and inadequacies before purchase. Companies also bought ships that had been managed by other companies, but usually only with prior experience of the ship type.

The standard fast cargo ships were bought in the 1946 sale. Buyers were Royal Mail, Canadian Pacific, Union-Castle, Prince Line, P&O, Eastern & Australian Steamship Company and Lamport & Holt, with just two going overseas:

Empire Camp (1943) was built by Short Brothers at Sunderland as a modified C-type ship. After the war she was bought by Cunard White Star and renamed *Valacia*, passing into the ownership of the Cunard Steamship Company in 1949. Bristol City Steamships bought her in 1951 and operated her for the next four years as *New York City*. She then went to owners in Glasgow and ended her days under the Turkish flag, before being sold for demolition in 1971. (AUTHOR COLLECTION)

Empire Life (1945) was one of twelve standard fast cargo liners with accommodation for a few passengers and was of 12,000 tons deadweight capacity. She was bought by the Union-Castle Line in 1946 and given the name *Good Hope Castle*, as seen here, and served that company's southern African trades until she was sold for demolition in 1959. (A DUNCAN)

Empire Rawlinson became *Monkay* for the French government, and *Empire Gala* became *Bir Hakeim* for Cie des Messageries Maritimes. One other fast cargo ship was converted on the stocks into a troop transport for Chandris/Charlton Steam Shipping Company and renamed *Charlton Pride*. The fast refrigerated ships went to Shaw, Savill & Albion, Blue Star, Port Line, New Zealand Shipping Company and Clan Line.

Many of the tramp ships were sold overseas, as well as to UK owners. Transfers had been made to the occupied countries during the war, those to Belgium adopting a nomenclature with the first word *Belgian*. The ships were offered at fixed prices with a differential for British owners. Liner companies were keen to buy them, including Clan Line, Harrison, Blue Star and Houlder Brothers. The South Georgia Company also bought one, *Empire Rhodes*, as a store supply ship for its whaling operations. The traditional tramp ship companies also bought, including Ropner, Court Line, King Line, Hogarth, Reardon Smith, Cairn Line, Bank Line and Graig Shipping. A large number were bought by companies registered in Norway, Holland, Belgium and France, and some went to the French government.

The Clan Line steamer *Clan Angus* (1942) was built by the Caledon Shipbuilding & Engineering Company as *Empire Prince*, one of the standard Y-type tramp steamers characterised by split superstructure. She served briefly as *Umkuzi* for Bullard, King & Company between 1956 and 1959, before again serving as *Clan Angus*, until she was sold for scrap in 1962. (AUTHOR COLLECTION)

The tankers essentially went to the oil company-owned fleets, mainly British registered, but also some to Norwegian flag companies. Two, *Empire Opal* and *Empire Collins*, became whale oil storage and transport tankers as *Southern Opal* and *Southern Collins*. The Athel company also bought *Empire Benefit* and *Empire Flint* to use as the molasses carriers *Athelqueen* and *Athelstane*. However, all the thirteen standard fast-type tankers became naval auxiliaries, with the first word of their new name becoming *Wave*, as in *Wave Ruler*, *Wave Victor*, etc.

The coasters and tugs were similarly disposed of. Many of the coasters built for Far Eastern service were sold to owners in Hong Kong and Singapore. The Straits Shipping Company, Singapore, for example, bought a block of eighteen dry-cargo motor ships of the shelter-deck type. These smaller ships became familiar sights at UK ports, the coasters then in the colours of F T Everard & Sons and the other major coastal fleets. The colliers were employed on the east-coast coal routes, and the tugs were resplendent in civilian colours, such as, for example, those of Clyde Shipping Company and Steele & Bennie on the Clyde, as well as all the other major regional tug fleets.

Some of the British liner companies did not partake in the big sell-off. One such was Manchester Liners, which had been fortunate to obtain licences during the war to build two of its *Manchester Port*-type group of ships. In 1946 it placed an order for a further vessel with an option of one more, which turned out to be *Manchester Merchant*, completed in 1951. The attraction of this was that the company had a

Empire Cadet-type coastal tanker *Empire Lass* (1941) was sold in 1946 to Esso Petroleum Company and registered at Grangemouth as *Esso Juniata*, and resold in 1956 to F T Everard & Sons, who renamed her *Argosity*. *Argosity* is seen at the layby berth at Barton on the Manchester Ship Canal in May 1961. She was sold for demolition in May 1969. (AUTHOR COLLECTION)

A variation in the profile of the coastwise tug was *Empire Sara* (1943), built by Cochrane & Sons, Selby. She became *Presto* for Ellerman's Wilson Line in 1946, and is seen here off the King George Dock entrance at Hull in August 1967, just before she was sold for demolition during the following year. (AUTHOR COLLECTION)

post-war fleet of ships built especially for its Manchester-based trades to east-coast Canadian and American ports. But, more importantly, it had a fleet with a consistent service speed of 13 to 14 knots, its two slowest and oldest vessels, the 1918-built *Manchester Division* and the 1925-built *Manchester Commerce* being disposed of in the early 1950s.

The entire fleet of Canada's Park Steamships Company was sold after the war, the last disposal taking place in 1947. A number of the Lend-Lease Forts were returned by Britain to the United States Maritime Commission (who had paid for them in the first instance) and were laid up in the Reserve Fleet or sold on. A large tranche of Parks and a few Forts were bought by Counties Ship Management of London, an Anglo-Greek-owned company, and put onto the tramp shipping market. Canadian companies bought some of these larger ships, but bought heavily into the smaller Lakers. The Ottawa-type coasters also went to Canadian owners, although the B type, designed for Far Eastern duties, mostly ended up in that region.

Many of the ships were modified to suit the commercial owners' needs. For example, nearly all the Liberty ships had their stump masts replaced by taller, more functional masts. The cargo-handling gear was upgraded, both in load capacity and by replacing steam cargo winches with more efficient electric winches. Some were adapted to serve the special requirements of a specific service as reported in *The Ships that came to Manchester*:

During 1947 Furness Pacific bid for five surplus wartime standard ships; four of them were the slow 11 knot steam reciprocating engined Liberty ships, the *Samcalia*, *Samavon*, *Samdaring* and *Samtredy* which respectively adopted the names *Pacific Liberty*, *Pacific Nomad*, *Pacific Ranger* and *Pacific Importer* … The fifth ship was the faster steam turbine powered Victory ship *Tusculum Victory* which was renamed *Pacific Stronghold*. Faster and, therefore, more suitable for the Pacific coast run she might have been but, as built, her air draught prevented her – and any other Victory ship – from going up the Manchester Ship Canal. Modifications were carried out to her before she entered service with Furness Pacific so that she received telescopic topmasts set into the crosstrees, which in turn were reduced in elevation from the deck. She also had a new shorter funnel. As such she was one of only a very few Victory ships which were altered in this way to come up to Manchester. The four Liberty ships were viewed very much as stopgaps until new purpose-built tonnage could be built, whereas the *Pacific Stronghold* was a longer-term investment.

There were numerous peacetime casualties. That of the American C1-type *Flying Enterprise* is perhaps the best remembered (see Chapter 7). The casualty rate increased with time, as ships became older and as standards became more relaxed once ships were flagged out to Panama,

Pacific Stronghold (1945) was built at the Bethlehem Fairfield Shipyard at Baltimore as *Tusculum Victory*, and managed for the Ministry of War Transport by Furness Withy as part of the Lend-Lease scheme. At the end of the war, Furness Withy bought the ship and placed her on the Furness Pacific service from Manchester and Liverpool to the Pacific coast of America and Canada. She was one of only a few Victory ships to be modified so that her air draught was reduced to fit the fixed bridges on the Manchester Ship Canal. (JOHN CLARKSON)

Greece, Liberia, and other flags of convenience. The loss of the Panamanian-flagged, British-built, Type B tramp ship *Faustus* at the entrance to the New Waterway at the Hook of Holland in November 1952 is one of the many strandings that should never have happened.

In May 1950 the role of the United States Maritime Commission was ceded to the newly formed Maritime Administration (MARAD) within the Department of Commerce. Concerns over the lack of fast cargo ships available during the Korean War led MARAD towards an experimental programme, which began in 1953, to investigate the feasibility of upgrading the Liberty-type ship to the same speed and capacity as a C3-class cargo ship, or at least a C2 type. Four Liberty ships were taken out of the Reserve Fleet. The first, *Benjamin Chew*, was fitted with Victory ship-type steam turbine machinery, following successful tank tests to ascertain the likely attainable speed and manoeuvring characteristics of the Liberty hull fitted with the steam turbine machinery. However, at speeds greater than 14 knots, she became difficult to steer, and her draught had to be reduced to attain the desired speeds.

Consequently, the other three ships were all lengthened by 25ft and a new, finer-shaped bow section fitted and the stern plates reinforced. Each ship had a different type of machinery installed: one, *Thomas Nelson*, had geared oil engines and served on the Atlantic run for the United States Lines for four years; *William Patterson* had gas generators and twin gas turbines

geared to a single shaft; and *John Sergeant* had an open cycle gas turbine with a combustion system compressor driven by the high-pressure turbine, and the propeller driven by the low-pressure turbine. The latter ship was also fitted with a 17ft 6in controllable pitch propeller. This was the largest controllable pitch propeller in existence at that time and was an essential prerequisite, as the gas turbine, unlike a steam system, cannot be reversed, although it could be operated at different speeds; *John Sergeant* was also the fastest of the four ships, attaining 18 knots on trials. But at a conversion cost of $3.5 million, even *John Sergeant* could barely be described as a success. The programme was not pursued.

Nevertheless there were a lot of lessons learnt. There was a great deal of hype over the trials of *John Sergeant*, probably in defence of the costs involved. Typical was a press release from MARAD issued in September 1956:

> The *John Sergeant*, first large merchant ship in the world pushed along solely by a gas turbine, yesterday was described as 'finest thing ever … the greatest advance in prime movers since the introduction of diesel engines' by J J McMullen, Chief Officer of the Maritime Administration's bureau of ship construction and repair.
>
> The ship scheduled for delivery 21 September will be operated by the United States Lines. She is one of four wartime Liberty ships involved in an experimental

Faustus (1943) was built as the Type B tramp ship *Empire Prospero* by Bartram & Sons at Sunderland. She became one of many peacetime losses of standard ships. In 1947 she was bought by W H Cockerline & Company of Hull and given that company's traditional name *Corinthic*. She was sold to London owners in 1951 and quickly resold to the Panamanian flag. As the Panamanian *Faustus*, she struck the North Pier entrance to the New Waterway in heavy weather on the night of 6 November 1952. She was inbound to Rotterdam with a cargo of coal from Hampton Roads. (AUTHOR COLLECTION)

conversion program under Maritime Administration auspices. The administration is attempting to determine the possibility of modernizing the country's huge fleet of wartime Liberty ships to meet present day national defense standards.

In the event, *John Sergeant* survived in service for just three years. The gas turbine machinery had worked perfectly well, and at an economic cost, while burning bunker Type C fuel. However, each year the ship had to be taken out of service for six weeks to have her propeller blade seatings replaced. Nevertheless, a great deal was learnt about the performance of the marine gas-turbine propulsion system, and the construction of a robust and long-lasting variable-pitch propeller.

The MARAD conversion programme did have one successful aspect to it. While the three lengthened ships were being converted, they were all fitted with a variety of new improved cargo-handling equipment, and one even had folding 'tween decks. Many of these ideas were translated to Liberty ships in commercial service but, in due course, the four experimental ships retreated back to the Reserve Fleet.

Back in the real world of commerce, the numerous standard-type ships maintained their routine services, alongside an increasingly modern and better equipped array of post-war-built shipping. Remarkably the 'five-year ship', the Liberty, was still trading profitably twenty years down the line. Many of the ships had migrated from European and American registration to cheaper tax and lower safety standard regimes under the flags of convenience, but nevertheless were to be found in ports throughout the world well into the 1960s.

Many of the ships stayed with one owner up and until their fifth survey. This was the critical fifth four-year, or twenty-year, survey, beyond which they became expensive units to keep in class. Other ships, for example, the Liberty ships acquired by the liner companies as post-war stopgap measures, were sold on quite quickly: as many as eight hundred of them flying the Greek flag at various times through the 1950s and 1960s.

The Victory ships were a better investment for getting through the twenty-year survey, and many lasted several more years. Four Victory ships, for example, the former *Saginaw Victory*, *Jackson Victory*, *Rutland Victory* and *Kelso Victory* were acquired by Transpacific Container Services and registered in Monrovia in 1969. During

1969 and 1970 they were converted at Hong Kong into cellular container ships and given the names *Oriental Express*, *Oriental Comet*, *Oriental Arrow* and *Oriental Dispatcher*, respectively. This gave them a new lease of life until February 1976 when the thirty-one-year-old former *Rutland Victory* sprang a leak on a voyage from Seattle to Kobe and foundered. The remaining trio were withdrawn a few months later and scrapped.

The commercially operated American C2 standard ships were profitable well into the early 1970s, with disposal only commencing around 1968. Again, several of this class were converted into container ships: three ships dating from 1942 and 1943 were so converted in 1957 and 1958, *Azalea City*, *Bienville* and *Raphael Semmes*. All three ships had been owned by the Waterman Steamship Company when it was taken over by McLean Securities, a company that was a leading champion of containerisation. Four more, *Wacosta*, *Warrior*, *Fairland* and *Afoundria*, were converted in 1966 for what had then become the Waterman Corporation. The last of these ships was scrapped in 1978. Several were lengthened, Sea-Land operating a number of C4-S-A1-type ships, lengthened and converted into container ships, and as such *Galveston*, *Long Beach*, *Oakland* and *Panama* were only disposed of in 1987. Very few C2-type ships as originally configured remained in service after 1972. The last, both registered in Beirut, were *Whistler*, which was scrapped, and *Spitfire*, wrecked, both in 1975.

There were two oddly configured engines- and accommodation-aft container ships that lasted in the Sea-Land fleet into the 1980s – as described in *Sea Breezes*, January 1988:

> … the *San Pedro*, 18,420 gross tons, was built as the *Marine Cardinal*. She became the *Baltimore* of Sea-Land in 1967, underwent surgery in 1970 for a new forward section built at San Pedro and was then herself renamed *San Pedro*. Her old forward section was joined to the after section of the T2 class tanker *Roanoke*, built at Chester Pennsylvania, in 1944 as the *Esso Roanoke*, and as the container ship *Baltimore* this vessel sailed for the Monterey Transportation Company, Wilmington, Delaware, until sold to Taiwan breakers in February 1985.
>
> … the *Pittsburgh* … ex-*Seattle*, ex-*Mobile*, ex-*Dorothy* was built at Chester as the C4-S-B1/B2 trooper *Marine Fox*. She became the *Pittsburgh* in 1969 when she was given a

new forward section built at Richmond, California. The old forward section was then joined to the after section of the T2 class tanker *Petrolite*, built at Chester in 1944 as the *Hanging Rock*, the end product of this operation entering service as the container ship *Seattle* owned by Littan Industries Leasing Corporation of Wilmington.

The fast C3 ships became expensive to operate as fuel oil became more costly following the Arab Israeli conflict in 1973, and few survived much beyond that period. The same applied to the smaller C1 ships, although many of these were disposed of by the late 1960s. The T2 and T3 tankers tended to get overtaken by economy of scale as tankers grew in size, and in the 1960s many were withdrawn and scrapped, while some were lengthened to increase their deadweight capacity. About sixteen of the T2 tankers were taken in hand in the 1960s and converted into container ships or roll-on roll-off railway waggon carriers, so gaining a second lease of life. Others were converted for use as bulk dry-cargo ships, again becoming competitive in their new trade, whereas they were barely profitable as tankers. However, by the mid-1970s there were very few of them left in commercial service.

All the ships had provided an invaluable service to the Allies during and immediately after the war. For the next twenty years, they were the backbone of the world's merchant navies, and some remained in profitable employment even longer. All in all, it was a remarkable performance that was down to the skill and expertise of the naval architects and shipyard managers and workers who built the ships while working under the most arduous and difficult conditions.

A few standard military vessels also came into post-war commercial service. The Landing Ship, Tanks (LST), were built in large numbers, including a few steamships, the LST(1) type, in Britain and Canada, and a much larger number of diesel-powered LST(2)-type ships in the United States. The prototype was three shallow-draught Lake Maracaibo tankers, *Bachaquero*, *Misoa* and the slightly smaller *Tasajero*, which were stripped out, their bow cut off and a loading ramp built in its place. During the war 1,051 LSTs were built, of which 113 came to Britain under the Lend-Lease scheme, and four went to Greece. Many survived the war to be mothballed for further service during the Suez Crisis, or chartered for commercial use as pioneer roll-on roll-off ferries.

Frank Bustard's Atlantic Steamship Company was established using LSTs chartered from the Board of Trade at very cheap rates. These were equipped with two triple-expansion steam engines and twin screws. The service started in September 1946 between London (Tilbury) and Rotterdam or Antwerp, initially with military hardware and stores to support the army in Germany, but soon attracting and developing a wider commercial customer base. A service between Preston and Larne was added in September 1948. In 1954 the company was taken over by the British Transport Commission as part of the nationalised shipping fleet and, shortly afterwards, purpose-built ships were developed, and two American surplus LSTs joined the fleet. The pioneering roll-on roll-off services using Board of Trade craft on charter were set to revolutionise the coastal shipping industry, with big company names such as Coast Lines and General Steam Navigation Company disappearing when they failed to keep abreast of the new technology.

A LST(1)-type Landing Ship, Tanks, *Empire Nordic* (1945), was one of Frank Bustard's Atlantic Steam Navigation Company ships, here seen arriving at Preston from Larne in August 1966. She had twin steam engines and a massive deadweight capacity of 4,800 tons. She was originally designated *LST 3026*, renamed *Charger* in 1946, and eventually decommissioned from the Royal Navy in 1955. (NICK ROBINS)

This LST(2) type Landing Ship, Tanks started life as *LST 1081* (1945) in the United States Navy and was renamed *Pima County* in 1955. She was equipped with twin oil engines that gave her a speed of 11½ knots, and had a deadweight of 4,080 tons. Surplus to requirements by 1965, she was put up for auction, acquired by the Atlantic Steam Navigation Company and refitted for commercial duties as *Baltic Ferry*. She is seen here at Stranraer in August 1970 working for Sealink, ie one nationalised company working for another. She was sold in 1972 for offshore servicing duties and eventually broken up following a fire in 1979. (NICK ROBINS)

In 1949 the American-owned LST(2)-type *Mowbray Road* was chartered from Seafreeze Industries, Rhode Island, by British Railways to carry railway containers on small trailers between Barrow-in-Furness and Belfast. *Mowbray Road* had been built in 1942 by the Bethlehem Shipbuilding Corporation as *LST 365* for use by the United States Army. She had two oil engines connected to twin shafts. The new railway operated service, however, was not a success and the charter was terminated after only twelve months; the small standard railway containers reverted to transhipment between Heysham and Belfast aboard conventional cargo steamers.

The British LST *Empire Shearwater* was chartered in 1959 by European Ferries (Townsend Brothers) from the Board of Trade to run between Dover and Calais. The idea was to operate a low-cost, roll-on roll-off commer-

The Isle of Wight ferry *Norris Castle* (1942) started life as *LCT 828*. Surplus to requirements after the war, she was bought by the Southampton, Isle of Wight and South of England Royal Mail Steam Packet Company in 1948 and converted for commercial use. She served as a car and goods ferry until 1962, when she was sold for further service in the Greek Islands. (AMBROSE GREENWAY COLLECTION)

cial ferry service between the two ports in competition with the London-based services offered by Frank Bustard. Unfortunately, the idea was ahead of its time and failed after only six months.

Five small Landing Craft, Tanks (LCT) Mark 4-type ships, which were just 180ft long by 38ft beam, were converted as British inshore ferries. *Norris Castle* was converted in 1948 for the Red Funnel service between Southampton and Cowes. Four others were converted for ferry duties between Granton, Edinburgh, and Burntisland in Fife: *Bonnie Prince Charlie, Flora Mac-donald, Glenfinnan* and *Eriskay*. This service, operated by Forth Ferries, only lasted from April 1951 until December 1952.

LSTs were not just used as ferries. They were suited to a variety of roles and used in North America and elsewhere as adaptable platforms for many different types of commercial activity. Other standard military vessels were also bought and adapted for commercial roles: for example, a number of small craft, such as the numerous Fairmile B and HDML launches, were used widely after the war as excursion ships, local ferries, and even as prestigious motor yachts.

Landing Ship, Tanks, from an article by Brian Macdermott in *Sea Breezes*, July 1992

It was Winston Churchill who, in June 1940, called for vessels to be built which could carry and land tanks directly onto beaches. By October 1940, the prototype tank landing craft was on trial but the design restricted her use to cross-Channel or short sea operations. Churchill stated the need for a ship to carry 60 tanks to an enemy shore and told the Admiralty to produce such ships. The Director of Naval Construction replied that such a vessel would not be practicable and suggested one to carry 20 to 25 tanks. Plans were made for what became the LST(1) *Boxer* class …

The pace of shipbuilding activity heightened when America entered the war following the Japanese attack on Pearl Harbor and with the passing of the Lend-Lease Act it was arranged for LST(2)s to be built entirely in the USA. Using an all welded construction method, they were 328 feet long with a 50 feet beam, powered by two 12 cylinder General Motors 12-567 diesel engines, 900 horsepower each, with a speed of around 10 knots. The urgency of production meant that many were launched before the first LST(1). A total of 115 LST(2)s were transferred to the Royal Navy …

Although the LST idea was British the design [of the LST(2)] was prepared by John Neidermair of the US Bureau of Ships. Neidermair had a background in submarine design and this was put to good use in LSTs by devising a system of ballast tanks. For ocean crossings they would take on ballast giving them a draught of around 7 feet forward and 13 feet 6 inches aft. For beaching, the draught would be reduced to around 3 feet forward and 9 feet 6 inches aft.

Official documents describe the LST(2) as consisting of a tank garage under a parking place and over ballast compartments flanked by storerooms, the garage and parking place communicating by means of a lift. The metacentric height (unloaded) was extremely high which resulted in heavy rolling with a short period – 20 to 25° roll was reported in a period of nine seconds.

15 THE INFLUENCE OF STANDARD SHIP DESIGN ON THE EVOLUTION OF NAVAL ARCHITECTURE

The greatest advances during the wartime emergency shipbuilding programmes were those of prefabrication and widespread use of welding. Welding was controversial in that there were inherent structural weaknesses in some ships, so much so that a British investigation reported in 1944 that 407 Liberty ships, nine Ocean ships, seventy-six T2 tankers and sixty-seven 'miscellaneous' vessels, including American-built LSTs, had been involved in some kind of structural failure that needed to be reported. It was believed that there were many failures that were not reported for a variety of reasons, and that incidents were, therefore, far greater in number. Three ships built by the Sun Shipbuilding Corporation at Chester had the highest number of recorded failure incidents, as high as nine: they were the T2 tanker *Conastoga* and two C2 cargo ships, *Shooting Star* and *Lightning*. The highest number of failure incidents in Liberty ships was six in each of two ships built at Kaiser's yards at Richmond in California.

Various theories were presented, but none altogether hit the mark. Milton Forman in a technical paper published in *Welding Journal* in 1945 acknowledged a likely contributory factor:

When the war began, the tasks and quotas set for the shipbuilding industry seemed beyond realisation. However, new yards sprang up all over the country, old yards expanded manifold, and the quotas were fulfilled and surpassed. This unprecedented expansion of the shipbuilding industry, coupled with the demands of the Armed Forces, left the shipyards with inadequate supervision and a large proportion of unskilled workers. In addition to this, the urgent demand that the ships be delivered now, meant that quality of workmanship was sacrificed to quantity production.

Launch of the C2-type *Lightning* on 23 August 1941. This press photo caption reads 'The 8,800 ton freighter *Lightning*, first of five C2 freighters built at the Sun Shipbuilding and Dry Dock Company is shown as it slid down the ways. Named for a famed American clipper ship of the 1850s, it was christened by Roberta Quirk of Chevy Chase'. *Lightning* had nine serious fracture incidents in the hull and main deck plating, the worst case for any C2- and T2-type ship. She was government-owned throughout her career and served the United States Department of Commerce after the war, until she was sold for demolition in 1971. (ACME NEWSPICTURES)

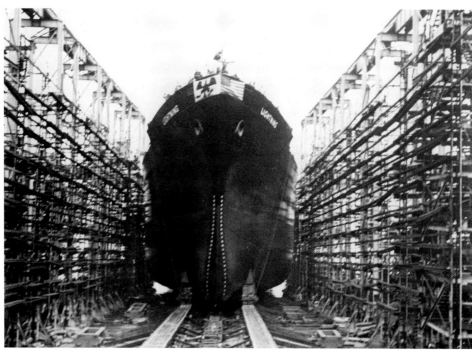

Schenectady (1942) was a T2-S-A1-type tanker, the first built at the Kaiser yard at Portland. She cracked open in two parts with a loud report just aft of her bridge on 14 January 1943, while berthed at the shipyard following completion of sea trials. She was repaired and in service by April 1943, and after a long and successful career was eventually sold for demolition in 1962. (AUTHOR COLLECTION)

One of the more notorious failures occurred in January 1943 when the T2 tanker *Schenectady* broke in half with an explosive crack. She was lying alongside in ballast, prior to her maiden voyage. The steel was tested and found to be of the specified grade, the probable stresses were below one-sixth the breaking strength of the metal and, most interesting of all, the failure may have originated at a weld, but soon took a straight line around the ship through the plates. Explanations there were none. A second T2 tanker broke in half while approaching New York ten weeks later. This was *Esso Manhattan* which, in a light sea in sub-zero temperatures, experienced a loud crack accompanied by failure abreast No. 6 tank, again across the deck and down both sides of the hull. Eventually, the ship split apart, but the two halves were later salvaged and rejoined without further incident.

Five Liberty ships were lost at sea, apparently as a result of a similar type of failure. *Thomas Hooker* cracked abreast No. 3 hatch in very cold weather off Newfoundland. The crack crossed the main deck plating and penetrated down each side of the hull to the level of the 'tween deck. The second was *J L M Curry*, which cracked simultaneously in at least two places in very heavy seas off the Norwegian coast in a Russian convoy. Again, the weather was bitterly cold and as the ship started to articulate she was abandoned. But the third loss occurred in mild weather, albeit in heavy seas, when *John P Gaines* cracked explosively in the vicinity of No. 3 hatch when she was between the crests of swells.

She was on passage from the Aleutian Islands to Seattle in July 1943 when she broke in two. All personnel were safely evacuated from the floating after-part of the vessel, but one lifeboat with eleven men aboard was lost, presumably swamped. Similar incidents happened to *Joseph Smith* and *Samuel Dexter*. A further failure was that of the Russian-flagged Liberty, *Valeri Chkalov*, which broke in two while at sea, although both parts were salvaged and later reunited.

Theories were abundant, and included welding residual stresses, locked-in stresses, strain concentrations, discontinuities and notch-sensitive materials. It was also apparent that ships built in low-temperature environments, such as, for example, those built at Portland in Maine, coupled with low operational temperatures, were most liable to failure.

There would be no place for the all-welded ship in the post-war shipbuilding industry unless the problems could be identified and addressed. Intensive programmes of investigation and research were carried out on both sides of the Atlantic into why a supposedly ductile material like mild steel should occasionally suffer from catastrophic brittle failure. Leading the British enquiries, Professor Frank Bull posed three questions:

1. How do riveted ships differ from welded ships in their structural behaviour?
2. What influence do the stresses locked into the structure during the welding process have on the incidence of failure?

Welding taking place on a prefabricated section of shell plating at the Kaiser shipyard at Richmond. Multiple welding taking place just yards apart can generate locked-in stresses. Nevertheless, the job was done and done quickly. (THE PERMANENTE METALS CORPORATION)

3. What is the nature and circumstances of the breakdown of ductile mild steel which causes brittle fracture?

To answer these questions a variety of sea-going and static measurements and tests were carried out, but the results all appeared inconclusive. As more information was gathered, the researchers started to look elsewhere and it was metallurgy that ultimately provided the answers. Dr Constance Tipper, working at Cambridge University, realised that the American mild steels were more notch-sensitive than British steels, which had a much higher magnesium to carbon ratio. Notches in steel cannot be seen by the naked eye and use of X-ray scanning is needed to find them. It also became apparent that one major steel manufacturer in the United States had been continuously falsifying test results on ductile failure and providing the yards with defective steel plate.

There was another unanswered question. Why did the British-manned Liberty ships not suffer any significant brittle fractures? The answer to this one was put down to likely good seamanship from officers who were better ex-perienced than the many newly qualified men in the United States merchant navy. Divisive though this supposition may be, it was given as the reason, and was supported by many seamen describing the difficulties they had experienced in handling Liberty ships in rough conditions when the ship was in ballast.

Professor Bull concluded:

The problem was not riveting versus welding, but ductile steel versus notch sensitive steel. Presumably the Americans would have got into as much trouble if they had used rivets (although there is an additional saving grace in a riveted joint, in that cracks tend to stop at a plate edge, and rarely continue on through a riveted joint). Similarly, the British steels should have shown a superior performance even when used on welded ships, and this was indeed the case, as the few welded ships produced in the United Kingdom had a much better record than those produced in the United States.

Welding and prefabrication were finally saved from possible obscurity and soon became normal practice in shipyards the world over. Greater care was taken over specifying and maintaining the grade of steel; in welding practice, as much of the structure that could be was machine-welded, and ships were carefully part-loaded or ballasted to ensure limitations of stress concentration. Frank Bull did qualify his conclusions by stating that understanding of the behaviour of the steel structure of very large hulls remains unknown, particularly in heavy weather with wave crest separation less than the length of the ship. This remark came back to haunt naval architects when the British bulk carrier *Derbyshire* was lost due to hull failure in September 1980; she was just one of 279 very large ships lost at sea between 1975 and 1990, a loss totalling 6 million gross tons of shipping, much of which, it is believed, was due to structural failure or caused by other design features.

The Victory ships were largely unaffected by failure, poor-quality steel or not, due to built-in stress arresters at the known points of weakness identified in the Liberty ships. The Victories also had a less rigid hull than the Liberties due to their wider frame spacing. The lessons learnt from these various factors were fundamental to the post-war emergence of the modern ship-building industry.

While the emergency shipyards in the United States closed down and workers were laid off, the British shipbuilding industry still remained cautious about the new American construction techniques. Duncan Burn observed in his book *The structure of British industry*, published in 1958:

> At the end of the war controversy was still acute as to the relative advantages and disadvantages of the all-welded ship; the backing that welding had received from the Admiralty and from the shipbuilders co-opted into government service had hastened on a change which in normal circumstances would have proceeded much more slowly. Even ten years after the end of the war, the all-welded ship has not found unqualified and universal acceptance with all shipbuilders, shipowners, or classification societies. In spite of evidence to the contrary, the belief that some riveted joints help to reduce the rigidities of a welded structure die hard ... Any doubts about welded connexions are more likely to lead to an improvement in the technique of welded construction than to a reversion to the extensive use of riveted connections.

Parkinson wrote on the slow take-up of all-welded construction in Britain in his book *The economics of shipbuilding in the United Kingdom*:

> As it is, shipbuilders have been able to convince most shipowners of the essential soundness and reliability of welded ships, and there has been an opportunity for both sides to see that welded ships are more economical to run and cheaper to produce than their riveted counterparts. One of the reasons why a welded ship is less costly to produce and operate is that it requires less steel and consequently is lighter and easier to drive through the water. With riveted connections the various parts of the structure must overlap in order that the rivets can be driven through all the members to be joined together; with welding, however, butt joints are used for plating so that overlaps are eliminated and welded [toe-on] rolled sections are used instead of flanges; there is also a minor saving in the steel used for rivets, since the weight of steel deposited for a welded connection is less than that of the rivets which it replaces.

It is also noteworthy that the rivets protruding from the hull of a large vessel could reduce the efficiency of propulsion by up to 10 per cent compared to a smooth-hulled equivalent all-welded ship.

Although it took time to convince the more conservative shipowners, all-welded hull construction did become the preferred method by the late 1950s. British yards began to find competition severe, as they had not retooled sufficiently to keep abreast of this change. Some had to close a slipway in order to make way for fabrication shops, but found that they could still produce as many ships in a set period because the hulls occupied the remaining slipways for a shorter period of time. It is ironical that Allied help to Germany and Japan in rebuilding their shipyards created a state-of-the-art industry overseas, which Britain could not compete with, having been denied similar financial aid both during and after the war.

The wartime standard ships did not only contribute the all-welded hull to the advancement of shipbuilding, but they also demonstrated the need for efficient machinery; efficiency both in fuel economy and in weight and volume, which otherwise eroded volume and deadweight carrying capacity. Of course, the

This C3-S-A1 ship was ordered by Moore McCormack Lines and launched with the name *Mormacgulf*, but completed as the flat-top aircraft carrier USS *Breton* (1942), before being reflagged as HMS *Chaser* later the same year. She was returned to the United States in 1946, and in 1947 purchased and rebuilt as the cargo ship *Aagtekerk* for NV Vereenigde Neder- landsche Scheepvaart Maatshappij. (AM- BROSE GREENWAY COLLECTION)

big old-fashioned Liberty ship steam engines did none of these things, but the modern steam turbines used in the C- and T- class ships built for the United States Maritime Commission and the double compound Lentz engine with the Bauer Wach exhaust turbine installed in the German Hansa-class standard ships were, in- deed, state of the art. So too were some of the oil engines developed for specific classes of stan- dard ship.

It was the United States Maritime Commis- sion's C- and T-class vessels that provided the optimum standard for all the wartime emer- gency merchant ships. The C3 fast cargo ships and T3 fast tankers offered shipbuilders the world over with a challenge – equal this or do better. As it happened, of course, American de-

sign and shipbuilding technology was soon to be overtaken by others, including the Germans and the Japanese.

The standard ships highlighted the need for efficiency, ease of operation and maintenance. The Liberty ship's main engine was modern in design, but it was big and heavy. This class of ship did, however, highlight the value of oil-fired boilers, where there was need for a smaller num- ber of firemen than in a coal-fired ship. The conservatism of many British shipowners caused a slow adoption of oil-firing, many having vested interests in the coal industry. Neverthe- less, the tramp ship industry based in northeast England was surprisingly well advanced before the war, with many owners experimenting with the Doxford and other oil engines. Several of

Mormacdawn (1946) was a C3-S-A5-type ship, the ultimate in design of the stan- dard ship types, built to the order of Moore McCormack Lines Incorporated. She had a service speed of 16½ knots and served her own- ers until 1970. (AMBROSE GREENWAY COLLECTION)

these owners went straight from coal-fired steam reciprocating engines to modern oil engines, reverting back to steam again when the surplus standard ships were offered on the post-war market.

It was the exposure of many shipowners to the oil engine, both in Britain and the United States, which provided the biggest advance in this means of propulsion. Shipowners managed a variety of ships for the British Ministry of War Transport and the United States Maritime Commission, and a number of them were put in charge of motor ships; not because they had experience of managing oil-engined ships, but because they had engineers with both steam and motor certification already in their employ. Almost without exception, the experience with the motor ship was positive and any lasting reservations were put aside.

The last important lesson from the wartime standard ships was that of economy derived from repeat building. The optimum number of ships built to a single design was six. Six ships built to one set of drawings provided a suitable spread of the set-up costs to bring the amortised cost of each ship to a minimum price. Gains beyond six were also possible, but on an exponentially decreasing scale, and British shipowners

were very much aware of these cost savings when they rebuilt their fleets after the war. For example, Alfred Holt & Company's Blue Funnel Line had the A-class motor ships built post-war, with five separate sub-classes – Mark I, Mark II and so on. The total amounted to twenty-five ships built by a variety of builders, but all to the same basic design. The first was *Calchas*, completed in 1947; the last, *Ajax*, completed in 1958. One of the other large classes of cargo liner was the British-India C-class, shelter-deck motor ships based on a design developed in the war, and which ran to a total of eleven near-identical ships, all built by Barclay, Curle at Whiteinch, Glasgow. The last of the C class were *Chakrata* and *Chinkoa*, being completed in 1952.

Ellerman Lines also had its own 'standard' post-war design and, interestingly, it stuck to tried and tested steam turbine machinery. James Taylor wrote in his history of the company:

In 1946 the *City of New York* was brought into service as the first of a new class, followed by the *City of London*, *City of Hull*, *City of Pretoria* and *City of Johannesburg*. Of these only the last named was a motor ship [and a hybrid of the class], which appeared to indicate that there had been a tentative

City of Hull (1947), seen at Birkenhead in August 1963, was one of a class of five cargo ships and a precursor to a further series of similar ships built for Ellerman Lines. *City of Hull* was propelled by an oil-fired steam turbine engine, and all but one of the twenty or so ships built to this or similar design post-war were steamships. (NICK ROBINS)

Haustellum (1954) was one of the first of the post-war Shell H-class, 18,000-ton deadweight cargo capacity tankers operated by Shell Bermuda (Overseas) of London. Shell commissioned fifty-two of these ships, all to near-identical specifications. (JOHN CLARKSON)

re-examination of this form of ship propulsion. Since the end of the war the small number of motor ships in the growing replacement fleet had been increased when the *City of Poona*, *City of Khartoum* and *City of Swansea* were obtained from the Ministry, but there followed a return to steam and conservatism when during 1948–1950, ten ships of the *City of Oxford* class were built all with steam turbines. These were followed during 1950–1951 by four of the *City of Birkenhead* class with similar engines … During the early years following the end of the war, it is of course possible that the sit-

uation was influenced by the fact that diesel engines were both expensive and in short supply, but whatever the cause, the effect was to prove expensive in future fuel bills.

Many of the British C- and D-type ships of the Second World War had transom sterns to facilitate construction. *Lagos Palm* (1947) was the very last D-type ship to be completed, and she is seen showing off her flat triangular stern in this picture. She was laid down at the Shipbuilding Corporation yard at Sunderland as *Empire Ronaldsay* and launched on 28 April 1947 as *Lagosian* for the United Africa Company, becoming the Palm Line's *Lagos Palm* in 1949. (AUTHOR COLLECTION)

The biggest post-war standard classes were those of the oil-tanker fleets. Tanker numbers had been greatly depleted during the war and, although the wartime standard tankers had replaced many of the losses, there was a post-war shortage of tonnage. The Anglo-American Oil Company fleet, for example, had been reduced from twenty-seven ships in 1939 to just fifteen at the end of the war. The British Tanker Company (later BP Tankers), as with other tanker companies, embarked on major building programme by commissioning over forty ships to a standard 12,200–12,400dwt design between 1946 and 1951. Tankers soon grew ever larger and Shell, for example, had a class of fifty-two motor ships of 18,000dwt, introduced into service between 1954 and 1960, including the celebrated H-class tankers, *Haustellum*, *Haustrum*, etc) operated by Shell Bermuda (Overseas) of London. These were soon to be outmoded, as the closure of the Suez Canal in 1956 required ships to travel via the Cape route, and larger and ever larger tankers had to be constructed, again built in quite large batches.

It is interesting to note that the transom stern of many emergency standard ships has nowadays become something of the norm. Both in the Great War and the Second World War the transom stern was much maligned by seafarers. Today, the massive container ships and large vehicle carriers all have transom sterns in order to maintain the maximum breadth of the ship almost to the stern. It is nice to muse that the old Great War National-class ships could have influenced modern day naval architects in this way!

Towards the end of the life of the Liberty ship in the 1960s, a number of shipbuilders introduced new standard ships designed to succeed them in the tramp and bulk trades. Austin & Pickersgill introduced a large standard bulk carrier in 1959. This proved popular with shipowners, but it also kicked off a flurry of Liberty ship replacement projects around the world. Austin & Pickersgill's managing director, Ken Douglas, instructed his team to start thinking about a ship that would be large and fast enough to upgrade from the Liberty-type ship, but of dimensions that would allow it into the smaller ports that the big bulk carriers could not use. Austin & Pickergill was partly owned by London & Overseas Freighters, formerly Counties Ship Management, who had bought a fleet of Canadian Park-type ships after the Second World War.

After much deliberation and consultation with potential buyers, Austin & Pickersgill

One of the GLR-type standard ships built in Germany by Bremer Vulkan was *Nile* (1972) which also traded as *Nedlloyd Nile*. This class had a deadweight capacity of 12,400 tons and a service speed of 16 knots. *Nile* had several subsequent owners and was broken up in 1996. (MIKE GRIFFITHS)

eventually opted for a 14-knot, shelter-deck type of ship, 14,000dwt, with engines and accommodation aft to maximise the volume of the holds. The plans were finalised in 1965 for the SD14 (Shelter Deck 14,000dwt) Liberty ship replacement. The intention was that the ship should take just eight weeks from keel-laying to launching and be fitted out in another six weeks. This they did; the first SD14 ship was built for London & Overseas Freighters' subsidiary General Freighters Corporation; she was launched in December 1967 and named *Nicola*. In total, 211 ships and seventeen derivatives of the SD14 were built at yards on the Wear, or under licence at other yards at home and overseas. Licence agreements were made with Hellenic Shipyards, Skaramanga, in 1967; Compania Comercio E Navagacao, Rio de Janeiro, in 1971; Robb Caledon, Dundee, in 1973; Smiths Dock, Middlesbrough, and Astilleros Fabricas Navales del Estado (Afne), Ensenada, in 1977.

The 126th, and last, SD14 to be built at Sunderland was completed in 1984 and the last British-built SD14 followed two years later from Smith's Dock, Middlesbrough. In 1988, twenty years after the delivery of *Nicola*, the last two ships were completed at Rio de Janeiro.

Other Liberty ship replacement types were offered by the Japanese and the Germans, but none were as successful as the SD14 type. The 14,000dwt, 14-knot, Freedom 1 type was built by Ishikawajima Harima Heavy Industries, and

designed by Canadian naval architect G T E Campbell. The first of the Freedom type, *Khian Captain*, was delivered to the Greek shipowner Carras in July 1967. The Japanese yard built 176 Freedoms. They were also built under licence in Spain as the Freedom Hispania type. The Japanese yard also developed the Fortune-type ships, of which sixty-two were constructed. Standard ships were also designed and built by several other Japanese yards, including Hitachi, Mitsui, Mitsubishi and NKK. The downside with the Japanese option was that the ships took nine months from keel-laying to delivery.

The GLR type was the best known German Liberty ship replacement. A total of fifty-two ships were built by Flensburger Schiffbau in Flensburg, Bremer Vulkan in Bremen and Rickmers Werft in Bremerhaven. These were all 15-knot ships with a deadweight capacity of 15,000 tons. The first of the fifty-two ships was *Dirk Mittmann*, which was delivered in May 1968. In addition, AG Weser of Bremen designed the Seebeck Type 36 cargo ship, which was a 16,000dwt dry-cargo ship with a speed of 16 knots. However, most of the sixty-one Seebeck-type ships were built under licence elsewhere.

Although the Liberty ship replacements were successful to an extent, they generally did not stay in service as long as the Liberty ships themselves. The new standard types coincided with the tramp ship being superseded by the dedicated bulk carrier, and the cargo liner by the container ship. The British SD14s in the liner trades, such as the ships in the P&O fleet, *Strathdirk* and her sisters, Lamport & Holt and the Larrinaga Steamship Company, did not stay long with their original owners and were soon sold on to foreign buyers. Nevertheless, a number of the SD14 and Seebeck ships remained in service with Far Eastern owners until quite recently, having served for thirty years and more.

Did the standard ships have an effect on marine engineering development?
By Ian Ramsay, CENG, FRINA, FIES, formerly Secretary of the Institution of Engineers and Shipbuilders in Scotland

At the start of the Great War, the triple-expansion engine was the means of propulsion for the world's general cargo ships. The *War*-named standard cargo ships of the emergency programme ordered by the British government, both at home and abroad, were propelled by this type of machinery. The exceptions were the 10,000–12,500dwt types ordered by Britain from American shipbuilders which were fast turbine steamers, although few were delivered to Britain as they were requisitioned by America when they entered the war in 1917.

During the 1930s, certain of the northeast England tramp shipowners had begun to take an interest in the oil engine, mainly the local Doxford type, but despite this interest, the ship selected by Cyril Thomson as the prototype of the Liberty ship for mass production in America was propelled by a steam engine – although of the most up-to-date design from North Eastern Marine Engineering Company. The ubiquitous triple-expansion steam engine had to be fitted in the Liberty ships because the American builders of large, slow-speed oil engines could not provide them in sufficient quantity to meet the proposed shipbuilding programme. This decision allowed the American locomotive building and heavy engineering companies to make their successful contribution to the Liberty ship programme with the manufacture of triple-expansion engines, water-tube boilers and simple steam auxiliaries.

While all this planning for merchant-ship production was going on, the Royal Navy were finding that the reliability and availability of their Parsons turbine-driven warships were showing a poor comparison with their US Navy counterparts. Their turbines were not specially designed for marine use, but were adapted from types used for electrical generation in power stations. This disturbing comparison was a wake-up call to the Admiralty, who set about designing a new turbine power package in conjunction with the English Electric Company, which contributed its vast power generation expertise.

As part of this development, the British marine turbine builders were kept informed, as many of them were also warship builders who manufactured the turbines for the ships they built, a fact that the Admiralty could not afford to ignore. This liaison resulted in the British turbine builders forming with Parsons Marine, the Parsons and Marine Engineers Turbine Research and Development Association – PAMETRADA for short. Whilst the slow-speed oil engines were being progressively developed to an ever greater power output, the PAMETRADA-designed steam turbines were the chosen means of powering the fast passenger and cargo liners, and the first generation of very large crude oil carriers in the post-war era. These turbines proved to be the reliable means of propulsion for those ship types until the early 1970s.

During the Second World War, development of the large marine oil engine had been continued by Sulzer in Switzerland. However, it is doubtful if Burmeister & Wain in Copenhagen did much development work lest it proved to be of use to their German occupiers. However, after cessation of hostilities Burmeister & Wain, along with their British licensee, Harland & Wolff, lost no time in starting to develop oil engines with an ever-increasing horsepower output that would eventually match the steam turbine for power output. Meanwhile, Doxford, Britain's sole indigenous designer and builder of large, slow-speed oil engines, was gradually left behind in this ever-increasing power output development.

Thus a significant contribution by the marine engineering industry to the design of merchant ships after World War Two was the development of the PAMETRADA steam turbine, with its much improved efficiency and performance. Although the use of steam turbines was not a lasting one, they did play a crucial part in the post-war years, when considerable shaft horsepower was required for the propulsion of both large and fast ships. On the debit side, the availability of the reciprocating steam-engined Liberty ship after the Second World War, in significant numbers at bargain prices, resulted in the delayed introduction of British built and owned oil-engined vessels until the early 1950s; this was particularly applicable to general cargo and tramp ships.

16 SUCCESSES AND FAILURES – AN UNPARALLELED ACHIEVEMENT

The RAF won the Battle of Britain and the Royal Navy, the Battle of the Atlantic, but the Liberty ship won the war. The impact of the American emergency shipbuilding programme in the Second World War was global. This was not only with regard to the outcome of the war, but also that its prefabricated Liberty ships, Victory ships, and fast C- and T-class cargo ships and tankers became a core part of the global merchant marine for the next two decades. The American shipbuilding programme also had an important post-war impact after the Great War, as well as after the Second World War, as Brian Cudahy reported in his book *Box boats*:

> An important advancement in cargo ship development took place as the United States mobilized for possible participation in World War I. Under the aegis of a federal agency called the United States Shipping Board, established in 1916, a flotilla of merchant ships was designed and built to support the nation's possible entry into the Great War and address whatever logistical challenges would be involved in sustaining American Expeditionary Forces fighting across the North Atlantic in the fields of France. Armistice came too quickly for the well-intentioned effort to have any substantial impact on the outcome of the conflict. By war's end, 470 vessels had been completed, while an additional 1,300, or so, hulls were delivered between 1918 and 1922. These vessels became the heart and soul of the country's post-war merchant marine. Various classes of standard wartime designs, the most notable among them being the colourfully named Hog Islanders, worked for such US steamship companies as the Grace Line, Lykes Brothers, Moore-McCormack and the Ward Line. During this era there were dozens of steamship companies operating deep-water merchant vessels that flew the US flag. By most accountings, at the end of World War I the US merchant fleet was second only to that of Great Britain in the number of ocean-going ships it owned and operated.

The unparalleled success of the American shipbuilding programmes in both world wars cannot be overstated. Although the Liberty ship was by no means the most up-to-date cargo ship in the 1940s, its genius was that it could be built in only a few weeks. Indeed, in the Second World War, Admiral Dönitz recognised the American shipbuilders as the biggest enemy of the U-boat,

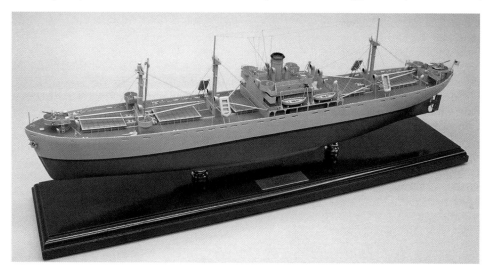

The iconic shape of the Liberty ship – adored by modelmakers. The American-built Liberty-type emergency shipbuilding programme contributed to the Allied effort in World War II such that it ensured victory over Nazi Germany. (AUTHOR COLLECTION)

even before the United States entered the war. Admiral Land of the United States Maritime Commission said in 1943:

> The Liberty ship is a product of war use. It can be classed with the tank, the fighting plane and other materials of war. It was produced to be expendable if necessary. If expended, it had served its purpose.

But it was not just the United States that built the standard wartime emergency ships. Britain too and Canada and Australia also contributed ships built within their own capability: some welded, some part-welded, some prefabricated, and some built conventionally, but all had the Allied war effort in common.

Meanwhile, the Axis countries were also busy with their own emergency shipbuilding programmes. These were nothing like on the massive scale of the American programmes, but were undertaken for exactly the same reason, as an emergency measure to compensate for losses. In the Second World War, Germany built two basic types of ship, the flimsy F-lighter and the hastily constructed KT ships at the bottom end of a scale of best practical ship design and construction practice, while the sophisticated Hansa A- and Hansa B-class ships were at the top end

of that scale. The Germans had nothing to match the Liberty ship, the design and construction of which lay firmly in the middle of this scale. The Japanese also built at the extreme bottom end of the scale, ultimately producing ships that were so poorly constructed that they were unable to comply with the requirements of the classification societies. But, for the most part, the ships contributed to the Axis war effort, although many of the proposed Hansa B cargo ships and all but one of the larger Hansa C-type ships were only commissioned after the war was long over. The Hansa B and C types were fitted with steam reciprocating machinery in association with the highly efficient Bauer Wach exhaust steam turbine. The latter machines were in short supply, and this delayed completion of many of these ships.

Without a doubt, all the emergency wartime ships were successful in one way or another. The Liberty was successful, if for no other reason, because it was built in volume; one British convoy commodore reported that out of a total of 106 merchant ships in a single Atlantic convoy, eighty-nine of them were Liberty ships. Whilst no single class of ship can be described a failure, the German Hansa C type falls nearest to this category, as it was over-designed and built too late in the Second World War to be effective.

Changing shift at the Permanente Metals Corporation shipyard at Richmond, California, during the Second World War. The Kaiser shipyards were worked twenty-four hours a day, seven days a week, on an eight-hour shift basis. Note the large number of women in the crowd. (THE PERMANENTE METALS CORPORATION)

It is easy to criticise the Japanese strategy for building ships that were not even acceptable for classification. However, it must be remembered that the Japanese programme was initiated as a desperate measure, rather than an emergency one, and the ships that were produced were built rapidly to provide quantity rather than meet quality requirements and, as such, were 'fit for purpose'. As time went on, the quality standard of the ships built in the second and third phases of construction greatly decreased, as the plight of Japan worsened.

Many of the standard emergency classes of ships were disparaged at the time of their introduction, not least the Liberty ship. Perhaps egged on by German initiative, seamen on both sides of the Atlantic feared the dreaded rupture across the aft end of No. 3 hatch which, 'like a crack of thunder', could instantly destroy the ship. But, despite occasional structural failures, it was a robust and feisty ship, as reported by Douglas Peel in *Sea Breezes*, May 1987:

> It was while in convoy in 1944 that the *Edward Bruce* encountered what was later described by the US Coast Guard as being the worst hurricane to hit the eastern seaboard of the United States for over 20 years. The convoy had to disperse and on just one four hour watch the *Edward Bruce* was blown

backwards on her course over 60 miles, just keeping her bow into the seas. The two large steel lifeboats on the weather side of the boat deck were stove in by the massive waves coming aboard and made completely useless, but the Liberty took it well.

One of the more stirring accounts of the Second World War was the Malta convoy WS21S, known as the Santa Marija convoy in Malta. It was officially part of the Operation Pedestal supply line to Malta. Heavily escorted, the convoy contained fourteen fast merchant ships, including *Empire Hope*, of the fast refrigerated cargo liner class built in 1941 and 1942, the American C2-type cargo ships *Santa Elisa* of the Grace Line and *Almeria Lykes* from Lykes Brothers, and the tanker *Ohio*, which was on loan to the Ministry of War Transport. Only five of the fourteen ships arrived at Malta: *Empire Hope* and the two American C2-type cargo ships were both sunk by torpedoes and bombs. The Union-Castle cargo liner *Rochester Castle* was torpedoed at 3.30 in the morning of 13 August on the approaches to Malta, but managed to stay afloat and rejoin the convoy, which got to the safety of Valletta harbour in the early evening; in that same attack, seven of the merchantmen were lost. But the most celebrated survivor was the tanker *Ohio*, loaded with fuel oil and vital aviation fuel.

Almeria Lykes (1940) depicted on the seventieth anniversary postage stamp of Operation Pedestal, Malta Convoy WS21S (the Santa Marija Convoy). The stamp was issued by Malta in August 2012. (AUTHOR COLLECTION)

In the morning of 12 June, *Ohio* was torpedoed amidships and set on fire. The inrush of sea water soon extinguished the flames, and the ship was patched up and able to attain 13 knots to rejoin the comparative safety of the convoy.

At 8am on 13 August, burning wreckage from the Shaw Savill Line's *Waimarama* rekindled the fires aboard *Ohio*, and later a burning enemy aircraft crashed onto the forecastle and burst into flames. Near-misses astern eventually flooded the engine room, and *Ohio* slowly lost way, and at the same time aviation fuel in tank No. 4 caught fire. She was abandoned at 2pm that afternoon. But as the fires subsided, an attempt to tow the ship was made by the minesweeper HMS *Rye*, an earlier attempt having been abandoned. The crew rejoined their ship, and slowly the two vessels headed towards Malta. A final attack was made on 14 August, when the big tanker lost her rudder. With at best only 3ft freeboard, the wallowing tanker eventually made Grand Harbour in the morning of 15 August, where she was greeted by a large crowd as the decks finally became submerged by water. Her remaining 14,000 tons of fuel were safely pumped ashore, and the wreck abandoned to settle on the bottom. She never sailed again, but ship and crew are to this day something of a legend.

A terrible incident occurred at Bari on the Adriatic coast of Italy involving the liberty ship *John Harvey*. The incident had horrendous implications for the Allied Expeditionary Force in Europe. *John Harvey* sailed from Baltimore in November 1943 with a cargo of munitions, part of which was designated as 'secret'. She arrived at the Italian port on 28 November and moored stern-on to the outer eastern mole to await her turn for discharge. Only the master, Captain Elvin Knowles, his cargo officer, Lieutenant Thomas Richardson, and Lieutenant Howard Beckstrom of the army, who was accompanying the cargo, knew that the secret cargo was canisters of mustard gas. Neither the port authorities nor General Eisenhower's headquarters in Algeria knew of the consignment. It had become customary to store mustard gas behind the lines as a potential retaliatory measure should the enemy use it, as they had in the Great War. That the mustard gas was available to the Allied troops was a well-kept 'top secret' by 'those that need to know': that is, until December 1943.

The port of Bari came under attack from German Junkers bombers on 2 December. Almost immediately the attack began, the Liberty ship *Joseph Wheeler*, moored nearby, blew up in a ball of fire, killing the entire ship's company. Liberty ships *John L Motley*, *Samuel J Tilden* and,

One of the five survivors of Malta Convoy WS21S was the Union-Castle Line's cargo liner *Rochester Castle* (1937). She had a remarkable survival, being torpedoed off Malta, but able to struggle on with the convoy to reach the safety of Grand Harbour. The famous American tanker *Ohio* came into harbour two days later. *Rochester Castle* is seen in her twilight years, arriving at Southampton in June 1969. (Nick Robins)

later, *John Bascom*, also caught fire and sank, with many men now in the water. Nearby, the Canadian-built *Fort Athabaska*, managed for the Ministry of War Transport by J & C Harrison, suffered a similar fate when forty-six of her crew were killed. Finally, *John Harvey* was caught in the inferno and exploded with incredible force, discharging smoke and mustard gas into the air and liquid mustard gas into the sea, there to mix with oil and light fuels in a toxic brew. Many died of the poison, others were burnt and blinded; the casualty list was appalling.

But for the moment the secret was kept, and Churchill even stated to the House of Commons in January: 'I do not believe that there were any mustard gas casualties at Bari on the night of 2 December 1943.' But so many people now knew the truth, including the surviving townspeople of Bari, that another statement was issued to the effect that the mustard gas was imported to Italy as a contingency should the retreating German army initiate its use. The Germans, of course, never did. Many years later, the United States Navy Department released the information that another Liberty ship in the port that night, *Lyman Abbott*, which survived with little damage, was also carrying mustard gas. Her crew survived that night as they had been issued with gas masks and ordered to flee the ship and port area, even though *Lyman Abbott* remained sound and seaworthy.

One of the most catastrophic incidents involving a standard ship was the disaster that befell the Canadian-built *Fort Stikine*. She arrived at Bombay from Liverpool on 12 April 1944 with a cargo of crated aircraft, shells, torpedoes, mines and bombs, totalling 1,400 tons of explosives. She docked 400yds from her sister ship, *Fort Crevier*. Bizarrely, this dangerous cargo also included a large consignment of gold bars. Drums of oil had been loaded at Karachi, and it was later found that some were leaking onto a large consignment of cotton and other goods destined for the return trip. Smoke was seen coming from the No. 2 hold ventilators before discharge at Bombay commenced, but the alarm was not raised. As discharge commenced, it was finally realised that the cotton cargo was ablaze. By mid-afternoon the ship was well and truly on fire, and just after 4pm the explosive cargo blew up with a tremendous roar. The after part of the ship initially remained afloat, but this too blew up half an hour later; the consignment of gold was vaporised in the blast. The resulting devastation was incredible, with various ships on fire and one large cargo liner lifted onto the quayside with a broken back. The whole dock estate, and part of the city, was destroyed, along with ten ships, including *Fort Crevier*. The dead and casualty list ran into many thousands. This was an incident that would not have happened under peacetime regulations, but the needs of wartime meant that many safety precautions were overlooked.

The peak of the standard ships' wartime efforts, and particularly those of the Liberty ships, was the offensive landings that took place at various wartime arenas. The first was in northwest Africa in November 1942, called Operation Torch, and consisted of 240 merchant ships that had sailed from Britain and another 112 ships from the United States, all with heavy escort guard. A large part of the merchant fleet were almost brand-new ships that had been built under the emergency standard shipbuilding programmes already initiated in Britain, Canada and the United States. In that initial sortie, there were forty-five Liberty ships, forty-six Parks and forty-two Oceans.

Operation Overlord, the Normandy landings, that took place in June 1944, was even larger. In the early stages of the landing some 864 merchant ships were involved, including forty Forts, twenty-two Lend-Lease Sam Liberty ships and eleven Oceans flying the Red Ensign, and numerous other Liberty ships under the Stars and Stripes. In addition, five badly damaged Liberty ships were among the fifty or so derelict ships towed to the beaches and scuttled as block ships to form the 'Gooseberry' breakwaters.

One of the Liberty ships at Normandy was *Jeremiah O'Brien*, now preserved at San Francisco. Walter Jaffee described some of the preparations aboard the ship ready for the landings in *Sea Breezes*, May 1994:

But even in war there were a few lighter moments which helped relieve the tension. While receiving gas training prior to the invasion of Normandy, Gunner's mate Morgan Williams recalls fishing for salmon while anchored in the Clyde. 'Waiting to go in, we were at anchor and we had a deck light hanging over the stern of the ship. When you looked down you could see all these salmon rolling under the light … So we rigged some lines and put a hook down with a rag or meat or anything on it and they'd bite it. We loaded up the whole ship, galley and everything, with 8 to 10 lb silver salmon.'

In Belfast the ship's mascot, a dog, was seen standing on the dock as the ship backed away. One of the crew hollered to the captain, 'The dog! Go back for the dog!' The rest of the crew picked up the chant, and soon the soldiers on deck took it up, all shouting, 'The dog! Get the dog!'. Captain de Smedt conferred with the pilot and they brought the ship back alongside long enough for one of the Armed Guard to scamper down a Jacob's ladder for the mascot ... The *Jeremiah O'Brien* made 11 crossings from Southampton to the beaches at Omaha and Utah, with one side trip to Belfast to load up part of Patton's Third Army.

Two Y1-type standard cargo ships built in 1941 at Port Glasgow by Lithgows as *Empire Ridley* and *Empire Baffin* demonstrated the versatility of many of the standard emergency ship types. In 1943 they were converted into the fuel pipeline-laying vessels HMS *Latimer* and HMS *Sancroft*. They were used to lay the Pluto pipelines between the Isle of Wight and Cherbourg following the Normandy landings in 1944. Both ships were converted back to a cargo role after the war and were sold in 1947, both remaining in commercial service until 1964.

The final wartime role of the Liberty ships was logistical support to the Pacific arena in 1944 and 1945. With VJ Day behind them, peace again reigned, and the wartime standard ships took up their new role as tramp ships and cargo liners. Peter Elphick wrote:

The importance of the Liberty ship did not end with the defeat of the Axis partners in 1945. So great was the need for shipping tonnage as the countries of the world dragged themselves back to normality after the war, that for many years after the conflict ended, the approximate 900 Liberty ships which were purchased from the United States at the end of the war, played key roles in the reformation of merchant fleets everywhere ... The last working Liberty ship, apart from a few altered and almost unrecognisable ones still being used as storage facilities, went to the breaker's yard in late 1998.

The Liberty ship is probably the best remembered of all the classes of emergency standard ships. Popular with both British and American modelmakers, it has also been the focus of preservation. *Jeremiah O'Brien*, present at the D-Day Normandy landings, is moored as a working museum ship at San Francisco, and *John W Brown* in a similar role at Baltimore, the former for many years laid up in the Reserve Fleet, while the latter had an educational role based in New York harbour. Both ships are now dedicated to teaching a new generation about the emergency standard wartime ships in World War Two. They also serve as reminders of the significant role that these ships had played during and after the Normandy landings in 1944.

Britain also has a Liberty ship, *Richard Montgomery*. Sadly, this one is lying submerged but for her mastheads at the confluence of the Medway and Thames estuaries, off the Isle of Grain in Kent. *Richard Montgomery* has become some-

HMS *Latimer* (1941) and HMS *Sancroft* (1941) were built as Y1-type standard cargo ships by Lithgow at Port Glasgow, as *Empire Ridley* and *Empire Baffin*. They were converted in 1943 to fuel pipeline-laying vessels, managed by the Admiralty and used to lay the Pluto pipelines between the Isle of Wight and Cherbourg in 1944. The photograph shows *Latimer* returning to the Isle of Wight after laying her first fuel pipeline to Cherbourg, a task that was completed in under ten hours. Both ships were converted back to cargo ships and sold in 1947.
(BRITISH OFFICIAL PHOTO FROM ACME, NEW YORK BUREAU)

The Liberty ship *Jeremiah O'Brien* (1943) steams out of the Reserve Fleet from her anchorage at Suisun Bay on 6 October 1979. She had been in the Reserve Fleet for thirty-three years and is now an operational museum ship berthed at San Francisco. In 1994 *Jeremiah O'Brien* crossed the Atlantic to take part in the fiftieth anniversary of the Normandy landings. (MARC PICHÉ)

thing of notoriety, as described by the Maritime and Coastguard Agency:

In August 1944 the ship was loaded with a cargo of some 7,000 tons of munitions and joined convoy HX 301 bound for the UK and then on to Cherbourg. On arrival in the Thames Estuary, the vessel was directed to anchor in the Great Nore anchorage off Sheerness. The ship was to await the formation of a convoy to continue the journey across the Channel. However, on the 20 August 1944, she dragged her anchor in the shallow water and grounded on a sandbank, running east from the Isle of Grain approximately 250 metres north of the Medway Approach Channel. The vessel grounded amidships on the crest of the sandbank. Intensive efforts began to unload her cargo. Unfortunately, by the next day, a crack appeared in the hull and the forward end began to flood. The salvage effort continued until the 25 September, by which time approximately half of the cargo had been successfully removed. The salvage effort had to be abandoned when the vessel finally flooded completely. The wreck of the

Richard Montgomery remains on the sandbank where she sank. The wreck lies across the tide close to the Medway Approach Channel and her masts are clearly visible above the water at all states of the tide. There are still approximately 1,400 tons of explosives contained within the forward holds.

There are also three Victory ships in preservation: *American Victory* is moored at Tampa Bay in Florida, *Lane Victory* at San Pedro, California, and *Red Oak Victory*, appropriately, at the Old Kaiser shipyard in Richmond, California. All three ships have spent an extensive period in the United States Reserve Fleet. *American Victory* and *Lane Victory* are both operational and carry out seasonal cruises.

The British are more modest in their preservation efforts and tend to prefer preserving the heyday of the coastal excursion steamer, such as the paddlers *Waverley* and *Kingswear Castle*. Almost by accident, however, there are some wartime standard ships still in existence in Britain. For example, there are three prefabricated TID-type tugs, *Brent*, built as *TID 159*, which spent much of her working life with the Port of London Authority dredging department

and now lies at Maldon in Essex; *TID 164*, which is at Chatham Dockyard, having spent much of her working life at Rosyth Dockyard; and *TID 172* is preserved on the River Stour. The steam tug *Cervia* , which spent much of her career serving William Watkins and latterly International Towing (which also operated *TID 164* as *Goliath* at that stage) was completed in 1945 as *Empire Raymond*, and now lies preserved at Ramsgate. *Empire Raymond* was built as part of the revised building programme ordered for the D-Day landings, although she was not completed until after the war had ended. Her 'invasion design' features include an armoured wheelhouse and gun emplacements.

Some ninety-eight VIC-type puffers (Victualling Inshore Craft) were built during the Second World War to the order of the Ministry of War Transport. Of these, four are preserved and two of them are regularly in steam. The first series of VIC puffers were based on a classic Scottish puffer design, of the type that worked around the Clyde, Western Isles and beyond. The first series of VIC craft had a length of 66ft, a 100-ton cargo capacity, a funnel in front of the wheelhouse, a simple cross fire-tube, or crane, boiler, and cramped accommodation for three or four of a crew. A second series with a length of 85ft, a cargo capacity of 120 tons, and a more efficient Cochrane multi-

Britain's 'preserved' Liberty ship, *Richard Montgomery* (1943), lies peacefully, but explosively, off the Kent coast off Sheerness. She was a product of the St Johns River Shipbuilding Company at Jacksonville, Florida. (AMBROSE GREENWAY)

The preserved but operational Victory ship *American Victory* (1945), seen on one of her twice-yearly day cruises out of Tampa. Her owners state that the museum is dedicated to 'honouring the men and women who built, sailed, protected and provided service, worldwide, through the American Merchant Fleet during times of peace and war'. (AMERICAN VICTORY SHIP MARINERS MEMORIAL MUSEUM)

tube vertical boiler, had accommodation for a crew of six, but lacked the sheer and ship-shaped hull of the earlier type, in favour of the hard chines and rectangular form of other wartime craft.

One of the last Canadian-built Fort Victory-type ships in British waters was **HMS** *Rame Head*, which had served as a submarine tender for many years. She finally went for demolition in Ghent in 2009, after being laid up in

Portsmouth harbour at Fareham Creek for some time. The Canadian wartime-built Landing Ship, Tanks, **HMS** *Stalker*, was in use as a submarine maintenance vessel, until she too was sold for demolition, the work being completed at Portsmouth in 2010. Neither ship was suitable for preservation because of the widespread application of asbestos in their original construction, the cost of removal being way beyond the means of any preservation society.

Aboard the preserved *Lane Victory* (1945), on one of her cruises from her base at San Pedro in California. (AMBROSE GREENWAY)

ABOVE: *Brent* (1945), seen searching the Thames for mines and other wartime debris in the late 1940s, was originally the prefabricated tug *TID 159*. Having spent much of her life working for the Port of London authority, she was intended to be scrapped in 1970, but was bought and restored by the Hall family of Maldon, Essex. The family used her as a 'yacht' for nearly forty years, until she finally had to be laid up as unseaworthy. She is now owned by the Steam Tug *Brent* Trust. (AUTHOR COLLECTION)

BELOW: *VIC 63* (1945), seen after 1956, when she was bought by James McNeil of Greenock and given the name *Colonsay*. She was one of the second type of VIC 'puffers'. *Colonsay* was wrecked at Barra in November 1960. (AUTHOR COLLECTION)

HMS *Rame Head* was the last Canadian Fort Victory-type ships in British waters. She was towed to Ghent for demolition in 2009, after being laid up at Fareham Creek for some time. She had served much of her career as a submarine tender. Her part-riveted hull plates and bridge front belie her pedigree. (AUTHOR COLLECTION)

The important role of the emergency standard ships of both the Great War and the Second World War underpinned the ultimate freedom of the Allied nations from Axis domination. The men and women that built the ships, including those famous American propaganda ladies 'Rosie the Riveter' and 'Wendy the Welder', are owed a deep debt of gratitude by so many, as are the men who sailed the ships across the most dangerous seas in history with U-boats taking every opportunity to pick the merchantmen off one by one. Australia also had its own modest emergency shipbuilding programme in the Second World War. The Axis powers too had emergency standard ships, neither so many nor built as efficiently as the Americans, but nevertheless of great help to their war efforts.

But the most remarkable aspect of all the shipbuilding programmes in both world wars was the longevity of the ships themselves. The Hog Islanders dominated the seas between the wars. The Liberty ships, the Victories, Forts and Parks, as well as the many British-built Empire ships, allowed world commerce to resume quickly after the Second World War. Indeed, the commercial service given in peacetime by all of these ship types was nothing less than astonishing. John Masefield, although writing about sailing ships, could equally have been talking about the emergency standard ships, particularly the Liberty ships, when he wrote: 'They mark our passing as a race of men, Earth will not see such ships as those again.'

Liberties with Harrison Line
By Captain Michael D R Jones

Having lost twenty-seven vessels through enemy action, The Charente Steamship Company (Thos and Jas Harrison Limited – Managers) along with every British shipping company, quickly needed suitable replacements in order to restore their former liner services. Of the various standard ships built during the war, Liberty ships were the most numerous and most suitable for liner service and eventually some eighty-four Liberty ships came into operation with British liner companies. Harrison Line owned and operated ten Liberty ships.

Compared with the last Harrison ship ordered before the war (the steamship *Trader*), the standard Liberty

ships were slightly larger in dimensions, deadweight and cubic capacity with the same speed of 11 knots and with a slightly greater purchase price. The Harrison Liberty ships were built of good-quality steel, had adequate cargo-handling gear and were very suitable for the Harrison trades, in particular with the trade of general cargo outward from the UK and cargoes such as sugar in bulk homeward. It did not matter if the sea passages took a day or two longer at the speed of the Liberty ship, which is why Liberty ships served with Harrisons until 1964. It is interesting that of the 127 Liberty ships owned under the British flag, almost all the British liner companies operated a number of Liberty ships, except, significantly, companies such as Manchester Liners, Canadian Pacific and Anchor Line, which all operated across the Atlantic, and only a small number of UK general traders (tramps) perhaps owned a single Liberty.

There were no structural problems with Harrison Liberty ships. This was possibly because the Liberty ships in the Harrison fleet were built by the Bethlehem-Fairfield shipyard in Baltimore, who had previously been shipbuilders before the Liberty ship programme and completed 384 Liberty ships, being some 14 per cent of all Liberty vessels built. In fact, Liberty ships from this shipyard were regarded by the marine world as the best built of the type, with good steel and, in fact, gained higher second-hand prices throughout. In addition, all Harrison 'Sam boats' as they were known, were fitted with a steel strap around the hull at sheerstrake level, as can be seen on many photographs, and also with other steel modifications to the hull, as were many other British Liberty ships. When being manoeuvred, both in port and at sea, they handled just as well as any low-powered ship of that size. The normal Harrison trades did not require the use of solid ballast, which did cause problems with some of this type.

As for the people who served with Harrison Liberty ships, it could not be said that these ships were not quite the favourite choice, but were certainly considered 'adequate'! Probably it was felt that the best feature of the type was the fact that the whole ship's complement lived in one block amidships. In other similar standard ships which the company purchased, being six of the coal-burning, 11-knot, Empire ships, and in previous Harrison classes, the deck officers lived under the bridge, and the engineer officers and the catering staff lived around the engine casing and funnel, this being separated from the bridge by No. 3 hatch. All the remaining crew lived aft on the poop, all separated by open decks. In a Liberty ship, a person could go from the engine room and reach all the accommodation and even up to the bridge, without stepping out on deck, this being a great advantage in creating a good team of 'shipmates', and a great advantage in bad weather. In addition, the accommodation was superior in many ways, with larger cabins and better furniture. In particular, these ships had showers for personnel hygiene, something not common in those days, although being rather open, privacy became a problem when wives were living on board. Ventilation was adequate, but the accommodation got rather hot when alongside in tropical ports.

For the deck department there was a fully enclosed wheelhouse, unlike the open style in Harrison tonnage, a gyro compass and good, and almost all-round, visibility from the bridge. Some masters insisted on using the open deck above the bridge when entering or leaving port, not something popular with junior officers, who had to keep logbooks going throughout the operation. The quality of the steel, in particular with the Bethlehem-built ship, reduced the amount of maintenance to keep a smart-looking ship.

Good stowage for the cargo was facilitated by wide hatchways, open decks and clear holds. There were two very good heavy-lift derricks of 60 and 40 tons safe working loads, with weighted cheeks of the lower purchase blocks, which avoided the necessity of overhauling the lower block by hand into the lower holds. All the cargo gear had much superior cargo blocks with roller bearings. As with many other British-flag Liberty ships, Harrisons fitted an additional set of derricks and winches at the aft end of No. 2 hatch.

The engineers were enthusiastic about the engine rooms with the very adequately fitted workshop and tool outfit, and good quality auxiliary machinery. Having the boilers and the main engine in the same space was not seen as a problem.

With the Harrison Line, their last Liberty left the fleet in 1964 after more than sixteen years of good service in peacetime with the company. The last Liberty of all left the UK Registry in 1967.

Author's Note:

It is heartening to read such a positive tribute to Harrison's Liberty ships from a seafarer with personal experience of their commercial operation during post-Second World War years. Despite the official reports and anecdotal stories of the poor-quality steel that was produced for the emergency shipbuilding programme, Captain Jones's comments on the general design of the Liberty ship, and the good build quality of those from the Bethlehem-Fairfield shipyard in Baltimore, may well be due to them being built by a subsidiary of a well-established shipbuilding company that was, in turn, a subsidiary of Bethlehem Steel, a major US company experienced in the production of ship-quality mild steel to meet classification societies' requirements; all quite unlike some of the newly established shipyards, who were sourcing their material from steel mills who were equally new suppliers to the emergency shipbuilding programme.

REFERENCES

Burns, D, 1958. *The structure of British industry*. Cambridge University Press, Cambridge.

Castro, F, 2008. 'In search of unique Iberian ship design concepts'. *Historical Archaeology* 42 (2), 63–87.

Chickering, R, & S Förster, 2006. *Great War, Total War; combat and mobilization on the Western Front, 1914–18*. Cambridge University Press, Cambridge.

Chida, T, & P N Davies, 2013. *The Japanese shipping and shipbuilding Industries; a history of their modern growth*. A & C Black, London.

Cudahy, B J, 2006. *Box Boats: how container ships changed the world*. Fordham University Press, New York, NY.

Donko, W, 2015. *Die Kriegstransporter KT1 – KT62 de Deutschen Kriegsmarine, Konzept, Einsatz und Versblieb*. Epubli GmbH, Berlin.

Elphick, P, 2001. *Liberty: the ships that won the war*. Chatham Publishing, London.

Forman, M, 1945. 'Some fundamentals in all-welded ship construction'. *Welding Journal* 58, 287–97.

Forwood, W B, 1920. *Reminiscences of a Liverpool Shipowner, 1850–1920*. Henry Young & Sons, Liverpool.

Friedman, N, 2014. *Fighting the Great War at Sea: strategy, tactics and technology*. Seaforth Publishing, Barnsley.

Goldberg, Mark H, 1991. *The 'Hog Islanders' – The Story of 122 American Ships*. American Merchant Marine Museum, Kings Point, New York

———, 1991. *The Shipping Board's 'Agency Ships', Part 1 The 'Sub Boats'*. American Merchant Marine Museum, Kings Point, New York

Granatstein, J L, & R D Cuff, 1974. 'The Hyde Park Declaration 1941: origins and significance'. *Canadian Historical Review* 55 (1), 72–9.

Hancock, W K, & M M Gowing, 1949. *British War Economy*. HMSO, London.

Heal, S, 2003. *Ugly Ducklings: Japan's WWII Liberty type standard ships*. Vanwell Publishing, St Catherines, Ontario.

Hennessy, F H, 2014. 'To market or to war: NATO shipping pools and the demise of the Canadian Navy', in G Kennedy (ed), *The Merchant Marine in International Affairs: 1850–1950*. Routledge, London.

Hope, R, 1990. *A New History of British Shipping*. John Murray Publishing, London.

Hopkins, F, 1994. 'Emergency Fleet Corporation ship construction in World War I in the Pacific Northwest'. *The Northern Mariner* 4, 15–22.

Jaffee, Walter W, 2006. *The Victory Ships from A (Aberdeen Victory) to Z (Zanesville Victory)*. The Glencannon Press, Palo Alto

Johnston, W, W G P Rawling, R H Gimblett, & J MacFarlane, 2011. *The Seaboard Coast: the official history of the Royal Canadian Navy 1867–1939, volume 1*. Dundurn Press, Toronto.

Knight, A, & M J Gaston, 1990. *Tugs and Towing: a worldwide survey of the vessels, techniques and development of the towage business*. Patrick Stephens Ltd, Wellingborough.

Lindberg, M, & D Todd, 2004. *Anglo-American Shipbuilding in World War II: a geographical perspective*. Praeger Publishing, Westport, CT.

Mitchell, W H, & L A Sawyer, 1965. *Empire ships of World War II*. The Journal of Commerce and Shipping Telegraph, Liverpool.

———, 1966. *Wartime Standard Ships, Volume 2: The Oceans, the Forts and the Parks*. The Journal of Commerce and Shipping Telegraph, Liverpool.

———, 1968. *Wartime Standard Ships volume 3: British standard ships of World War I*. The Journal of Commerce and Shipping Telegraph, Liverpool.

Miwa, Yoshima, 2015. *Japan's economic planning and mobilization in wartime – 1930s and 1940s*. Cambridge University Press, Cambridge.

Mowbray, Tate E, 1986. *Transpacific Steam: the story of steam navigation from the Pacific Coast of North America to the Far East and the Antipodes, 1867–1941*. Associated University Presses, Plainsboro, NJ.

Parkinson, J R, 1960. *The Economics of Shipbuilding in the United Kingdom*. Cambridge University Press, Cambridge.

Pritchard, J, 2011. *A Bridge of Ships: Canadian shipbuilding during the Second World War*. McGill-Queens University Press, Montreal and Kingston, Ontario

Robins, N S, 2015. *The Ships that Came to Manchester: from the Mersey and Weaver sailing flat to the mighty container ship*. Amberley Publishing, Stroud.

Sawyer, L A, & W H Mitchell, 1970. *The Liberty Ships: the history of the 'emergency' type cargo ships constructed in the United States during World War II*. David & Charles, Newton Abbot.

———, 1974. *Victory Ships and Tankers: the history of the 'Victory' type cargo ships and of the tankers built in the United States of America during World War II*. David & Charles, Newton Abbot.

Schwadtke, K H, undated. *Deutsche Standard Frachtschiffe des Zweiten Weltkrieges, die Hansa A, Hansa B, Hansa C frachter*. K H Schwadtke, Berlin.

Sturmey, S G, 1962. *British Shipping and World Competition*. University of London, Athlone Press, London.

Taylor, J, 1976. *Ellermans, a wealth of shipping*. Wilton House Gentry, London

Vernon Gibbs, C R, 1970. *The Western Ocean Passenger Lines and Liners, 1936–1969*. Brown, Son & Ferguson, Glasgow.

Witthöft, H J, 1968. *Das Hansa Bauprogramm*. J H Lehmanns Verlag, Munich.

INDEX

Original as-built ship names are indexed except where subsequent names are described in the text. Page numbers in italic refer to illustrations.